THE ENTREPRENEURIAL NUTRITIONIST

by

Kathy King Helm, RD

The Entrepreneurial Nutritionist, 2nd Edition

Cover design: Steve Mathis
Printing: Jarvis Press, Dallas, TX

First edition Copyright 1987 by Harper & Row and John Wiley & Sons

Second edition Copyright 1991 by Kathy King Helm

For information or to order books call or write:

Kathy King Helm, R.D.
P.O.Box 1295
Lake Dallas, TX 75065

(817) 497-3558

ISBN 0-9631033-0-X   (formerly ISBN 0-06-043662-X)

Table of Contents

Section 5 Managing Your Business

Section 6 Developing Your Professional Practice

Preface

Information on how to start your own business or become more entrepreneurial in your own setting fills bookstore shelves. It is becoming common knowledge, but it is still an area of fear or mystery to many. I personally can't imagine life without the thrill of the challenge it presents.

This book is written for dietitians and dietetic technicians to offer practical suggestions and guidelines on the development of money-making ventures. You can be successful as a private practitioner, consultant, or as an employed *intrapreneur*. My contributing authors and I hope to give a dietitian's insight into how to become more entrepreneurial.

The chapters follow the practical and logical stages that usually occur in the creation of a business. The book is designed for easy reading. This second edition tells more about business ventures in all areas of dietetic practice. There are answers to questions commonly asked at over 100 seminars and lectures conducted on this topic since 1979.

The opinions are obviously those of the author and contributors. They should provide a starting point or option for your personal research. In very few cases are there absolute right and wrong ways of doing things. It often depends on you and the circumstances. You must make the best decisions for your situation. It is important, therefore that you take calculated and well thought out risks.

I have been told by readers that the information in this book takes on new significance and meaning when the reader starts to seriously consider becoming an entrepreneur.

This book cannot guarantee success because even if your business is well run, other factors like the economy, a new competitor, or your personality and attitude, can undermine the best of financed and organized businesses.

In a survey I conducted in 1990 of dietetic educational institutions, of the 81 responding, 81 percent of the dietetic students and 65 percent of the dietetic technician students answered "yes or "maybe" to the question whether they would one day like to work in consulting, private practice, or business and industry. Those numbers indicate to me that the skills needed by the entrepreneur will be in greater demand in the future. This book should help students and instructors identify skills and knowledge to produce a strong business foundation.

Established practitioners will find that this new edition offers business strategies beyond the entry-level. It is imperative that our skills continue to grow as our markets and competition mature and become more sophisticated.

Acknowledgements go to all of the dietitians who have shared so much with me for this book and over the years. Their excitement, fears, and imaginative ideas have inspired me to do more. I want to thank Donna Smith, William H. Smith, Ph.D., and Iris and Lee King for their input into this manuscript.

I want to thank my mentors and friends like Jean Yancey, Polly Hering, Sue Bach Baird, Olga Satterwhite, Mary Hess and Lois Smith for sharing with me over the years.

My everlasting devotion and love go to my parents and siblings Iris and Lee King, Nelson King and Coleen Buckmaster who have for the last 20 years, licked labels, stood in booths, designed my logo, coauthored book concepts, copy edited manuscripts, and joined in the fun of my ventures, and I in theirs.

I want to thank my husband Carter, daughters Savannah and Cherokee, and step-son Stan for their love, enthusiastic support, and for embracing entrepreneurism as a way of thinking so that new ideas and ventures keep our lives interesting.

I dedicate this edition to my friend Jim Rose. His mind and enthusiasm inspired so many of us. He is really missed.

Introduction

The mere idea of starting a business venture of some sort was embraced by only a few maverick dietitians in the '1960s' and '70s'. More practitioners created new dietetic jobs and self-employment in the '1980s'. Today entrepreneurship is in the mainstream of dietetics.

The marketplaces where dietitians have traditionally worked are changing at alarming rates. This is happening at the same time more dietitians are looking for new career options and challenges. With nutrition's "window of opportunity" still wide open, opportunities in the field of nutrition will continue to grow for some time.

Smart employers today are learning how to keep top employees satisfied and productive by allowing more time and resources for the development of new ideas. Many new positions offer more freedom in scheduling to allow employed practitioners time to pursue outside, noncompeting interests, such as speaking, publishing or consulting.

Self-employment is not for everyone. If you decide to pursue it, it will surely be one of the most challenging and difficult projects you ever undertake. It may also be one of the most satisfying and exciting. Trial and error are part of every new business's growth. Becoming skilled requires study, practice, evaluation, more practice, and more time and money.

The dietitians who founded our profession were innovative, risk taking individuals. Many had been consultants, authors, or innovators who created their hospitals' and universities' first dietary departments.

The earliest known clinical private practice was begun by Eloise Treasher in 1949 in Baltimore, Maryland. As Eloise retired from work at The Johns Hopkins Hospital, many physicians wanted to continue sending their patients to her, and her business began. Eloise has stated that "private practice is not for everyone and not everyone will be good at it. But, if you offer quality, you will be in demand."

In 1953 Norma MacRae began her business in Seattle, Washington. Today she continues to update her successful cookbooks. When asked about her success, Norma stated, "I knew 'I had arrived' when physicians started coming to see me as patients."

Other pioneers include Virginia Bayles, R.D., a Consulting Nutritionist in Houston, Texas, and author Dorothy Revell, R.D., from Fargo, North Dakota. Carol Hunerlach, R.D., of Maryland is credited with spearheading the movement to organize the Consulting Nutritionists, a Council on Practice dietetic practice group in The American Dietetic Association.

The contributing authors or reviewers all have areas of specialty that distinguish them, and their chapters provide new insight to the readers:

Alanna Dittoe, R.D., began her practice in 1978 in the San Francisco area. She originally worked out of a physician's office. Her business grew into publishing patient education materials, and then full time independent practice. Today she has two very successful offices--one in downtown San Francisco and the other in Menlo Park. She uses a psychological approach to her nutrition counseling. Alanna teaches a class on entrepreneurism each year at U.C. Berkeley.

Karen Reznick Dolins, M.S., R.D., is the present chairman of the Sports and Cardiovascular Nutritionists Dietetic Practice Group of The American Dietetic Association. She is a cardiovascular nutritionist and also Nutrition Director for The Wall Street Nutrition Group in Battery Park City, New York.

Marianne Franz, MBA, R.D., is director of the AP4 program at Louisiana Tech University in Ruston, Louisiana. Before becoming a dietitian, she received a Master of Business Administration from SMU (Southern Methodist University) in Dallas, Texas. She teaches a graduate course in how to start a private practice or consulting business .

Cecilia Helton, MA, R.D., was a college instructor in Idaho and a participant on their College of Education Microcomputer Team at the time this chapter was written. Cecilia has been a teacher, consultant to nursing homes, and clinical dietitian. Her major area of interest is education media.

Paulette Lambert, R.D., has a very successful private practice in Tarzana, California. Her clients include a predominance of executives and professionals and their families. She specializes in using behavior modification techniques with patients who have eating disorder and weight control problems. Paulette now has a partner and junior partner working with her.

Susan Tornetta Magrann, M.S., R.D., is a published writer, lecturer, and consulting nutritionist in Villa Grove, California. Today she is a nutrition education specialist for the SPIN Project (school program). She has been a consultant to Vons supermarkets and a contributing writer to *Sporting Times, Women's Track World, The Jogger, Gemco Courier, and Muscle Digest.* She is past president of the Orange County, California, Dietetic Association.

Becky McCully, M.S., R.D., has been a popular private practitioner in Oklahoma City since 1978. She writes a weekly nutrition column for the *Daily Oklahoman* newspaper and appears as a guest on local radio and television. Today, she works full time with a group of cardiologists, teaching cooking classes and instructing patients. She developed a cooking video for heart patients which has been sold in retail stores across the U.S. She

iv

is past chairperson of the Consulting Nutritionists dietetic practice group of The American Dietetic Association.

Olga Dominguez Satterwhite, R.D., began her private practice, Nutrition Consultant Services of Houston, in 1976. She is bilingual and first marketed her services to the Spanish surname physicians in and around the Texas Medical Center area for their local and foreign patients. Before opening her business doors, she had contacted over 200 physicians. She secured a personal loan and opened a well-financed, full-fledged office with a part-time secretary in a medical complex. Today, she appears regularly on the media, she publishes a successful weight loss program, she subcontracts to fourteen other practitioners, and has six employed dietitians on staff. Her clients include private patients, restaurants, HMOs, renal dialysis units, and medical clinics. Much of Olga's time is spent in negotiating contracts and in management of accounts and people.

Marilyn Schorin, Ph.D, R.D., is Director of Nutrition for Weight Watchers, Int. in Jericho, New York. She formerly worked with the MR FIT program and is coauthor of a booklet, "A Recipe for Fitness," for Best Foods. In 1981 she designed and produced a program for nutrition and sports for Johnson & Johnson's "Live for Life" program. In 1982 Marilyn was a scientific consultant for "Upjohn Healthworks." She is past chairperson and cofounder of the Sports and Cardiovascular Nutritionists dietetic practice group.

Jan Thayer, R.D., is an accomplished businesswoman, media personality, and community leader from Grand Island, Nebraska. Jan is the owner and chairman of the board of two retirement homes and co-owner of Excel Management and Development Services. She sits on the Boards of more than five organizations for health care and business. Jan is past chair of the Consultant Dietitians in Health Care Facilities.

I graduated in Food Science and Nutrition from Colorado State University and completed a dietetic internship at Beth Israel Hospital in Boston. After practicing two years as a clinical dietitian, I began my business in 1972 in Denver, Colorado.

I was frustrated with the lack of patient teaching in the hospital setting at that time, and excited by the future of preventive nutrition. I decided to keep my investment and overhead low, work day and night for a year, and then reevaluate. These decisions were not hard to come by since I was single and had nothing of value to borrow against--but I had the time and dedication.

My business was located in several physicians' offices in the area near the hospital where I had worked. One physician paid me a retainer two days per week. I consulted at six other medical offices by appointment. I spent a lot of time in transit and trying to market my services to physicians.

The first year I charged $7 for the initial visit and $2 for revisits--and still had complaints about fees! I supported myself from the start, supplementing my income with cleaning houses and sewing. For every hour of generated income, I usually worked three hours on paperwork, marketing, or projects with no guaranteed income.

Before one year was up, I knew the concept worked. I decided to borrow $1000 (not a sufficient amount even then) and opened an office in a new local medical building. I loved it. Patients came to me. I raised my prices a little to cover the increased overhead and it started to look like a legitimate business.

During my third year I decided to sublease the office two days per week to a speech therapist. That freed me to take consultant positions on the side and start a masters degree in exercise physiology to broaden my expertise. It also gave me a change of pace from constant counseling.

To promote my business I usually gave several free talks per week. I appeared weekly on NBC TV's "NoonDay" and monthly on KMGH TV's "Blinky's Fun Club" for a total of eight years. I volunteered with the state dietetic association so that other dietitians would get to know me and I them. Soon, over half of my new accounts were referred to me by other dietitians.

To learn more about sports nutrition, I volunteered for three years to the exercise physiology department of the University of Denver. I was their "on call" nutritionist for visiting athletes, girls' gymnastic team, and guest speaker. I invented in 1976, with the aid of the Herty-Peck Company of Indianapolis, a natural sports drink that was way ahead of its time, but that's another story of its own.

Sports consulting with the Bronco Football Team and Denver Avalanche Soccer Team, paid media work, lecturing, and writing started to come my way as my expertise and reputation grew. My approach to nutrition was from a wellness point of view, so when the trend finally hit Denver, I was ready to grow with it. I taught wellness nutrition to physicians, nurses, hospital administrators, as well as the public.

My commitment to dietetics grew as I was elected President of the Colorado Dietetic Association, and spent five years in the leadership of the Council on Practice, two on ADA's Board of Directors and one year in ADA's House of Delegates.

When I married and moved to Texas in 1983, I didn't want to start over again building a group of clinical offices. Instead, I authored or coauthored several books and numerous articles. I helped develop a hospital-based wellness program, consulted at The Greenhouse Spa, acted as a media spokesperson, hosted a weekly nationally syndicated radio talk show, and traveled some giving lectures and seminars. In between I stayed home with two little girls to play "mommy."

From my business experience, I have learned that when the tough decisions have to be made no one can do it better than I. I have stopped looking for that expert on a white horse. I find it still takes time and patience to break into new business arenas where I am unknown. I and the entrepreneurs I know continue in business because we love the chance to be creative, to work with people, and the freedom. The difficulty of the challenge makes us appreciate the rewards even more.

Kathy King Helm, R.D., L.D.

section 1

The Beginning

Words of Wisdom:

"Do not follow where the path may lead. Go instead where there is no path and leave a trail."

"Many of life's failures are men who did not realize how close they were to success when they gave up."

"Choice, not chance determines destiny."

Chapter 1

The Entrepreneurial Spirit

Many dietitians are doing what has not been done before. They embody the entrepreneurial spirit. Their ingenuity, creative verve, and aggressiveness are leading them and the dietetic profession into new fields of experiences.

Dietitians are best selling authors, hosts of media talk shows, and sports nutritionists whom at times travel with their teams and consult worldwide. They own public relations firms, publishing houses, and nursing homes. Some are vice presidents of worldwide equipment companies, or hospital systems. A few invent products like fruit-sweetened cookies, diet card games, educational videos, and multi-million dollar computer databases. Dietitians are culinary and nutrition consultants to restaurants and other food services. Others offer management expertise that teaches hospitals how to reduce the incidence of malnutrition.

THE ENTREPRENEURIAL EXPLOSION

Entrepreneurism is thriving in America. Today, more than thirteen million people are running their own businesses and millions more are considering it. More than 700,000 new businesses will be started this year with women starting businesses at twice the rate of men (1). Women owned thirty-one percent of all small businesses in 1987; by the year 2000, it is expected that women will own fifty percent of all small businesses (2).

In his book, *Innovation and Entrepreneurship,* Peter Drucker, veteran business consultant and management philosopher, suggests that America and American business are entering upon an "Entrepreneurial Society." Drucker says the *entrepreneurial spirit* is based on the premise that change is normal, healthy, and desirable, that "it sees the major task in society, and especially in the economy, as doing something different rather than doing better what is already being done" (3). Entrepreneurism is a way of thinking where you see the possibilities of an idea before you dwell on its limitations.

Rosabeth Moss Kanter, editor of the *Harvard Business Review* and author of *Change Masters,* a book based on her study of fifty corporations, concludes that those companies on a downward slope are there because of "the quiet suffocation of the entrepreneurial spirit" (4). There is a close relationship between entrepreneurship and innovation, not just in product or service development, but also in meeting new customers needs, increasing job satisfaction, devising new work methods, and improving quality (5). New ideas are essential.

1

Kanter states, "A new kind of leader is emerging who is very energetic, very impatient, and willing to stand the traditional system on its head. They're willing to do it all very differently" (4). These people are or will be our employers, peers, and competitors. To keep pace with the flood of new ideas and new competition, the health care market where most dietitians are employed is having to change. Dietitians with an interest in entrepreneurism no longer have to leave their employee settings to try out their new ideas. Many managers want their employees to think of new ways to generate revenue or improve their public relations or their cost/benefit ratio. They are just waiting for dietitians to come forward. The term "intrapreneur" was coined to identify the employed entrepreneur.

In *The Atlantic Monthly,* authors Stephen Pollan and Mark Levine made observations about today's small business environment (6):

- During the past decade, small businesses created *eighty percent* of all new jobs.

- Small businesses run by one person or married spouses have income that is *growing at a faster rate* than corporate profits and salaries.

- Small businesses have been so successful that large, hungry corporations have been moving into areas traditionally left to entrepreneurs, like child care. As big businesses move, entrepreneurs are moving into areas that once were thought beyond their scope, like manufacturing for global markets.

- Creativity and innovation remain the province of the entrepreneur. More than half the major inventions since World War II have come from small business people.

- Technology--in particular computerization and information processing and retrieval--is lowering the start-up costs associated with small business and helping them seize chances, which they are better at doing than large businesses.

- Since two-income families are becoming the norm, more women than ever are entering business, often as entrepreneurs. According to the SBA, women-owned businesses have a better rate of survival than those owned by men.

- Government at all levels, realizing that small businesses are the primary creators of jobs, are offering incentives to encourage entrepreneurs into their communities.

- The current tax situation makes it clear to Americans that owning one's own business is one of the few opportunities people have to create wealth.

CHANGES IN THE EMPLOYMENT ENVIRONMENT

Twenty-six million Americans work at home, either full or part time, and that number is expected to reach thirty-one million by 1992 (7). Working at home

2

is a growing option, especially for people who consult, write, publish, make home visits, speak or use the computer for the bulk of their work. A home office keeps the overhead low, reduces travel time, allows more time with your family, and offers scheduling flexibility. Unless you are careful it can overwhelm your personal and family life. Any negative stigma associated with working at home for men and women is quickly disappearing.

Job loyalty is changing. As more companies cut costs, merge and consolidate, an increasing number of highly educated or highly experienced people will be let go (8). Business experts see a trend toward replacing many employees with a staff of subcontractors and consultants who will only be used on an on-call or per-project basis---no fringe benefits and no regular paychecks, but more pay per hour. This will hit the Baby Boomers especially hard since so many will be vying for the too few good top level positions that their years of experience and expertise warrant.

The majority of employers do not want to be responsible for their employees' careers, and the work force is just beginning to realize the full implications of that new independence---sometimes less job security, no guarantees, and fewer fringe benefits. However, in areas where too few dietitians are available, these job benefits will be used to entice new employees to work.

The average American changes jobs about every four years due to a better job opportunity, boredom, cutbacks, spouse transfers, or other reasons (9). For some the change is unsettling, but others see it as an opportunity to grow, meet new people, and try new ideas.

With the number of white males retiring from the work force over the next ten to twenty years, management styles will change, and the faces in the work place will be more female and males of many races. It takes approximately thirty-five years in the corporate pipelines before a person is considered ready for the CEO position of major businesses, according to Regina Herzlinger, professor of business administration at Harvard (8). Therefore, the next fifteen years should see more women reaching that level and bringing with them a collaborative, people-oriented management style. It's predicted organizational charts will flatten with fewer middle levels of authority, or many will try a circle or spider-web structure to make people and departments intercommunicate and collaborate more.

The global market will change our competitive environment in America. In his newspaper column, Tom Peters, author of *In Search of Excellence,* reported that through robotics, computers, and subcontractors, instead of employees, global corporations are able to produce $5 billion in gross revenue with 6,000 employees while U.S. companies on average need 50,000 employees to do the same thing. He writes that several large professional firms in London are subcontracting their typing to Taipei 9,000 miles away using telecommunications in order to get bargain prices. To compete, London typists are improving the level of their skills and offering services with more sophisticated software and equipment.

Here at home the single greatest change in the work force has been the number of women who now work. In 1970 it was forty-nine percent of the women between the ages of twenty and sixty-four years; in 1988 it was sixty-seven percent and by the year 2000, it is expected to reach eighty-one percent (10). Economists believe, however, that there is starting to be a change in attitude and behavior in women. After so many years of sacrificing their quality of life, many women are no longer willing to conduct business as it has "always" been done. A recent study by Wick & Co. of Wilmington, DE, found that women are not leaving middle management in droves to go home or to find better child care. Seventy-three percent quit to go to firms where they perceive they'll have a better chance of advancement; thirteen percent start their own businesses in order to make their own rules (11).

Dietitians who anticipate trends, keep their knowledge and skills on the cutting edge, and actively become involved in change by learning the tools of communication in business will fare the best. Those working in volatile markets where funding is not always assured, cutbacks are common, or employers' expectations, or new regulations, effect job satisfaction must approach their jobs more creatively or change jobs altogether.

ENTREPRENEURIAL/ INTRAPRENEURIAL R.D.

The 1990 membership survey of The American Dietetic Association revealed that 97.7 percent of ADA's members are women and that 69.6 percent are under the age of forty-six years. Eighty-four percent of dietitians are employed or work for themselves (12). For most dietitians their jobs are necessities, not just interesting diversions. They take their jobs very seriously.

Many dietitians who reach the top of their professional ladders look for new ways to grow. They want to be successful, recognized, and well paid for their expertise. Jean Yancey, a small business consultant in Denver, calls this their "X-Point" where they arrive at a decisive point and they feel they want/must do something different. It almost feels like starting over again, but this time on a much higher level of expertise.

Many new graduates see nutrition's potential In the marketplace and want to try something different.   They eagerly watch and listen to the role models who are blazing new trails, or they see markets and trails that no one has tapped.

For some, the answer is entrepreneurship: the chance to be their own boss, schedule their own time, and try out new services or products to make a profit.   Decision-making is streamlined, thus faster and often more effective. Changes in the marketplace can be answered almost "overnight," as compared to the response of a large corporation with many levels of management.

Another reason dietitians turn to entrepreneurship is to stimulate productivity and relieve boredom. A study by Robert Half International, reported in *USA Today* in 1990, that executives who remained in the same job for as little as two years showed a drop in creativity, energy, and performance. This problem is often remedied by seeking lateral career moves and periodic changes of responsibilities---running a business venture leaves little time to be bored.

The human qualities that are usually identified with entrepreneurs or intrapreneurs are creativity, ability to take risks, openness to experiences, and self-confidence. You not only want to keep up with the competition, you

4

want to lead it (13). You see business as a game---one that you will play to win. A survey called "What Sparks Entrepreneurs" in *USA Today* in September 1990, found that sixty-four percent start their own business to be their own boss, thirty-three percent did it to have more control in their lives over their work quality, schedules, and families, and three percent did it for the money. A survey in July 1991 *Home-Office Computing* reported that being boss was number one, but over sixty percent wanted more control, and over thirty-five percent became entrepreneurs to earn more money.

Self-employment with its uncertainties, is not for everyone. The majority of dietitians still prefer to work where the economic risk is more limited, where fringe benefits are offered, and where support systems function well enough to allow the dietitian freedom to do what she or he does best. Thus, many have chosen intrapreneurship---to work as employees while pursuing new opportunities for revenue generation, improved public relations, or meeting the needs of their customers better. The dietetic profession needs both in today's competitive markets.

The following chapters will give insights into what employed intrapreneurs are doing in hospital-based clinical practice, food service, public health, education, and in nontraditional dietetic careers. They will explain the logical steps in creating a business venture, give examples to illustrate points, and answer questions commonly asked by new and seasoned entrepreneurs. The term "entrepreneur" will be used to identify both self-employed and employed businesspeople.

THE FUTURE

Presently, the marketing window of opportunity for nutrition is wide open. Nutrition has never been a "hotter" topic and it will remain so for some years to come. How fortunate and exciting that this should happen during our professional careers! However, as with all great ideas and trends, it too will fade as our very large target markets become saturated with nutrition information and products.

Nonetheless, there always will be an ongoing need for good nutritional information as each new generation goes out for sports, has babies, fights obesity, prevents or recovers from illness through good eating, and wants to stay healthy as it grows older.

Career avenues for dietitians who distinguish themselves will abound. Competing successfully in the new markets of the future may require experience and education outside the required nutrition curriculum and traditional career settings. Today, dietitians are learning about media broadcasting, advanced business management, exercise physiology, law, marketing and sales, product manufacturing, professional writing, highly effective patient counseling skills, and public speaking to top organizations. As is often said when faced with so much opportunity, only the person's imagination and energy will limit what she or he can do.

In a speech to undergraduates at Cornell University in 1990, Tom Peters gave advice that fits this topic well. He said (14):

5

1. **Don't think, do.** You only really know if something works after you try it, so don't spend all your time and energy planning. You will never make all of the right decisions before you start something. Things get better as you go and apply what you learn.

2. **Fail with flair.** Novelist Tom Robbins: "If you've any sense at all you must have learned by now that we pay just as dearly for our triumphs as we do for our defeats. Go ahead and fail. But fail with wit, fail with grace, fail with style." Sadly, all too many newly minted college grads, and forty year olds, fear failure--that in the end is to fear living itself.

3. **Listen naively.** Don't just listen, but also "hear." Hearing is about empathy and taking the time to respect others. If you are not empathetic (by this point), I don't know what to tell you-- except, don't be the boss.

4. **Ask dumb questions.** You couldn't possibly know all the answers, so ask and improve your ability to solve problems.

5. **Get others involved.** It takes time to listen, hear, trust, and gain commitment, but it is time well spent. Others come to us with motivation and then we go about destroying it with demeaning attitudes and humiliating rules instead of enthusiasm for new ideas.

6. **Go where the action is.** The best, most successful chiefs and generals spend their most time at the firing line, and the least in the office.

7. **Make it fun.** All human endeavor is about emotion--zest, joy, pride, fun, and even crying are near the heart of any successful enterprise.

8. **Be Interesting!** Life's too short to waste time suppressing emotions, trying to be like the others, fearing rebuffs, or being fired. You will never please everyone.

So go nurture some very interesting failures and even better successes!

REFERENCES

1. Ciabattari, Jane: "When You Start Your Own Business," *Parade Magazine,* August 21, 1988.
2. Stacy, Carey: "Taking Issue," *Entrepreneurial Woman,* May/June, 1990.
3. Drucker, Peter: *Innovations and Entrepreneurship,* Harper & Row, New York, 1985.
4. Kanter, Rosabeth: *Change Masters: Innovation for Productivity in the American Corporation,* Simon & Schuster, New York, 1985.
5. Feinberg, Mortimer R. : "The Entrepreneurial Spirit," *Restaurant Business,* January 1986.
6. Pollan, Stephen and Mark Levine: "Playing To Win," *The Atlantic Monthly,* Fall 1988.
7. Brabec, Barbara: "Who's The Boss Now?," *OMNI Magazine,* March 1990.
8. Kunde, Diana: "Striking Out On Their Own," *The Dallas Morning News,* February 19, 1991.
9. Bolles, R. N.: *The 1989 What Color Is Your Parachute?,* Ten Speed Press, Berkeley, CA,1989.
10. Mathews, K.A. and J. Rodin: "Women's Changing Work Roles: Impact on Health, Family and Public Policy," *Am. Psycho.,* 44:1389-1393, 1989.
11. Lawlor, Julia: "Experience, Demographics in Their Favor," *USA Today,* June 1, 1991.
12. Selected information from the 1990 Membership Survey, The American Dietetic Association, *JADA,* September 1991.
13. Helm, Kathy King: *Becoming An Entrepreneur In Your Own Setting,* ADA Study Kit, 1991.
14. Peters, Tom: "Some Advice: Do. Fail. Laugh. Weep. And Be Interesting," *Dallas Business Journal,* February 12, 1990.

section 2

Business Ventures in Dietetic Practice

Words of Wisdom:

"We cannot direct the wind...But we can adjust the sails."

"Do not let what you cannot do interfere with what you can do."

John Wooden

Chapter 2

Hospital-based Clinical

Hospitals still employ the largest number of dietitians (40.9 percent) according to the 1990 census (1). The hospital environment is in a state of flux with mergers, funding cutbacks, turf protection, uninsured patients, and in some areas of the country, staff shortages. Any dietitian who shows leadership, a perception of the "whole" picture (not just their own department) and solutions to problems (not just awareness of them) is becoming highly prized.

Joan Ullrich, R.D., CNSD, director of clinical nutrition program development at UCLA Medical Center in Los Angeles, says that, "the most successful clinical dietitians are putting more emphasis in public relations, political networking, and interaction with other allied health professionals. Through publications, promotions, and coordination of hospital programs and national symposiums, these people work hard. Whatever they do is always an 'event' not an incident " (2). These are the people whom hospitals prize, promote, and stand behind.

Hospitals can offer dietitians the opportunity to use their nutrition knowledge and skills to help ill patients recover. Hospitals are a theater of excitement, high emotions and short time lines. Ideally, they are meeting places where highly educated professionals of varying health-related degrees come together, collaborate, and carry out treatments for the benefit of the resident patients. That business marketing philosophy is now changing to include patients who return home, or enter extended care facilities or hospices. It may include patients that can be rehabilitated at home without first entering the hospital. Many hospitals are also creating community and corporate outreach programs with health fairs and wellness or fitness themes. Others are publishing consumer newsletters, patient education materials, or opening Age Wave libraries for self-help reading for seniors.

Twenty years ago much of the clinical dietitian's day centered on routine tasks involved in passing and picking up and then checking over menus. Today, most clinical dietitians delegate the tasks that do not require their advanced level of education to dietetic technicians, diet aids, or computers. These dietitians are then free to spend the bulk of their time on the floors with the patients, their physicians, and the nursing staff. Depending upon their initiative, and encouragement or discouragement from above, clinical dietitians also become involved in a myriad of other projects. At times these sideline projects turn into full time positions highly prized by us all.

Clinical dietitians have helped develop hospital-based renal units, cardiac or sports rehabilitation centers, research units, and critical care institutes. Many have improved food delivery systems, and initiated diabetes, geriatric and prenatal education programs. Others created parenteral and enteral care teams, corporate and in-house wellness and weight loss programs, community health fairs, and nutrition assessment software. They have written diet manuals, cookbooks for their patients, educational booklets and software programs, and produced audio and video tapes for patient education. Clinical dietitians at St. Paul Medical Center in Dallas rotate taking an eight-day cruise in the Caribbean each year with diabetes or arthritis patients and provide entertaining nutrition classes (3).

To improve the nutritional status of their patients, clinical dietitians have created many new business ventures. The outpatient nutrition clinic is the most common addition to an inpatient nutrition department. It can serve two purposes: first, to follow up the progress of former inpatients with special nutritional needs, and second, for the community as a source of good preventive nutrition counseling. The clinic may be attached to the hospital. It may be in a store-front shopping area at a satellite emergency care clinic, or in a hospital-owned HMO somewhere else in the community.

Another business idea is the development of a nutrition component for a hospital-run home health care service or extended care facility. Developed to follow former patients, this service also cares for patients with long term, chronic illnesses like AIDs, cancer, eating disorders, dependency on tube feedings, or when patients are unable to care for themselves while recovering from illness or injury. Hospices also use the services of experienced clinical dietitians.

Hospital-based child care and elder care centers for well and ill clients are other business opportunities that include a dietitian's input. Usually day care centers will not allow children to come if they are running a fever or are sick. When an elderly parent or live-in relative is sick there is concern. This keeps many nurses, dietitians, and the rest of the hospital staff from coming to work, so hospitals are considering and a few have started day care for ill relatives. Some extend their programs to the community at large; others do not.

A hospital in Denton, Texas offers a program called "Lov'n Care" where staff and community residents sign up their children in advance. When a child is sick and the parents must go to work, the child can be taken to a special area in the hospital for the day (for a fee of $3/ hour with a four-hour minimum, and they even take credit cards).

Learning from her own experience and recognizing the need to market the clinical dietitian, Alice Smith, R.D., director of clinical dietetics and food service at Children's Memorial Medical Center in Chicago and her husband Phil, created a consultant service and manual how to inform and train hospitals to use their dietitians better. They show how an adequate number of trained clinical nutritionists on staff leads to more aggressive assessment and nutrition therapy. This results in fewer patients with malnutrition. A malnourished patient usually costs twice as much or more to care for as a patient who is not malnourished. Patients recover better and stay fewer days in the hospital, which can mean a big financial savings when the patient is uninsured or covered by DRGs. Some hospitals have gone out of business because of too many unpaid patient days.

Kathy Stephens, Ph.D., R.D., is director of food and nutrition service at Harris Hospital in Ft. Worth, Texas. She is successful in using her business and negotiating skills to sign several local HMOs, PPOs and private physician groups to contracts with the hospital's outpatient nutrition clinic. She approaches the process as a business agreement in which all parties benefit. Physicians' patients are cared for nutritionally at a time when they need the help most and the clinic has a steadier flow of patients that uses its staff better and generates a profit.

Most dietitians in the clinical setting, whether they are pursuing a business venture or just doing their regular duties, benefit from knowing and using more marketing strategies to promote themselves and their services, department, and profession. As they incorporate more cost/benefit analysis information and business communication tools, like proposals and financial projections, dietitians are often taken more seriously by management.

When asked why hospital-based clinical dietetics is changing and maturing, Judy Klopfenstein, M.S., R.D., director of food and nutrition services at Iowa Methodist Medical Center in Des Moines, Iowa, states, "personal initiative. If dietetic professionals find a specialty they enjoy, I encourage them to dig in and visibly show a real commitment to that interest. Our staff provides quality services and communicates this fact to everyone" (3). It is equally important to have supervisors like Judy who lead and encourage without micromanaging.

Given the right mix of adequate pay, adequate staff, and good support for creative, revenue-producing ideas, hospital dietitians could be in one of the most exciting practice areas of the 1990s.

REFERENCES

1. 1990 Census, The American Dietetic Association, *JADA,* September 1991.
2. FYI section, *JADA,* vol. 90, Jan. 1990.
3. *Courier,* The American Dietetic Association, February 1991.

Chapter 3

Food and Food Service

Dietitians who work directly with food are starting a very exciting time. As never before the public wants healthy food. Jobs associated with food from agriculture, hydroponic gardening and ranching, to food processing, marketing, retailing and food services are all experiencing profound change because of the public's interest in nutritious food.

Successful food service dietitians are coupling their knowledge of how to cook healthy with culinary skills to make the food look and taste wonderful. Others are finding new ways to reach their customers through improved marketing. Entrepreneurs find new twists to service such as home or office delivery, drive-thru, carry out, parking lot kiosks, and gift baskets. For people with their own line of food products, catalog sales and gourmet sections in grocery stores are reaching many new customers.

BUSINESS VENTURES

Practitioners with special interest in foods are writing cookbooks, teaching cooking classes, starting restaurants, and manufacturing foods. They are starting bakeries, delicatessens, catering businesses, room service for patients, low-cost senior meals in their cafeterias, Meals-on-Wheels, co-op groceries, and farmers' markets. They are manufacturing frozen healthy entrees. Others are creating computer management and recipe or menu analysis software programs. Dietitians are hired by food brokers and public relations firms to help market their food accounts' products.

To give some perspective on the potential in foods, consider the following examples of what other people are doing. A twenty-two-year-old homemaker in Tennessee saw a show on TV in 1982 on how cheesecakes are popular desserts. She took a week to perfect a recipe and nine years later she and her husband sell 1,500 cheesecakes per month (1). In 1986 a Missouri farmer sent a sample of his gourmet homemade mustard to a friend in the food business who immediately ordered 100,000 jars in thirty days. Although he couldn't deliver that fast, he did go into the food manufacturing and popcorn business and grossed over $1 million in 1989 (1). In 1986 a former executive with Beatrice Foods quit her job to start the first food company to prepackage meals for kids called My Own Meal, Inc. Four years later her company grossed over $5 million in sales (1).

Franchising is the fastest growing type of business venture in the food business. Joyce and Ted Rice invented T.J. Cinnamons Bakeries where you can watch fresh baked cinnamon rolls being made. Joyce was a

11

home economics teacher and Ted was a TV camera operator, and they wanted to do something that would give them an early retirement. In 1985 they invested all their savings in a custom van with a large window that Joyce could use during the summer to attend fairs, rodeos and flea markets to sell cinnamon rolls. She made so much the first summer that she quit her job and opened a store with a large window in a local mall at the base of glass elevators. Between the smell of the cinnamon and the interest at the window, they had people waiting out the door and down the mall. Five years later they have over 170 franchises nationwide.

CAREER PATHS IN FOOD and FOODSERVICE

Don Miller, R.D., CEC (Certified Executive Chef), president of Don Miller and Associates, says that, "Culinary skills are the missing link for dramatic success in dietetics. A hospital food service can produce food and service like a four-star restaurant. " His method for achieving such results includes empowering, training, and compensating his staff well, cooking fresh foods in smaller batches, increasing variety in the cafeteria, serving with flair, and changing the appearance of the dining room, patient trays and foods. Because he has built a reputation on renovating and turning hospital food services into money-making operations, he is called when a hospital is ready for that step.

Cheryl Hartsough-MacNeill, R.D., a certified chef apprentice, has used her expertise to consult at the Doral Spa Resort.   Spas are no longer seen as "fat farms," but instead most clients visit them to learn about healthy living, new ways of eating and fitting exercise into their lives.   Some spas use dietitians as guest speakers or food service consultants while others employ them as integral parts of their daily programs where every guest is individually counseled.

According to the American Culinary Federation, in 1990 there were 250,000 jobs available for trained chefs, and not enough graduates to fill the positions. This growing shortage means restaurants, hotels, and hospitals will resort to wooing chefs away from their current posts. The average starting pay for a chef is now $18,500, while average wages run about $37,500; however, executive chefs make as much as $210,000. A dietitian with a particular flair for cooking or baking might consider this complementary career option which should grow in interest given the public's desire for healthy food.

Another dietitian has created a career path for herself by becoming an expert in fish and shellfish. Dr. Joyce Nettleton, D.Sc., R.D., is a lecturer at Tufts University, a writer and consultant. The public's interest in fish has opened doors for cookbook authors, chefs, nutrition experts, researchers, and others.

Judy Ford Stokes, R.D., has built a business out of Atlanta that today offers management consulting services and kitchen design for major client accounts like convention centers and large correction facilities.   Her company hires registered dietitians and architects to help carry out the contracts. In addition to her business, Judy has held elected offices in

ADA's Council on Practice (COP) and served as president of ADA's Foundation.

Jim Rose, M.S., R.D., was a food service director who excelled in management and writing. He was ADA's most published author with seven books, six years as editor of Aspen's *Hospital Food and Nutrition Focus* newsletters, and hundreds of published articles. He was an accomplished speaker. He was a person who was happy when he had a lot of exciting things working simultaneously. He would often get up at 2 AM and have 10-20 pages written on a book, article, or speech before he left for work. At one hospital where he was the food service director, his contract specified that thirty percent of his time could be spent on creative projects and holding professional offices such as being elected COP Division of Management Chair and president of the American Hospital Association's American Society of Hospital Food Service Administrators.

Dietitians also work for food brokers in sales to food accounts, on healthy food marketing campaigns, in customer service, and in professional or health care marketing. Pharmacuetical companies use dietitians in sales, marketing, and research for their line of meal replacement products and formulas.

Annette Briggs, R.D., Irving Health Care System, Dallas, TX, started a hospital-based catering service as a result of positive feedback at catered hospital events. When asked what advice she would have for dietetic professionals starting a money-making project in an institution she stated, "Communicate your thoughts to administrators early and keep them informed at all times. Research your ideas and come up with a business plan. Monitor costs and revenues closely (2)."

Wolf Rinke, Ph.D., R.D., recently became an entrepreneur after thirty years in the food service industry. He is taking his skills in speaking, motivation and writing on the road with a lecture series, one or more books, and audio tape program on "winning." Consulting, writing and speaking are natural extensions of a person's career when he or she is ready to grow in new directions or have a change of scenery.

Dietitians with special skills in food marketing, service and technology can generate increased revenue, public relations, and goodwill for their employers through successful ventures. Given good ideas and management, adequate financing, great staff support, and a lot of work a new food venture could be "an overnight success."

REFERENCES

1. *Entrepreneur* magazine, June 1990.
2. For Your Information, *JADA,*, vol. 91 no.1, January 1991.

HERMAN

"You the guy who ordered the 'Breakfast Special'?"

Chapter 4

Public Health

The need to "sell" their ideas is not new to public health dietitians. Some have had to become highly motivated as they experience budget cuts that threaten to eliminate popular, highly successful services. Others generate revenue to help cover their departmental budgets. Taking the challenge, community-based dietitians create many marketable services and products, including educational materials, wellness programs, school-teaching tools, lecture series, community food banks, and farmers' markets.

ENTREPRENEURIAL NUTRITIONISTS

Bettie Thomas, R.D., a WIC nutritionist in Alabama, created a very comprehensive, innovative breastfeeding program in 1989. In 1991 she estimates they reached five hundred new mothers for a fiscal expenditure of $120. Bettie invites pregnant women interested in breastfeeding to a monthly social at a local library where they are given an introduction to breastfeeding.

Women are matched with BEST Friends (BEST stands for Breastfeeding Education and Support Team), WIC clerks trained to reinforce, support, and make referrals (based on a modified version of the Tennessee Nutrition Project). A match also is made with a BEST Buddy, a WIC mother that breastfed her infant. The Buddy provides support throughout the prenatal, hospital, and postpartum phases. Funding cuts for group classes and limited time for individual consults makes this support system invaluable.

Along with support, Bettie developed a fun public relations and goodwill project. She visits each new breastfeeding mother at the hospital and gives her a new pair of crocheted baby booties. The booties are handmade by elderly shut-ins on the Food Share program who work two hours for the community in return for earning a coupon that lets them pay $13 for $36 worth of groceries. Yarn shops and private citizens donate the yarn. The new mothers also receive a baby's blanket (donated by a local hospital for their patients) with machine sewn border (by Bettie) in blue and pink and a hand-stenciled design that reads "Best Fed." Each letter is painted a different pastel color of fabric paint from a craft store. This idea won the "1990 Governor's Award" and an award from the Center for Disease Control. It shows that you can do unbelievable things with a dedicated leader.

15

Anita Owen, M.A., R.D., is an innovative, entrepreneurial community-based dietitian. Her early work in public health led to the development of the first statewide WIC program in the nation. One of her initial contributions to ADA was the development of the first National Nutrition Week (now Month) (1). Anita has a knack for knowing how and where to network so that changes can be negotiated and made for the improvement of the public health.

Many public health nutritionists are going into the public arena to educate the more well-off, healthy population. In Knoxville, Tennessee over five years ago, the public health nutritionists were marketing lecture series and competing for wellness programs with dietitians in private practice. They had the skill, ability, and flair to be very successful.

Some public health nutritionists in Florida have written educational materials for different target markets that they sell to hospitals, schools, and private physicians. Others have written wellness programs that they market to hospitals and corporations.

WHAT MAKES AN ENTREPRENEURIAL PROJECT WORK?

In a marketing workshop with the Georgia public health nutritionists in 1991, dietitians identified five characteristics that made their entrepreneurial projects successful. **First,** the clients' needs are being satisfied, not the administrator's or the dietitian's. **Second,** they have a multidisciplined power base. In other words, the physician(s), nurses, and significant others buy into the idea. **Third,** the more fun or interesting the project is, the better---for clients and staff. **Fourth,** although there are exceptions like the earlier example, money is often a limiting factor. Of course there are alternative sources like grants, private and corporate donations, and charging the client---and those may become far more important alternatives in the future. **Fifth,** adequate promotion is essential so people know about it.

Public relations is free publicity that is a valuable promotional tool in social marketing. Exciting public health messages attract air time and print space. Planned activities with celebrities, corporate backing, and media coverage all tied to a health message are commonplace today.

Government funding that comes and goes often thwarts program planning by public health nutritionists. In the future perhaps the lean times will be tempered with more outside funding for projects, and revenue generated by exciting, highly competitive products or services.

REFERENCES

1. C. Vickery and N. Cotugna: *Legends and Legacies: Pacesetters in the Profession of Dietetics,* Kendall Hunt, Dubuque, Iowa, 1990.

Chapter 5

Education

Entrepreneurial dietetic educators are authors, lecturers, consultant, or business owners. Many conduct market research to decide the needs of their present students and those of new target markets. With fewer college-age students in the population, educators are coming up with very innovative ways to attract new students. Business-oriented educators are covering business and marketing skills in their curricula. Student community rotations and seminars include dietitians who are business owners, inventors, publishers, and other innovative role models, along with more traditional ones.

INNOVATIVE EDUCATORS

Barbara Taylor, R.D., internship director at Presbyterian Hospital in Dallas, developed a rotation in their interns' program that includes a week at The Greenhouse spa, commonly associated with Neiman-Marcus. The interns also spend six days at the Fairmont Hotel, and one day each with a pharmaceutical sales dietitian, the ARA contract food company, and dietitians at Cooper's Aerobic Center.

Nell Robinson, Ph.D., R.D., at Texas Christian University, Ft. Worth, and Nancy Wellman, Ph.D., R.D. at Florida International University in Miami, were successful in having their institutions give science credit for their nutrition course for nonmajors. Similarly, it was reported at a Competitive Edge marketing seminar several years ago that one nutrition educator wrote a note to everyone in her course for non-nutrition majors who earned a "A" or "B." The note said she was proud of their work and wondered if they had thought of majoring in nutrition since they obviously had ability in the subject. It worked.

Sara Parks, MBA, R.D., associate dean, Pennsylvania State University, in University Park, has been innovative and entrepreneurial all of her career. She wrote, along with several others, the first "extended" associate degree for diet technicians. This enabled students to continue working and complete the course in their off time without coming to campus. For over twenty years she has taught a senior year course that forces students to bring all of their acquired knowledge and skill together to design a hospitality or health care operation for the year 2010 (1).

Libby Piner, R.D., former director of a dietetic technician program in Denver used her food service talents and her son's programming knowledge to produce a software program for menu planning that they are marketing to dietitians and the foodservice industry.

Vel Rae Burkholder, M.S., R.D., associate professor at North Dakota University, Fargo, has spent the last year or so working with a dietetic graduate student to develop nutrition assessment tools specifically for senior citizens who live in extended care facilities. Such tools will become even more important and in demand as the American population ages (2).

Sonja Connor, R.D., researcher in the Lipid-Atherosclerosis study at the Oregon Health Sciences University's Department of Medicine, in Portland, developed a unique eating habits questionnaire to help dietitians quickly evaluate the composition of a patient's diet (2). She co-authored, along with William Connor, M.D., the best selling book, *The New American Diet.*

The dental curricula at Tuft's University in Boston has included nutrition for many years. For many dental programs and practicing dentists, nutrition is still a new, controversial addition to their practice. The key to bringing nutrition into dental practice, according to nutritionist Carole Palmer, Ed.D., associate professor at Tufts, "is making it relevant to dentistry" (3).

HOW EDUCATORS BRING ENTREPRENEURISM INTO THE CLASSROOM

Nutrition is the body of knowledge we possess that makes our profession unique. Where dietitians need help is in developing the skills that act as vehicles to exploit the full potential of our knowledge. Those vehicles include communication skills that are unique and exciting, and a knack for presenting nutrition in "new" ways. Marketing knowledge and experience are crucial to the development of services and products that sell because they fit the needs of their markets and the markets know about them. Business skills help dietitians get funding and political support for their projects. They help dietitians know how to protect their intellectual properties in order to build worth, as well as plan, manage, and fiscally control projects. Through understanding more about how businesses function, a dietitian becomes more of an asset to any organization, whether as an employee or consultant.

Educators are exposing students to new skills through including the information in existing courses and by adding rotations in less traditional settings. They invite guest speakers to class and act as role models by becoming entrepreneurs themselves. Students will grasp bits and pieces about entrepreneurism using these ideas, but they will learn it best by creating an idea of their own. By developing a new idea from embryonic conception through the business and marketing plans into implementation, business with all of its excitement and challenges will come to life.

Alanna Dittoe, R.D., a private practitioner in the San Francisco area has taught a course on entrepreneurism at U.C. Berkeley the past several years. Her course has four sessions of didactic information, followed by lectures by guest dietitians, class discussion, and solving typical scenarios that arise in business. Students bring news and magazine clippings that

18

show changes in the business climate, or new venture ideas or fads in nutrition.

FUNDING BEING CUT ?   HERE IS A SUGGESTION

In Stephen Covey's book, *The Seven Habits of Highly Effective People,* pages 224-226, he tells of his experience with a large banking institution that asked him to evaluate and improve their management training program (4). It was supported by an annual budget of $750,000. New college graduates were put through twelve two-week assignments over a six month period in order to learn a working sense of the industry. At the end of the training they were assigned as assistant managers at various branch banks.

The most difficult part of the evaluation was trying to get a clear picture of the desired results. They asked top executives, "What should these people be able to do when they finish the program?" The answers were vague and often contradictory. The training program dealt with methods, not results.

Covey suggested a pilot program based on "learner-controlled instruction." This was a win/win agreement that involved identifying specific objectives and criteria that would demonstrate the trainees' accomplishment. It also identified the guidelines, resources, accountability, and consequences that would result when the objectives were met. The consequences in this case were earning a higher salary and becoming an assistant manager.

It took a lot of work to hammer out the objectives. Covey asked,"What is it you want them to understand about accounting, or marketing, and so on?" Finally thirty-nine behavioral objectives with criteria attached were identified. The trainees were highly motivated and finished all the objectives in three-and-a-half weeks.

The top managers were resistant because they felt the new people would not be "seasoned," and besides it seemed too easy. So eight additional, very tough criteria, were added in order to give the executives the assurance that the people were adequately prepared. The new trainees cooperated with each other and met with managers one-on-one to ask for help. They finished the additional objectives in one-and-a-half weeks. The whole program was reduced from six months into five weeks!

There is a difference between this example where employees stay inside the system to get more on-the-job training and our dietetic internships where we give the hands-on training before sending graduates into the world. But, there may be a lesson to be learned here that could apply to our dietetic programs that could revolutionize our training. This concept may only save two or three months on a nine-month or year long program, but that savings could save an internship program.

REFERENCES

1. C. Vickery and N. Cotugna: *Legends and Legacies: Pacesetters in the Profession of Dietetics,* Kendall Hunt, Iowa, 1990.
2. Dietitians develop innovative nutrition assessment tools: *Courier, ADA,* March 1991.
3. Dietitians focus on the role of nutrition in dentistry: *Courier,* ADA, August 1991.
4. Covey, S.: *Seven Habits of Highly Effective People,* Simon and Schuster, New York, 1989.

Chapter 6

Nontraditional Jobs in Dietetics

(Adapted from "Finding Nontraditional Jobs in Dietetics" by Kathy King Helm, RD, April 1991 *JADA*. Reprinted by permission of The American Dietetic Association, copyright 1991.)

Interest in nontraditional dietetic jobs is increasing. Twenty years ago when a dietitian became an RD, there was only a handful of employment arenas. Today, the "well" population, with its interest in fitness and healthy foods, has a seemingly insatiable desire for nutrition information. This has opened the door to employment at spas and fitness centers and business and industry, product invention, media and marketing, consulting, book publishing, sports nutrition, speaking, and private practice.

A wave of curiosity always surges through an audience of dietitians and dietetic technicians when a peer mentions an unusual, especially a challenging or higher-paying, job. At ADA Annual Meeting the past two years, sessions on new career avenues and entrepreneurship have had standing-room-only audiences.

WHY THE GROWING INTEREST?

Many practitioners and students are drawn to the excitement and challenge of new jobs with less routine and structure. Others enjoy the wellness philosophy, and still others like working with athletes and sports or educating the public.

It is understandable that dietitians are reexamining their options considering the uncertainties in today's job markets, the relatively few traditional positions with lateral career mobility; and the fact that dietetics ranked the "worst paying profession for the amount of required education" among the 250 U.S. professions listed in *The Jobs Rated Almanac* (1). Dietetics was ranked overall *above* nursing, social work and physical therapy, however, because there is less stress and physical demands on the job and the working environment is better. The dietetics profession tied with protestant ministers in total points!

In the 1990 ADA Membership Survey, of the 30,199 dietitians who answered the question on their primary employment setting, 8,088 or 26.7%, *over one quarter of the membership,* indicated settings other than employed food service, education, public health, and hospital inpatient or extended-care facility. Sixty-one percent indicated they work in consultation, private practice, for an HMO, physician, clinic or ambulatory-care center, or for a for-profit organization (food company, public relation firm, television station, and other settings) as their secondary place of work. Of the 1,539 dietetic technicians answering the question on primary work setting, 118 or 7.6%, indicated the above less traditional settings. Eleven DTRs even indicated they were in private practice (2).

In a survey I conducted in 1990 of dietetic education institutions and their students, 58% of the dietetics students said "yes" and 23% said "maybe" they would like to pursue nontraditional dietetics careers eventually. Dietetic technician students answered 30% "yes" and 35% "maybe."

In the same survey, however, only three of the eighty-one institutions responding offered a course on dietetic business or entrepreneurial skills, which may be useful to those pursuing nontraditional jobs. Eleven offered some of the information in other courses, and twenty-one reported that business courses are offered by their institutions. Twelve dietetics departments (15%) were considering adding a course on these topics in 1990-1991.

WHAT OTHER KNOWLEDGE OR SKILLS MAY BE NEEDED?

Consultant accounts, employers, and business peers want a dietitian with the same personal qualities that make a dietitian successful in a traditional job and one who keeps up with the cutting-edge information in her or his area of specialty, but they also want someone who is self-confident and self-motivated.

It also helps to have a working knowledge of the tools of business such as letters of agreement and contracts, financial balance sheets and budgets, and business and marketing plans. Previous business experience is beneficial, but most learn it along the way. Each experience, whether positive or negative, usually has something of value to offer the entrepreneurial dietitian.

Next, business demands skills that set the dietitian or dietetic technician apart from the crowd. It could be exceptional speaking or writing ability; counseling skills; negotiation or selling expertise; computer, financial, or research background; or the ability to manage a venture or business. The value of a practitioner's personality should not be underestimated, and neither should the skills acquired from experience.

Gail Levey, R.D., ADA Ambassador and media spokesperson states, "To get started in media you have to jump at everything even when you aren't sure you can do it. When you are in unfamiliar territory, you just have to be more prepared. When someone calls and wants you to do something, be honest if you have never done it, but let them know you would love to give it a try."

Dawn Schiffhauer, R.D., together with Dr. Theodore Van Itallie developed a multimillion- dollar weight loss company based in New York City with five sites. Dawn became vice president and directed the entire start up of the business including the program development, planning, hiring, and training of 150 employees and opening the new sites. She credits her supervisory skills to the fact she was the oldest of six children and had experience since a young age (3).

Bettye Nowlin, R.D., is program director of the Dairy Council of California, and a member of ADA's Board of Directors. Her employer is known for its innovative programming and training of professionals. For the past 22 years she has grown with the organization using her background in home economics education, dietetics, and public health (3).

Gail Becker, R.D., is owner of Gail Becker Associates, Inc., a New York public relations firm which employs seventeen people, including four dietitians. Gail admits that she uses her skills in managing employees, creating marketing campaigns, and building interpersonal relationships, as much as she uses her nutrition skills.

Elaine Chaney, M.S., R.D., is vice president of worldwide marketing for Groen, a kitchen equipment and services company. Her exceptional skill in managing projects from inception to successful roll-out and eventual financial success has made her an asset to her employer.

WHERE DO YOU FIND THESE NEW JOBS?

Often the skill that distinguishes a person the most is her or his ability for self-promotion, because, in the nontraditional job arena, communication links are less formal and structured. People learn about qualified practitioners through resumes, personal interviews, mutual friends, and acquaintances; through membership in organizations and on committees; through networking, publishing, and speaking. Dietitians find jobs by looking around, talking to people, becoming known, and marketing their particular area of expertise.

Using her years of food service experience, Char Norton, R.D., president of Norton and Associates in Houston, consults to food service operations on staffing considerations, evaluation of bids and contracts, and general trouble-shooting. Her clients are from all over the United States, therefore, she has special marketing needs for high visibility on a national basis. Her national office as a COP Division Chair allowed peers to get to know her and the quality of her work. Networking is especially important for dietitians who pursue consulting and other nontraditional careers where communication channels are more informal.

Leni Reed, R.D., originator of Supermarket Savvy and its related products, has a knack for networking. This has proven to be very beneficial in the development and promotion of her business, especially with people in the media and food industries and with dietitians.

Most independent practitioners will tell you that their good jobs came to them upon referral---career experts suggest that 70-80 percent of employment opportunities actually come from referrals. How do you get the referrals? **Become known and become known for doing something very well! Networking, contacts, and excellent output attracts others to you.**

New markets don't always know the range of a dietitian's expertise, so part of a practitioner's time is spent teaching new markets how to use the services the dietitian offers. In an article in *JADA*, Sneed and Burkhalter stress that registered dietitians need to market their skills to restaurants and restaurant corporations (4). Talk to people and let them get to know you. Join professional and trade groups outside of dietetics. Go talk to the people who can hire you in new markets.

Carolyn O'Neil, M.S., R.D., of Cable News Network, Atlanta, had to sell herself and her potential in braodcasting to the management in order to get her job. After she got it, she worked long hours with very little support staff until her segments became established. She was willing to do it to start on the ground floor of a new, exciting venture.

In the Dallas area, a few of us are trying the concept of peer mentoring. Three or four of us try to meet or talk monthly to go over recent projects and ask for advice. We all have different areas of interest and expertise, but not so different that we can't share and advise the others on how to negotiate an agreement or attract a new target market. Sometimes there's just simple phone calls to ask about the wording in a brochure or to choose between a number of possible trade names for a new project. Each of us has our own trade secrets. We ethically respect each other's trade secrets and yet share openly, which has proved extremely supportive and productive.

HOW CAN YOU PREPARE FOR NONTRADITIONAL JOBS?

Access into new career avenues is different for each job and each dietitian. For some, it's as simple as being at the right place at the right time. Other positions are the result of calculated, progressive growth. It sometimes comes with a large financial investment in advanced education, media training, volunteer hours to learn the ropes, self-promotion campaigns, writing for publications, and seminar and organization fees to learn new markets and skills.

Mentors and peers, along with paid and volunteer small business counselors, can help practitioners determine how to get where they want to go professionally. Several national and state dietetic practice and interest groups are implementing mentoring systems in order to facilitate members helping members.

In business, it is very common to have several mentors or wise peers to call upon in different areas of expertise to act as sounding boards. In return, that person reciprocates with time, friendship, loyalty, or whatever it is that satisfies the other party.

Traditional dietetic education gives a good background in clinical nutrition, nutrition assessment, general management, and foodservice management. Smith and Wellman, in their *JADA* article, "Spas: New practice setting for dietitians," suggest that "educational programs should include more opportunities for development of contemporary skills to ensure that graduates can compete successfully in today's job market" (5).

Robin Spencer Palmisano, R.D., is an attorney in the health-care division of a law firm in New Orleans. After becoming a dietitian, she decided she wanted to become more specialized so she started a law degree instead of a masters in nutrition. Her father was a lawyer and she had always respected the field. She represents health-care providers, physicians, medical group practices and cases involving management of hazardous/infectious waste. Advanced education helped her find the kind of job that keeps her challenged (3).

23

Jackie Berning, Ph.D., R.D., is a consultant to the U.S. Swimming Team and the Denver Broncos Football Team. She just recently completed her advanced degree that gave her exposure to exercise physiologists, sports teams and athletes. Jackie initially volunteered her services in order to get to know people.

Barry Wishner, R.D., a Woodside, California speaker and soon to be published author, says, "Other published authors told me to only plan to write one major book in my life, but have it the very best I can do. They said that to really sell in the '1990s' a book or speach can't be homogenized from everyone else's ideas and publications. It needs to have original ideas and news. Do your own research to make your work unique. One good book and its publicity should open doors in speaking and consulting for many years to come." To that end, Barry and his staff are currently interviewing over 1,200 corporate CEOs in preparation for his book manuscript.

BECOMING A CONSULTANT

Becoming a consultant in any practice area of dietetics is a growing career alternative for dietitians. You may even find that you can generate a larger income, sooner, by pursuing contracts as a consultant to food companies, public relations firms, nursing homes, small rural hospitals, wellness programs, sports and cardiac rehabilitation centers, and so on.

Several factors influence your chances of becoming a consultant who is in demand. While many consultants prosper and enjoy high incomes, others are just getting by. Besides having specialized experience or training, success in the consulting business is a function of effective marketing, according to Howard Shenson, a recognized authority on marketing consultant services (6). His surveys have found that as important as specialty, location, contacts, education, and other factors may be, they really do not have as great an impact on your consulting profits as marketing does. His five marketing strategies for building a successful consulting practice are (6):

- **Know the market.** What is the market willing to pay for? Do market research. Be widely read. Read the news and consider how it will effect your clients. What opportunities or threats does it reveal?

- **Make a commitment to target and niche marketing.** There is no universal product that everyone will want to buy. Divide your markets into segments that you can reach easily and affordably.

- **Make your services cost-effective for the client.** Position yourself so your clients either save money or perceive your value to be higher than your fee.

- **Be a troubleshooter.** Take problems that your clients may or may not know they have, and give your clients a proposal on what you could do for them.

- **Create an image and a reputation**. These cause clients to think of you first when they have a problem or need.

24

Shenson found that the type of marketing strategies used by people who made over $110,000 per year versus under $55,000 per year varied greatly (6). The top performers promoted themselves through:

1. Prospects referred by clients

2. Lectures to civic, trade and professional audiences

3. Writing articles, books, newsletters for trade, professional, and civic audiences.

The people who made below $55,000 marketed themselves primarily through:

1. Cold personal calls

2. Direct mail brochures or sales letters

3. No -charge consultations to pre-qualified leads

Successful consultants learn to work well with their clients so that the client feels he is getting the best service available for the money. Good consultants are careful to discuss with clients the expected outcomes before and during a project. Communication is open and frequent with possible problems being top agenda items. It is imperative that clients be satisfied.

Locally, consultants can offer program development, nutrition presentations, in-service training, computer programming, set up, or system analysis, recipe development, kitchen design, writing, individual or group counseling, management, or sales.

For dietitians who want to consult to nursing homes, Ann Hunter, M.S., R.D., author of *Policies and Procedures for Long Term Care Dietetic Services (7)*, suggests that a practitioner can read sources like her book and *Nutrition in Long Term Care Facilities* by Anna C. Jernigan, M.S., R.D., from ADA to understand what is expected of you for that type of consultant work.

On a national scale consulting is especially suited to experienced practitioners with established professional networks and contacts. Those with recognized reputations as experts in their fields. Consultant positions on this scale could include program development, media work or nutrition education materials for spa chains, government, hospital and business agencies, the food or pharmaceutical industries, public relations firms, national or state health-related services and so on.

As formerly stable positions in dietetics are cut due to budgetary or philosophical changes, many dietitians are rethinking what they have to offer. Employers can keep their especially qualified and upwardly mobile dietitians happier in their work perhaps by allowing more flexibility in their scheduling, which could include outside consulting with noncompeting accounts.

SPEAKING

Speaking is one of the best promotion tools an entrepreneur can use. However, it does not come easily to many people. Controlling and yet exciting a large group while one speaks is even more challenging. Following are some preplanning ideas that will make speaking engagements more predictable and enjoyable for you.

Ask for a speaking fee. When a group pays for a speaker, it often spends more time and effort in promoting the speech and the turnout is better. When you are paid to speak, you often put the talk as a higher priority, come better prepared, and give a better presentation.

Set minimums on the size of the group you will speak to. If a group in your area wants you to speak, and by reputation you know that their turnouts are poor, especially if the fee is low, state that you request groups to have at least twenty people (or whatever number) present. If they still want to have you, they will accept the commitment. We have all had the experience where we drive across town at night to find an obscure building and give an elaborate presentation to three people.

Find out as much as you can about the group you are going to speak to. What is the range in ages? What are the percentages of men, women, and children? What are their educational backgrounds and do they know much about nutrition, weight loss, fads, or whatever? Will other speakers be on the program with you, or speak the week before or after on a similar subject? What specifically do they want you to speak on and highlight? *What are some human interest items about the group or individuals that will personalize the talk without embarrassing anyone?*

Find out about the building, the room, audiovisual capabilities, and reprinting of handouts. Request a letter of confirmation on the time, date, place, topic, expense reimbursement, and fee. People who speak regularly usually ask that a one week (or two) cancellation clause be added for local talks and thirty days for national ones. In case you become ill keep names of substitute speakers available. Be sure to state that you want to have your business cards, brochures, and order blanks for your book or whatever available at the speech.

Before accepting a speaking engagement to school groups, find out about the groups and the school policies. The last ten years willing speakers have reported frustrating experiences while trying to teach teenagers and children who were not adequately disciplined or prepared to hear the topic. Substitute teachers are not always welcomed unless someone with authority is also present for the talk. Presentations before kids are challenging and enlightening. Props, student involvement, and question and answer sessions are always welcomed more than a straight oral presentation. It can be great fun!

Be sure to get the name and phone number of the person contacting you and write the date down in your calendar.

If you are really serious about becoming a speaker and you seem to have some flair for it, consider joining a local speaking group like Toastmasters, or get training from a professional speaker or drama coach. Consider joining the National Speakers Association and attending their conventions.

Look at the topics you choose to speak on. For more exposure and money, consider speaking on topics that are of interest to all allied health professionals, or to business people on longevity, energy, disease prevention, or whatever, through nutrition. What could you teach other groups about management, employee relations, juggling family and career, or other originally researched topic?

Consider what elements you could add to your speeches to make them entertaining and memorable. For example, could you write a self-assessment questionnaire, or offer a variety of media (audio tapes, video, slides, overheads, etc.), or use audience interaction, or problem-solving scenarios. What props could you use? What elements of humor or fun can you interject?

LEAD, FOLLOW, OR GET OUT OF THE WAY

Innovative practitioners will continue to lead our profession into new, nontraditional job markets. We as a profession need to identify these trailblazers and let them teach us how to find these new career avenues. We should be willing to learn about new avenues of practice and act as mentors to our younger members. Or, recognize when someone is willing to take the risk and support that individual with your goodwill and enthusiasm. Or, get out of the way because we need that type of growth and experimentation to take place in dietetics today (8).

REFERENCES

1. Krantz, L.: *The Jobs Rated Almanac,* New World Almanac, New York, 1988.
2. Selected Information from 1990 ADA Membership Database, The American Dietetic Association, *JADA,*Chicago, September 1991.
3. "You've Come A Long Way, Baby!:" *Restaurants and Institutions,* October 16, 1989.
4. Sneed, J. and J.P. Burkhalter: "Marketing nutrition in restaurants: a survey of current practices and attitudes," *JADA,* April 1991.
5. Smith, J. and N. Wellman: "Spas: new practice setting for dietitians," *JADA,* April 1991.
6. Shenson, Howard: "Surefire Strategies For Making It As a Consultant," *Home-Office Computing,* April 1991.
7. Hunter, Ann: *Policies and Procedures For Long Term Care Dietetic Services,* Aspen Publishers, Inc., 1990.
8. Helm, Kathy King: "Risk taking isn't risky like it used to be," *JADA,* April 1989.

Chapter 7

Is Self-Employment For You?

We hear about individuals who start their own businesses "to fill a need for counseling outside the hospital" or "to concentrate on wellness"---but what makes these individuals want to do such a thing in the first place? What drives some to do it, while others only talk of it? What character traits distinguish entrepreneurs from employees? How do you tell if you're one of them?

There are few universal criteria that are common to all successful entrepreneurs. The personal qualities, experience, or financial resources that were necessary for one entrepreneur's success may be less important for another. Encouraging potential entrepreneurs merely to have years of experience in dietetics without regard to the type and quality of experience is not well founded.

WHAT DOES IT TAKE?

A successful entrepreneur has many areas of expertise that should be developed. These areas include a thorough working knowledge of how a business operates (often learned on the job), and an appreciation for marketing and financial management. Expertise in the areas of dietetics or foods that the business will offer and communication skills are essential. It is important that a businessperson develop his or her own unique areas of specialty.

The character of entrepreneurs is also extremely important. They need a fierce dedication to achievement. They must have perseverance and they must be willing to take risks. Enthusiasm is essential. They are usually intellectually curious and open to new ideas and methods of doing something better. Successful entrepreneurs know (or learn) how to be tough, how to accept criticism, and how to make quick decisions. Personal integrity is crucial. The most successful strive for short-term excellence on every project or they do not agree to do it. They must be able to accept responsibility and stick by commitments (1).

As a nutrition counselor it is important to be people oriented, empathetic, and exceptionally good in communicating with others. As media spokespersons, public speakers and consultants, dietitians must develop their verbal and nonverbal communication skills, and the powers to reason and organize.

28

There is no guarantee that a new business will show an immediate profit. Individuals starting their own business cannot be prone to discouragement or boredom. A successful entrepreneur is a realist as well as a dreamer---reaching for the stars, while maintaining a firm, earthly footing.

Successful entrepreneurs learn from others because so many new skills are unfamiliar, and because most new ventures are solo projects. Many will set up informal mentor relationships with highly respected authorities who have experience and insight beyond that of the entrepreneur. They then learn from and consult with those persons on major decisions. Others will network and share ideas and problems with other entrepreneurs.

WHY CHOOSE SELF-EMPLOYMENT?

Dietitians on the verge of leaving employee status for that of self-employment find that being an employee no longer gives them what they need. It is as if they have come to the end of a certain passage. They can no longer grow in the present environment. Venturing into the unknown becomes necessary in order to continue personal and career growth.

Other reasons for becoming self-employed are to gain flexibility of time, to be your own boss, or to be with small children at home. You might do it to follow patient care better, to create and implement programs, to do a variety of work, or to promote yourself for greater profit and recognition.

The potential exists to make it in a big way and if successful, to make much more money then you ever could as an employee in a traditional job at today's wages. There is a tremendous swelling of pride in your work and in yourself as you bring to fruition projects that you originate. In society as a whole, entrepreneurs receive the approval and respect of many people who realize the commitment and effort entrepreneurship exemplifies.

What Price Is Paid?

Many of the benefits granted the employee, for example, regular paychecks, paid sick leave, pension plans, health insurance programs, regular working hours, and vacation time are no longer givens when you are your own boss. It may dawn like a revelation for the new entrepreneur that if he doesn't work a day, he doesn't get paid. There are no benefits when self-employed except what you provide for yourself.

In logical and practical terms the possible risks of being an entrepreneur can include financial and emotional insecurity (at times), a large time and effort commitment, no paid benefits, a financial investment ($10,000-$40,000 or more initially), and family patience.

Not for Everyone

A point that needs to be made is you can't just assume that since you have good ideas, money, lots of energy, and the right credentials you *should* start

HERMAN

"Cold lunch today ... I'm going out."

your own business. You might also think about going into business and industry, catering, consulting, management, or other nontraditional employment avenues. As mentioned, good progressive corporations are starting to recognize the value of hiring more creative individuals who are looking for other career alternatives, but want paychecks and benefits.

Successful entrepreneurs agree that the positive aspects of being a business owner far outweigh the negative ones. However, most people who tried it and then stopped, state they did learn a lot, but the commitment had been too great for what they had to show. Starting a new small business is *certainly not for everyone* and it is *not* the only answer professionally. The dietetic profession needs both entrepreneurs and intrapreneurs.

The negative aspects of starting a business are very real but certainly not insurmountable when a nutritionist does careful research, and develops well thought-out solutions. The fear of the unknown is often more paralyzing than what really happens.

MAJOR REASONS WHY BUSINESSES FAIL

The major reasons businesses fail include:

1. **The product or service is not unique enough** and there is either no demand for what you're selling or the competition is too strong and you can't compete.

30

2. **You haven't borrowed or saved enough money** to run the business and pay living expenses. Or, you let your overhead get out of hand by having an expensive office, staff and equipment before you could afford them (2).

3. **By not advertising or promoting enough,** many businesses have gone under before they could start adequate money coming in (2).

4. **Joining forces with the wrong partner(s)**---the average partnership lasts less than two years---has destroyed many business ventures.

5. **You are not willing to put in the time and effort necessary** to nurture the start-up process. "What separates success from failure: You have to be willing to do *anything and everything* to get the business off the ground"(3).

6. Starting a business is a major lifestyle decision. **The business owner and her or his family must be committed to making the business succeed.** If not, the owner is under a lot of pressure that may jeopardize their venture (3).

RISK TAKING ISN'T RISKY LIKE IT USED TO BE

Risk taking has always involved fear of the unknown. In today's dietetic market, the status quo involves fear of the unknown. Change is happening at an alarming rate. Dietitians must grow just to stay even (4).

Risky ventures do not have to be so grandiose as starting a private practice. They can be as simple as changing the selection of food in the cafeteria to fit the Dietary Guidelines or asking to be included in a planning meeting at work. Traditionally, risky ventures thrust us into unfamiliar territory, where we could embarrass ourselves or, worse yet, fail. But in today's different market, embarrassments and failures can happen because we haven't taken any risks or tried anything new (4).

Smart people learn how to minimize their risks. In an article *Risky Business* by Bob Weinstein, he points out the difference between "dumb" and "smart" risks (5):

Dumb Risks

1. When the odds are staggeringly against you.

2. You've done little or no research.

3. It was an emotional decision.

4. You are about to change your life all at once.

5. You'll make a big effort for a small return.

Smart Risks

1. You've researched it for months.

2. The timing is right.

3. You've given it your undivided attention.

4. Experts support you.

5. It blends well with the rest of your life.

6. Your gut instinct tells you to go for it.

Six Steps To Success (4,5):

1. **Careful planning.** *Which* venture and *when* are extremely important questions. Markets change and trends come and go. Competitors' plans can open new doors for you or destroy your plans. Market research is essential.

2. **Keep your agendas private.** Share your ideas only with the people you need to. Those are the business trade secrets that will set you apart in the marketplace.

3. **Control the size of the risks.** Consider starting slow and building your business as revenues grow. Consider working part-time or securing consultant positions while waiting for your entrepreneurial venture to grow. Start with services or products that are familiar to you and try promoting them to new markets instead of inventing something totally new. Contact clients first who already know you and like your services instead of going after all new markets. Offer more than one service or product to each client you contact.

4. **Time your risk.** Learn more about the importance of the Product Life Cycle described in Chapter 8. You will be able to time the introduction of new items better than when you just allow them to "happen."

5. **Build a support system.** To get through tough times, surround yourself with people who support you in your risk taking. Look for role models, join groups where successful people meet and get to know one another. No one expects a person who is new to business not to make any mistakes. There is no excuse for repeated blunders when there are so many people and resources available to help the new business person.

6. **Keep cool under stress.** Learn to identify the amount of change and stress you can handle comfortably. Look for signs of having too much stress such as irritability, hyperactivity, shakiness, dry mouth, excessive smoking, overeating, or drinking, depression and forgetfulness. If these signs appear, consider delegating some of your "duties" and unnecessary busy work, take some time to relax and get away from the office.

Make a list of what you have to do and then set priorities. Get the most difficult thing done first.

COMMONALTIES IN PRIVATE PRACTICE

Although there is wide diversity in dietitians' businesses, the majority support themselves, especially initially, with one-to-one counseling (1). In private clinic practices there is a shift in the type of nutrition information that is used most---from acute medical diets to "chronic" or preventive nutrition with special emphasis in weight control. Many practitioners report that at least seventy percent of their clients have weight loss as a primary or secondary diagnosis. Fat controlled heart diets, diabetic, and allergy diets are also common(1).

Practitioners find that this business is seasonal with slack times occurring over the holidays and in late summer. It is important to remember that these times do exist. They are great times to do busy work and plan your own vacations but good times to avoid when planning group classes, mail outs, and grand openings of offices. In the weight control business there are two times of the year when major marketing efforts are most effective---fall and after the New Year.

Private clinical practitioners' relationships with other health professionals begin to mature to true member of the "health care team." Because patients are treated more for chronic problems instead of acute, life-threatening ones is surely one reason the interrelationships are more cooperative. As an entrepreneur, more time is given to patient instruction and follow-up than is traditionally available in a hospital setting. Therefore, the results may be far more impressive. Referring physicians, office nurses, and other employees become very supportive of effective nutritionists.

Practitioners realize the beginning pace can't be kept up forever. The need arises to develop projects that produce "passive" income. Some product or service that brings in revenue without the consultant's constant input. It could be publishing a book, selling copyrighted teaching materials or computer programs, inventing a product, or hiring other dietitians to cover your client contracts. This business strategy is responsible for some of the most financially successful businesses owned by dietitians.

Money takes on new meaning to new business owners. To survive they must generate more income than expenses. It doesn't take long before a new business owner learns how to call her or his "accounts receivables" to ask for payment. And in the beginning, the fun, creative work with great *future* financial potential may have to take a backseat to less exciting projects that make money now.

COMMON CONCERNS

I am afraid that I won't keep current without the input of other professionals around, for instance, in the hospital.
   Solution: This can be a problem. However, since your livelihood will depend upon staying up with, if not leading, the times you must develop some solutions. First, see if you can start an informal journal club with other

dietitian business owners who are in the same situation. Start subscribing to nutrition newsletters and journals or use a personal computer to do searches and access databases. Read the newspaper and business-related magazines regularly. Join The American Dietetic Association dietetic practice groups such as Consultant Nutritionists, Dietitians in Business and Communications, and any others that involve your areas of interest. Their newsletters, membership directories, and state and national programs can be very informative.

I've always had difficulty getting organized.
    Solution: This concern is extremely important, and it will take care of itself. You will either learn to do it yourself or hire someone to do it for you, if you want to stay in business. You alone are responsible for your output. There isn't an employer or supervisor looking over your shoulder telling you what to do and when to do it. If you work out of your home, it will be even more crucial that you establish control of your work space and schedule.
    Good time management is also essential. Start a notebook and begin writing lists of things to do and then set priorities for them and *date* them. Many people write lists, but fail to do the most important things on time because other items are easier or more fun.

ASSESSING WHETHER PRIVATE PRACTICE IS FOR YOU

As the saying goes, "If it's worth doing, it's worth doing well," so goes the effort put into starting your new business. Just wanting to try it may carry you far. How far and how well you go can be dependent upon how well you plan, organize, and carry out your ideas.
    Right now you may feel somewhat overwhelmed by the concept of self-employment. The best way to overcome that feeling is by breaking down the whole into manageable tasks and smaller, simpler goals. The information in this book will help guide you through the steps.
    Philosophically, any dietitian or dietetic technician can go into business. You will be most successful if the business is based upon your areas of expertise and personal interest (since it will be a labor of love). Your target markets must need or want what you have to sell.

Evaluating Your Strengths and Weaknesses

It is important that you look at your strengths and weaknesses objectively. You need to know what your strengths are because you will want to capitalize on them and base a lot of your business strengths on them. Knowing your weaknesses will show you where you could be vulnerable. You can seek help to supplement or retrain your weaker areas, such as public speaking, writing, marketing, typing or whatever. The less you are able to do for yourself, the more it will cost to operate a business. The cost of delegating responsibilities and retaining office staff must be weighed against the value of your time in generating income.

34

Education   Whether or not a dietitian's nutritional education is adequate to function in private practice is dependent upon the individual's level of competence and continued learning.   What seems to be lacking in our educational experience are business, communication, and psychology courses.

In a survey of successful clinical practitioners, Rodney Leonard found that, "If they had to do their schooling over again, they would choose a curriculum heavily weighted toward building communication skills and acquiring a basic knowledge of business practices. They would take public speaking, journalism, marketing, public relations . . . bookkeeping or accounting, economics " (1).

A dietetic technician is limited in the clinical areas of nutrition practice, but he or she is certainly more qualified than most of the lay counselors who work with the public in weight loss centers. By working in management or with "normal" nutrition, a dietetic technician could be successfully self-employed.

Graduate education should open more varied doors in business and improve a nutritionist's marketability. Besides nutrition, dietitians are taking advanced degrees in exercise physiology, communications, health promotion, food technology, business management, or marketing, to name a few.

Practitioners do not agree on the exact role that an advanced degree will play in an entrepreneur's career. Some feel that it is "an absolute necessity" that provides an edge in today's professional world and competitive market. Others feel that advanced degrees are perhaps only important in clinical settings, academia, and government positions. Everyone agrees that a Master's or Ph.D. will not compensate for a lack of ability, skill, or personality traits needed to succeed in business.

Reeducation is important when a dietitian has not remained current in the areas of nutrition that will be used in practice. Due to the growing nutrition awareness of the public and the sophistication of the competition, new business owners cannot afford to be outdated.

For dietitians who have not practiced for some time, do not underestimate what you know. However, you should consider taking updated dietetic courses, qualifying for dietetic registration (if you aren't registered), and perhaps working in a teaching or clinical setting for a while to refresh your education and improve your skills.

Experience/Expertise   Experience and expertise can be gained in a variety of ways---from working in a family-owned business, working as an employee, working as a volunteer, or trying a business venture of your own. The quality of the experience and the degree of involvement are usually as important as the number of years, but adequate time and exposure are necessary.

Dietetic experience past the internship or master's level is all but mandatory to gain composure, practical clinical knowledge, and to learn those things not taught in school. People presently in practice have recommended two to ten years of experience in a variety of dietetic positions before starting out on your own. A report published by the New York Academy of Medicine, "Statement on Physicians in Private Practice and Referrals to Consultant Dietitians" recommended that consultant dietitians be registered or meet the educational requirements to be registered, plus have a minimum of four years of recent clinical experience (6).

There are of course exceptions to every guideline, and there are dietitians who have started successful businesses directly out of school. But for the majority, the added years can be beneficial in learning new ways of doing things, trying out programs in institutions where resources are more readily available, and saving seed money for a new venture.

Commitment Limits You will need to decide on the amount of personal commitment you want to have to your business.

There are some major questions to ask yourself and decisions that need to be made. Will you work at private practice full- or part-time? Will you try to keep your other job? Will you have a medical, commercial or home office, share or sublease space? How much debt can you handle? Where can you get funding for the venture? If you have a family, how will you juggle your responsibilities there?

When determining your limits, recognize that having support for your venture from your family and friends can be very helpful on your road to success. Involving other people in your decision making may help solicit their support for your projects.

LEAVING YOUR OTHER JOB

How you leave your present job or how you handle your job while you start a new business on the side can be very important professionally. Your reputation either will precede or follow you in your new venture, so the past is never really gone. Try to leave as amicably and cordially as you can.

If you are starting a business on the side, keep it "on the side." Do not get fired because you used the photocopier to print all of your diets or solicited patients on the floors of the hospital. Also, be aware that many employers consider starting a private practice after hours as moonlighting, or conflict of interest, and it may jeopardize your job.

Several clinic dietitians have found that their employers were less than understanding when they established part-time private practices in the same community and offered services that competed with their clinic services. That is not a smart move. Put yourself in the employer's spot---wouldn't you make the dietitian decide which job she or he wanted more? Work in a different community or offer excellent, but noncompetitive services, such as group weight loss classes with an exercise specialist or diabetic cooking classes.

Your reputation and goodwill toward you will grow as you become known for your services. Your identity will grow separate from your employer's.

A common question dietitians ask when they quit their jobs is "What is mine when I quit?" Generally, the rule of thumb is: intangibles probably are yours (including the names of your contacts); tangible (patient records,

36

the Rolodex provided by the employer, etc.) probably are not. If you invented something on your salaried time, it belongs to your employer usually, unless you have another agreement. If you have written materials that you want to use later in your business, plan to write different ones with newer information.

A former employer cannot keep you from practicing your profession---unless you signed a noncompete contract---and that must still be within reason. An agreement may state that you can't solicit business from or work for your employer's client accounts (without the employer getting paid) for one year.

One practitioner reported that the food service company she worked for had her sign a contract when she first started. It stated she could not work as a dietitian for anyone for five years within a 100-mile radius of the large metropolitan area where she lived. Don't sign something like that! It's doubtful the agreement would stand up in court, but who wants the expense and bother of a court case? A good suggestion would be to mark through the clause and initial the change before you sign the contract If the employer insists on retaining the clause and you want the job, talk to a good lawyer about some negotiation options.

REFERENCES

1. Leonard, R.: "Private Practice: On Our Own," *Community Nutritionist*, Washington, DC, 1982.
2. Mancuso, Joseph: *How to Start, Finance and Manage Your Own Small Business,* Prentice-Hall, New York, 1990.
3. Ciabattari, Jane: "When You Start Your Own Business," *Parade* magazine, August 21, 1988.
4. Helm, Kathy King: "Risk Taking Isn't Risky Like It Used To Be," *JADA*, Chicago, 89:4.
5. Weinstein, Bob: "Risky Business," *Entrepreneurial Woman* magazine, May/June 1990.
6. New York Academy of Medicine: *"Statement on Physicians in Private Practice and Referrals to Consultant Dietitians, "* 1979.

section 3

Private Practice

Words of Wisdom:

"Every job is a self-portrait of the person who did it. Autograph your work with excellence."

"Quality is never an accident; it is always the result of high intention, sincere effort, intelligent direction and skillful execution; it represents the wise choice of many alternatives."

Willa A. Foster

Chapter 8

Business Strategies

THE BIG IDEA

At one time or another, we all have a "big" idea that we know will make us a million dollars if we would just pursue it. Truth is, not many people actually try to pursue their ideas. The patent office reports that out of the 1,400 new patents issued per week, only about five percent are ever manufactured.

In his book, *The Rejects,* Nathan Aaseng explores the difficulties and negative feedback that inventors of well known, highly successful products or services, had to endure in order to make their ideas successful (1). His examples included: Orville Redenbacher and his high priced but high quality popcorn; Frederick Smith and his idea for overnight delivery (Federal Express), and Clarence Birdseye, who drew upon his adventures in the Arctic, to invent a process to freeze vegetables successfully.

The small book is inspirational because it does *not* highlight the "overnight" success stories.   Instead it looks at the dedication and perseverance that is required when you believe in your idea, and it is *not* an instant hit. The reader sees that the thrill and satisfaction from an idea is in the intellectual challenge, creativity, comradery with the others involved with you, and the emotional highs along the way. Money is a good reward too, but for most entrepreneurs, it is the thrill of the challenge that makes them happiest.

What is it about an idea that makes it unique? It could be you and your association with it. It could be how you market it; its *message.* Usually, it is the fact that it was *first on the market,* or if not first, then it was *different and better.* There are many ideas that hit when the *timing* was right; they weren't first, but the public acted like they were. Miller Lite beer was actually the third or fourth lower calorie beer to hit the market, but when it hit, the timing was right and so was its *message,* "lighter and less filling," not "diet."

PRODUCT LIFE CYCLE

The product life cycle concept can be applied to products, services, market trends, and even careers and professions. Just as trends come and go, so does market potential. By understanding the graph (see Figure 8.1), an entrepreneurial dietitian can   better anticipate the levels of consumer demand and competition, and better estimate the amount of capital

Figure 8.1 Product Life Cycle

Product Life Cycle

Chart by Marty Waugh, MBA

needed to enter a market. The more established the competition, the more it will cost to create an identity for a new service or product. The concept helps explain why some new efforts have a better chance of succeeding than others (2).

As illustrated in **Stage One** of the chart, *Infancy* describes the period when a new trend is just emerging, when a new idea is at the cutting edge, as was wellness in the '1970s'. A few people are talking about the idea, but it does not have mass appeal. The dietitian who wants to become established as an expert at this stage does so at her or his own expense. However, it often doesn't take much money to become established at this point. True entrepreneurs love this stage. They thrive on the untapped potential of the emerging trend and engage in creative brainstorming. They often develop close professional and personal ties with other people they meet while actively pursuing the trend (2).

Stage Two begins when the idea becomes more popular and demand grows for the best services, products, and leaders from stage one. Profits rise, and the new idea starts to attract the attention of other possible providers (your competitors). Competitors copy or improve on the best ideas and add lots of marketing dollars. As the market matures, it becomes expensive to enter with a new product or service. Businesses experiment less at this stage. Ineffective and marginal services, products, staff, and marketing efforts are let go. The venture is honed to a lean, well-functioning, revenue-generating business (2).

Saturation becomes a problem in the mature **Stage Three,** as too many competitors vie for a piece of the market. Sales are at the highest level since the product or service was introduced, but growth declines. As James Rose, R.D., stated, "During stage three the business becomes fairly routine so many entrepreneurs lose interest. A person with good management skills is needed at this stage to keep the product or service consistent in quality and efficiently produced " (3). Marketing is especially competitive at this stage with each competitor trying to attract the same shrinking target

40

markets. There are fewer buyers because everyone who wanted the product or service has purchased it.

Finally, **Stage Four**, or *Decline,* arrives. The trend and its attractiveness to its present target markets is declining. Sales drop, and the product, service, practitioner, profession, or trend in its original form is no longer competitive. There are three options at this stage. The first is to continue the product or service for as long as it is profitable. The second is to reformulate and reintroduce it as a "new and improved" item. While either of those two options take place, you could invest a percentage of your resources into a new, cutting-edge concept in stage one or early stage two. Many businesses offer several products or services, each fitting into a different stage of the life cycle.

Although many trends may take years for stage four to evolve, when something dramatic happens like a new breakthrough product or widespread publicity, change can literally happen overnight. For example, when Oprah Winfrey announced that she lost weight on a liquid diet, it gave credibility and heaven-made exposure to that industry. Other weight loss programs based on more gradual diets could not attract enough participants to hold class---stage four happened in a matter of weeks. However, as often happens with fads, when news hit of the women suing a diet franchise because of gall bladder problems, liquid diet programs began to fold within weeks.

The keys to successful business are:

- Having products or services that sell

- Marketing that attracts buyers

- Good management

- Open-mindedness and flexibility to make changes when needed

- Credibility and shared loyalty with customers

- Perseverance and hard work

THE PROCESSES OF MANAGEMENT

Managers decide what is to be accomplished and how the process will work (4). The number one reason entrepreneurs begin their own businesses is to be their own boss. The majority of self-employed entrepreneurs will work by themselves. So, although they don't have employees to manage, the success of their business is still based on how well they manage. They must be self-motivated and have coordination in three critical areas (4):

- Planning: determining what is to be done

- Organizing: arranging how it is to be done

- Controlling: making sure it is done

Managers analyze a situation, determine what needs to be done, set priorities, decide on objectives, plan how objectives will be met,

41

implement action plans, and control the progression of events. Managers who pay attention to detail often produce a product or service that stands out in the crowd, but they may not have a prosperous business if the output is too slow and the price is too low. A good balance is necessary.

Business consultants suggest that good managers know when to micromanage a project and when to only set up check points along the way. They know they will never be able to guess all the right answers before a project begins, so they develop action plans based on their best research and then begin. They make corrective decisions along the way in order to stay on target to their goals. Entrepreneurs take risks, but they are calculated, well-researched, and closely managed.

Because entrepreneurs are so self-relient and independent, many have trouble delegating to anyone else. They fear loss of control or loss of quality output. This may cause problems: burnout in the entrepreneur, frustration for anyone who has to work or live around him or her, fear in any investors, red flags of warning for possible investors, and if the business is ready for expansion, it could stifle its growth. This situation is remedied by hiring or subcontracting to very qualified people, which will take the entrepreneur some research time to find. He or she should carefully communicate what is expected, and how it is to be done. Through evaluating along the way, the entrepreneur sets his or her mind at ease, and assures quality output. It may take several tries, but if the person(s) is right for the job, it should become apparent.

DESIGNING SERVICES THAT DELIVER

Even though they are intangible, services can be subjected to the same rigorous analysis as other management operations, according to Lynn Shostack, a senior vice president at Bankers Trust, in an article in the *Harvard Business Review (5)*. She uses a blueprint concept to develop new services, to decide the steps and stages of delivery, to identify problems, and potential for other market opportunities.

The development of new services is usually characterized by trial and error. However, there is no way to ensure quality or uniformity without a detailed design (5). Although a consultant's product may appear as a bound report, what the consumer bought was mental capability and knowledge, not paper and ink.

By adapting a work flow design and time-motion engineering, you can devise a blueprint that is nonsubjective and quantifiable, one that will allow you to work out details ahead of time (5). Simply identify all the steps of a service you might or presently provide, adding time and costs, including any preparation time. By illustrating what you do, or plan to do, you can find possible weak points where quality may be compromised. Or, you can use the example to train a subcontractor on the finer points of a service you provide that you want duplicated.

COMMON QUESTION: SUBCONTRACTING

I have a private practice that is going well after two years. Other dietitians are calling, wanting to work for me. I would like to expand my business and eventually make more money. How do I do it?

Expansion is not to be taken lightly. It must be well planned, adequately financed, and you must be willing to accept new additional responsibilities, especially management and leadership. Your accountant, lawyer, and business advisor(s) need to be consulted before any steps are taken in this direction.

The major component that must be present is a larger volume of business than you can handle yourself. Consult your business advisors to see if there are any untapped public relations or marketing avenues that you could pursue to increase the flow of clients. Contact nursing or drug rehabilitation homes, fitness centers, spas and other possible accounts to see if they need a nutrition consultant. Consider a new marketing campaign to your referring physicians.

Don't bring on a subcontractor to help you, if only your needs are presently being met. Don't jump prematurely. Many business advisors suggest having enough work for one and a half full-time dietitians before a part-time associate is added. The other option is to have a consultant work as needed to cover new projects, client accounts, or office patients in order to free your time to pursue new client accounts. First, get more business, then subcontract---in that order.

Dietitians who own businesses that subcontract to other dietitians report it is a big challenge. You cannot expect that other practitioners will have the same dedication as you do to your business. Many dietitians are not good patient counselors. Olga Satterwhite, R.D., owner of Nutrition Consultant Services of Houston, a business that subcontracts, says, "Out of every 25 people I interview, 24 will ask what I can give them, and *one* will sell me on the flair and expertise she or he can bring to the business." Guess which one gets the position?

If you think subcontracting to other practitioners will make you a lot of money fast, think again. It may take years to build the contacts where you will place subcontractors. You will spend more time in overseeing accounts and personnel, and thus, you personally, may have a resultant loss of income. Overhead expenses may increase for local travel, bad debts, added secretarial services, telephone, insurance, printed materials, bookkeeping, attorney fees and so on.

If you split the revenue generated by the subcontractor, for example 50-50 or 60-40 percent, after you deduct the added overhead, according to two business owners, you may make less than 10 percent on the money generated by a subcontractor. When you consider your earlier loss of income, and time spent managing, that could be breakeven.

According to these same experts, unless you can bill three times the hourly wage you pay the subcontractor, it is probably not worth the time to subcontract. In some industries, like public relations, media work, and consulting to business and industry, fees may be high enough. In areas of the country where dietitians' hourly wages are lower, it might also work financially, but where salaries are high and fees are low, it is difficult.

In his book on entrepreneurship, Joseph Mancuso discusses how to choose the team members that work best with an entrepreneur (6). The best choice is *not* an energetic, go-getter like the owner. This person may become frustrated and refuse to take orders or become an in-house competitor instead of an aide. You want to choose a "bright, lazy or other-wise committed (family, small children, etc.)" person who benefits your company through good ideas, loyalty, and team spirit. Dietitians have had luck with subcontractors who complement their own personality traits. If the owner loves to market or sell, the subcontractor may enjoy a more stable position counseling patients in a well-run office.

After a subcontractor is chosen, take time to make sure that she or he is adequately trained in your office policies, procedures, philosophies, successful teaching methods, and so on. She or he will be a representative of your business and as such could be a financial and professional blessing.

A contract or letter of agreement should be signed and reviewed by your lawyers. If a subcontractor is placed with a client's account, have the client agree to it in writing, and visit the client every four to six weeks. Replace the subcontractor if the client is unhappy instead of losing the account. Keep business as business, but remember if you made a good choice in a subcontractor, give her or him room to use his or her freedom, maturity, creativity, and expertise to both of your advantages.

Advisors will tell you that the advantages of having subcontractors over employees or partners are numerous:

- No employee benefits or taxes required, although you may wish to offer some benefits eventually (the IRS is very particular about who can be called contract labor, check with your account).

- Subcontractor hours can be cut back more easily when business is slow.

- Subcontractors often pay for their own malpractice insurance and continuing education.

- There is less paperwork using subcontractors than with either a partner or employee.

- Decision making is more expedient than when a partner is involved.

GROWING A PRODUCT-BASED BUSINESS

The profession of dietetics can point to some very successful members when it discusses people with product-based businesses. Merilyn Cummings, M.S., R.D., invented "The Diet to Lose & Win," a card-wallet system to control food intake using the diabetic exchanges. She had such a good concept, others used it too. She won a suit out of court against the very similar, Deal-A-Meal.

Ellyn Luros, R.D., is president and co-owner of Computrition, Inc., a supplier of food cost management and nutrition analysis software, and computerized cookbooks. In total they have over fifty different products for the food service and dietetic industries. Through aggressive marketing,

Computrition's products have become known as state-of-the-art in the food service arena. Sales in 1991 expect to reach $4 1/2 million. Ellyn says, "It takes about eighteen months for a product to be developed, tested, refined, and packaged for the market. It takes an additional twenty-seven months for it to breakeven, for us to recover our investment. Our company has about $10 million invested in its product development. But even with the high costs, having products to sell is the only way I know to make a lot of money in dietetics. Service-based businesses soon realize that there are only so many hours in the day to sell. After the start-up investment, products can sell and generate revenue without your heavy input of time like with service businesses."

Randye Worth, R.D., developed the fruit sweetened cookies you see in your grocery called R.W. Frookies and Animal Frackers. She wanted an all-natural cookie that was good for you. Two and a half years in development, with her husband's marketing and product experience, Randye started with four flavors and a concept for a free-standing display. She knows that with the competitive grocery market, her products must have mass appeal to be successful (7).

In a 1990 interview, product experts, John Luther and Jim McManus of the Marketing Corporation of America in Westport, Connecticut, gave advice to people with product-based businesses (8):

• Don't introduce a new product unless it has proprietary competitive advantages. If it's not unique, don't spend your time and money on it. If there is no barrier to a competitor entering the market with a product that is just as good or better than yours, you'll quickly be competing on price. You could have a marketing success, but you'll have a business failure if you can't sell it at a profit.

• Be simple and candid in your packaging and in your description to the trade. If you can't be, the product probably isn't very good.

• Don't bet the ranch. Always hold some assets in reserve.

• You test market by getting into the business. There is nothing theoretical about it. Just do focus groups in at least two geographic regions to get a reality check that you are on target. The old thinking was that you test market a product in a "representative" city and if they liked it, it would sell nationwide. That did not prove to be true.

Two very interesting books on product development are *How To Create Your Own Fad and Make a Million Dollars* by Ken Hakuta (9) and *Toyland: The High-Stakes Game of the Toy Industry* by Sydney Stern and Ted Schoenhaus (10). Although these two books talk about the toy industry, the manufacturing trials, competition, retail problems, and so on, are often similar to those in other markets.

The library will have many more references for you to read and consider before starting a product in any market. There are several universities in the U.S. that have departments that, for a $150-200 fee, will analyze your product and its marketing plan to determine whether they feel it has a chance for success. Products can be extremely successful, and they can be very time-consuming and expensive pastimes.

You ideas for your business may change many times as you conduct market research and talk to people. The most important point is to remain open-minded, but analytical and thorough in your quest.

REFERENCES

1. Aaseng, Nathan: *The Rejects,* Lerner Publications, Minneapolis, MN, 1989.
2. Helm, Kathy King: *Becoming An Entrepreneur In Your Own Setting,* The American Dietetic Association, 1991.
3. Rose, James C. from his Cooper Memorial Lecture at ADA Annual Meeting 1987.
4. Gagnon, Myrna author of "The Processes of Management," in *Managing Clinical Nutrition Service* by Norma Huyck and Margaret Rowe, Aspen, Maryland, 1990.
5. Shostack, G. Lynn: Designing services that deliver, *Harvard Business Review,* January-February, 1984.
6. Mancuso, Joseph: *How to Start, Finance and Manage Your Own Small Business,* Prentice-Hall, New Jersey, 1978.
7. *Courier:* Dietitian and Product Development, The American Dietetic Association, 1990.
8. Richman, Tom: How To Grow A Product-Based Business, *INC.,* April 1990.
9. Hakuta, Ken: *How To Create Your Own Fad and Make a Million Dollars,* Avon Books, New York, 1987.
10. Stern, Sydney and Schoenhaus, Ted: *Toyland: The High-Stakes Game of the Toy Industry,* Contemporary Books, 1990.

Chapter 9

Nurturing Creativity

Creativity remains the lifeblood of continued growth in a career. Creativity can mean a new invention or insight, or the ability to overcome obstacles by approaching them in novel ways.

Psychologists now believe we are born with creativity but allow it to atrophy as we grow older. They believe it is our social conditioning that teaches us to squelch curiosity, fear failure, and inhibit any new, nontraditional ideas. Eventually, we become so used to conforming that creative thought becomes uncomfortable. Ashley Montague once said that all man wants today is "a womb with a view " (1).

Many businesses are just beginning to recognize the importance of having new, exciting ideas. They are developing innovation committees, creative think-tanks, and rewarding new ideas. Some companies have been doing it for years. The 3M Company has allowed its researchers to spend fifteen percent of their time on whatever project interests them since the '1920s' (2). Corporations are sending their employees to training programs run by "creative consultants." Some business schools now teach creativity along with other basic courses.

INTELLIGENCE AND EDUCATION

As nutritionists with scientific training, we often discount the importance of creativity. Creative ideas may be seen as non-scientifically based. Could our entrenchment in this way of thinking be why so often we are hired to carry out a layman's new nutrition ideas? Why aren't more of us at the forefront of the nutrition trends?

Nobel Laureate, Jonas Salk, inventor of the polio vaccine once said, "When I became a scientist, I would picture myself as a virus, or a cancer cell, and try to sense what it would be like to be either "(3). He often referred to himself as both a scientist and an artist. Intelligence is by nature creative. Creativity helps develop ways to better use our intellectual capabilities (3).

By teaching and only using today's nutrition ideas and strategies, we are doomed to follow instead of lead in our field. Trying to make every dietitian think just the same is a grave mistake. Yet, so often we are hesitant to try new ideas ourselves or to support our peers when they try something new.

Personality

Creativity is not just a matter of intellect; it is a factor of personality (1). Experts describe a highly creative person as one willing to live with ambiguity. He does not need problems solved immediately and can afford to wait for the right idea. Creative people are often unconventional, curious, and are highly motivated, but easily bored (3).

Creative people are often depicted as leading chaotic lives. The truth is that business executives could learn a lot about organization from artists (4). According to Stephanie Winston, author of *The Organized Executive,* "Creative people are extremely disciplined in their use of time, very much in control of their environment, and capable of focusing their attention like a laser. They are essentially not distractible, whereas many of my business clients can be distracted by the drop of a pin (4)."

Creative people are sometimes perceived by others as being "different" or so ingenious as to be a "threat" to the comfortable status quo on a job. For a self-assured supervisor, these people won't pose a threat but instead an opportunity to have wonderful energy and new ideas coming into the system.

Often creative people work best while alone. They can also be productive in a supportive environment where other people with greater skills in management or technical expertise can refine and carry out their ideas. By complementing each other's areas of specialty, each person's capability for creativity can blossom. Work output is sometimes brilliant.

"Stuck"

The opposite of creativity is being "stuck" or habitual thinking. When a quick answer will not come for a problem, many people doggedly stick to the same problem-solving processes they have used all their lives (5).

When people are "stuck," they often jump to conclusions before they have full understanding of the situation. On the other hand, creativity allows a good problem-solver to look on all sides before committing to a solution (3).

MYTHS ABOUT CREATIVE GENIUS

In an article "Strokes of Genius," psychologist Perry Buffington, Ph.D., explores the myths around the idea that very creative people are "different" from the rest of us. He suggests that "genius may be nothing more than a certain style of thinking "(5).

Because most people do not feel they are capable of advanced thinking, they often fail to live up to their full potential. However, genius may be the result of using the creative potential of the brain instead of being born with a "special" brain (6).

When Albert Einstein's brain was donated to science, it was found that it did have more glial brain cells. It is thought that these cells contribute to the amalgamation of information from other areas of the brain. In fact, the extra brain development in Einstein may have been the result of his genius ways of working and thinking rather than the cause of it (7).

Myths about creative genius need to be explored in order to negate the powerful hold they have on our perceived ability to grow and be creative. **Buffington identified the following five myths (5):**

Myth: A Genius Creates Masterpieces or Invents Revolutionary Theories Overnight

This is not true. Much like the average person, a genius develops ideas via incremental critical thinking and a special type of worry. For example, there is no doubt that Ludwig von Beethovan was a genius. Yet, inspection of his sketch books with over 5,000 pages of preliminary musical scores make it clear Beethovan worked hard to perfect his work (5).

Inherent in this myth is the idea that creative ideas all of a sudden appear without any previous thought. According to Buffington, "It appears that efficient problem-solvers 'creatively worry' and carry a problem around with them mentally even while doing other tasks. Brief episodes of mulling over a problem are precursors to insight. What appears to be a sudden solution is actually the result of days or weeks of detailed thoughts, incremental changes, and critical evaluations eventually allowing the solution to arrive" (5).

Myth: Geniuses Are Born

Although slightly true, there is evidence to suggest that a genius' abilities are due to practice. Ten years of practice seems to be the amount required (5,6). A period of time is needed to learn the rules of the trade or field of study. Even a would-be genius must study and learn the necessary building blocks. For instance, a master chess player must develop at least 50,000 patterns, with four or five pieces in each pattern. These building blocks have been developed over time: ten years and 25,000 to 30,000 hours of creative worrying and actively studying chess (5).

Motivation and commitment are key variables in the definition of genius. Dr. John Ketteringham, co-author of the book *Breakthroughs!*, states that originators of great ideas "come from all strata of society, and can be anyone from distinguished research scientists to high school drop-outs "(8).

Myth: An Individual Genius is Consistently Creative Throughout His or Her Life

This is not true. For example, Einstein rejected the statistical laws of quantum mechanics as an explanation of how our universe works and as a result removed himself from the forefront of new thought in this area. In later years, Einstein himself stated that this inability to see far enough into the future made him and his views a "genuine old museum piece "(7).

Until recently, dietitians have had the image of being slow to accept or apply new ideas in nutrition. This slowness often has made our programs and business ideas "also-rans" instead of on the leading edge of nutrition innovation.

Myth: To Be A Genius, One Must Create Original Works

Often the creative genius lies in the ability to do a common thing "different or better." It is not necessary to create a "breakthrough" idea to be considered immensely successful in life.

A "breakthrough" is defined as a product or service that proves to be much more than a fad or trend. It can change the way people live, and can create huge new markets where none existed before (8).

Copying others' work is certainly not suggested since it shows lack of creative thought and respect of ownership. Learning from another is the way most ideas are developed.

Myth: Genius Is Always Respected And Acknowledged

Not so. The true worth of a person's ideas may be seen after the person's death or fall from popularity.

What is genius in one set of circumstances may be simple mediocrity in another. In other words, the acknowledgement of creative genius is an interaction between the artistic work or scientific theory and the current needs of the audience (7).

Dr. Ketteringham states that, "The popular myth is that inventors see a need in the marketplace and try to satisfy it. In most cases we found that they were driven by their own intellectual curiosity and personal need to solve a problem" (8).

CREATIVITY TRAINING

The purpose of creativity training is to help people avoid becoming "stuck" or escape from it to find better solutions. For years experts have been trying to find out how people come up with creative ideas.

The moment of creative insight often does not come when a person tries the hardest, but when he least expects it. In most cases, creative people had been grappling with the problem consciously and subconsciously for a long time before their sudden insight (1).

The major contributors to the development of creative thought are the commitment of adequate time, energy, and free flowing thoughts. Old barriers (time, money, resources, etc.) and old ways of doing things should not be allowed to influence the flow of ideas. Reality can be dealt with later after the full potential of the idea has come forth. Another idea to help stimulate creativity includes associating with other creative people who encourage new ideas to flow. When a person gets "stuck," he should change his pace, change the room, or go for a walk. Let his subconscious mind work with the problem while he does something else (3).

TECHNIQUES

Faced with the job of fostering new ideas on a daily basis, business people soon develop their own style. Some common techniques follow:

Brainstorming vs Creative Worrying

In the early '1950s', Alex Osborn developed the notion of brainstorming, initially designed to increase the creativity of American scientists and engineers. The technique allows any idea to be put on the table. Criticism is not allowed; bizarre ideas are welcome; quantity is encouraged; and no critiquing takes place until the ideas are generated (5).

Recent studies have compared brainstorming groups and critical thinking groups (creative worrying practiced by most geniuses). The result supports the genius way of thinking. Two groups of undergraduates were chosen as participants. Both groups were asked to invent brand names for a deodorant and an automobile. One group was allowed to use the brainstorming technique with no instructions. The other group, critical thinkers, were offered instructions that placed more emphasis on analyzing the ideas as they were produced. The names generated were then rated on a quality scale by another group of students. As was expected, the brainstorming group generated more ideas than the other group. However, upon closer inspection, they did not create as many "great" ideas. In other words, critical evaluation, or creative worrying, increases the quality of ideas. Critical judgment is essential from the moment the idea is conceived, and is what separates average ideas from genius-type ones (5).

HOW CAN BUSINESSES FOSTER CREATIVITY?

There is no set formula for fostering creativity. The company that designs a 'creative work place' has no more chance than any other company of engendering a breakthrough idea, according to Ketteringham. He states, "we found that breakthrough ideas grew in rich soil, poor soil, and no soil at all " (8).

Management can help by allowing teamwork and exchange of new ideas to take place. It also can help by not overmanaging a new idea. New ideas need to be given time and room to develop to their full potential.

THE CREATIVE DIETITIAN

Sarah and Paul Edwards, authors of *Making It On Your Own,* a book on how to start a business from home, give the following suggestions on "what to do when you don't know what to do " (9):

1. **Don't worry.** Decide instead that you need to solve the problem and then go after it.

2. **Trust your gut.** One way to make sure you do something right is to do it wrong first, but not for long. However, intuition can often be accurate and a very dependable barometer for how you really feel about something.

3. **Focus on the desired outcome.** If you're caught up in the problem, the solutions aren't readily apparent. Look at it objectively.

4. **Think of several solutions**. Generate as many options as possible before you decide which is best.

5. **Talk with an outsider**. Talk it through with someone, and then look or listen for new ideas or perspectives. Seek out people you respect who listen well and don't always agree with you. This may be a good time to consider talking to mentors, peer confidants, or professional advisors.

6. **Don't just stand there, do something.** Often lack of action sets you back as much as taking the wrong action. Try out an option in a small way if you can, to see if it works.

Every business venture has problems and every businessperson has times of indecision. The successful businessperson is the one who learns to solve problems, come up with new options, or react to situations that need feedback quickly and efficiently.

REFERENCES

1. Ingber, Dina: "Inside The Creative Mind," *Success,* New York, 1985.
2. Hoffer, William: "Innovators At Work," *Success,* New York, 1985.
3. Neimark, Jill: "Intelligence vs Creativity," *Success,* New York, 1985.
4. Feinberg, Andrew: "Artists of Organization," *Success,* New York, October 1987.
5. Buffington, Perry: "Strokes of Genius, " *Sky,* February 1987.
6. Weisberg, R.W.: *Genius and Other Myths,* W.H. Freeman and Co., New York, 1986.
7. Yulsman, T.: "Einstein Update: The Better Brain," *Science Digest,* July 1985.
8. *"For Members Only"* by American Express, interview with John Ketteringham, author of *Breakthroughs.*
9. Edwards, Paul and Sarah Edwards, *Making It On Your Own*, JP Tarcher, 1990.

Chapter 10

Building Your Credibility

Not being taken seriously is a common complaint of newly self-employed people. It is a problem if you work out of your home, or you look or sound very young. Institutions still discriminate against self-employed people. Most banks, for example, categorically refuse credit card merchant accounts to home-based businesses, and some temporary employment agencies won't send personnel to a home office (1).

THREE SOURCES OF POWER

In his book, *Games People Play,* Dr. Eric Berne, discribes the three sources of power that he feels lead to credibility (2):

Position power is authority and respect that you command because of the position you hold within an established organization.

- Refer to yourself as "President, Owner, Senior Partner or something similar"

- Highlight former position like "Former director of..." or "Former consultant to..."

- Take a part-time teaching position that will show authority "Instructor at..."

- Become active in trade and professional organizations and work to be elected to positions of authority and visibility

- Try to land a position on the media or as a columnist in a newspaper or magazine

Cultural power arises from the values of the culture within which you work. The academic degrees you hold, the schools you attended, the people you know, the clients you've served, the way you dress---each field and each community has its own set of expected credentials.

- Look the part. The successful people look and act a certain way. How you look and act is your business but if you want the approval of others in power, it helps to look successful.

- Become involved in business and business organizations so you know the unwritten way to do things. It will give you more power, more clout, and probably save you money.

Personal power is the authority you command by the force of your own personality and the results you produce. The other powers may get you in the door, but only if you produce results will your credibility grow.

CREDIBILITY IS THE GOAL (3)

Credibility is a perception others can have about you. It means they believe and trust you. Having credibility with others gives you freedom to act because others trust you will do it well.

Studies of the most important qualities in scientists, managers, leaders, and salespeople always put credibility at or near the top. Most executives believe that credibility is essential to their effectiveness.

Strong credibility can sustain a professional relationship even in severe adversity. Credibility is the basis of all lasting and fruitful human relationships. It forms the basis for open communication, teamwork, and mutual respect.

Strong credibility is difficult to build, but once established, it is very resistant to erosion. However, once destroyed, credibility possibly will never be reestablished.

Components of Credibility

Four basic terms act as building blocks in helping develop credibility. Those terms are: honesty, responsiveness, consistency or reliability, and forethought. Since having credibility is so important to a career, these four terms will be described in more detail.

Honesty

The primary building block of credibility is honesty or truthfulness. People must feel you are being honest with them. Credibility will never be built if others think, or even suspect you are lying. Credibility can be tarnished whether or not you knowingly tell an untruth.

As an example, a food service director may budget in and promise her employees a raise of $.20 an hour, and fully believe it is true. If the results do not come as promised, employees may perceive a lack of honesty. The dietitian's attempts at explanations may only make it worse.

The best way to build the perception of honesty is to be honest. Making a prediction about something over which she did not have final control was risky.

Honesty generates confidence. If people think you are telling the truth, they will tend to have confidence in what you say. If people (patients, clients, peers, employers etc.) have confidence in what you say, they do not need further verification beyond your word.

Confidence means people do not second guess you. You say it, and the matter is put to rest. There is not endless debate about what you "really meant." Where confidence does not exist, your statement is the beginning of the matter, not the end of it.

The perception of honesty means people believe you. Communication is clean, clear and efficient. Messages are taken at face

54

value, not analyzed and reprocessed. People listen for your content rather than your motive.

Responsiveness

Responsiveness occurs when others believe you will come through for them. They feel you have access to the resources needed and you have the intelligence, energy, and ability to make something happen.

Promises must be kept. Responsiveness is built on honesty, but it goes beyond honesty. When your weight loss proposal arrives at your client's office on Tuesday as promised, or when you increase your diet aide's salary as promised, your credibility is established. When you have to state honestly that the proposal was mailed on time and you don't know what delayed it, credibility tends to deteriorate.

The perception of unresponsiveness, sometimes seen as irresponsibility, is deadly to credibility. Others often perceive you as being half-hearted or only giving "lip service."

On the positive side, responsiveness generates loyalty. If others think you will "come through" for them, they will do so for you. Responsiveness is actually a form of loyalty, the best form. If people perceive you have that kind of loyalty, they will return it.

This is not a loyalty born of obligation. This is a reasoned loyalty, earned loyalty, loyalty rooted in legitimate self-interest. If credibility is strong this loyalty will endure. Others will stay with you in a crisis, in other words, you have a right to make a claim on their loyalty when times become rough for you.

The basis of very strong relationships is seen when others pay for your responsiveness with their loyalty. A dietitian who offers extra time or energy to an employer or client shows responsiveness, and of course, expects loyalty in return. If loyalty is not forthcoming, credibility is lost, and the dietitian may not choose to be responsive in the future.

Following is a good example of how responsiveness works in brief encounters: if a patient requests an appointment for a diet consultation at 7:00 AM, but the patient fails to show up, it is doubtful the dietitian will agree to reschedule again. Loyalty was not returned and therefore the patient's credibility was compromised.

Consistency or Reliability

When you are consistent and reliable, others believe they can depend on you. They believe you will not give your support one day and retract it the next day. You do not change styles or behave erratically in other peoples' opinions.

Your credibility will suffer if you constantly change career courses or begin a new job before adequately finishing the last. It will suffer if you switch loyalties too often. Someone given a task should not have to be concerned that you will change course and leave them with many hours of wasted energy.

Sometimes reliable simply means that you are available, present. Reliability adds depth to responsiveness over time.

Trust is generated by consistency and reliability. Others trust you. They trust the course you have chosen. There is a quality of constancy about your working relationship.

Others have access to you; they can find you. You will not scare them off with mood changes or messages that you are too busy for them.

Credibility not only means that others believe what you say. They also believe what you say today, you will say tomorrow. This quality is really stability, a decision-making process that reaches conclusions sound enough that frequent changes of mind do not happen.

Forethought

Forethought means what you say makes sense to other people. The things you say seem to be based on sound suppositions, on researched information, and logic. You show a command of the topic or situation. You seem to understand the way things really are. This aspect of credibility is often overlooked, yet its absence erodes credibility. It appears that a person does not use forethought when quick off the cuff remarks are made, or the statements show poor awareness of the real situation. Comments also may be poor due to the speaker's lack of expertise, knowledge, or intelligence.

Forethought generates respect. Respect is really a sense of security. Others feel secure you know what you are doing.

Respect also means other people feel you understand enough about a situation to make intelligent statements on it. Dietitians who do not know enough about sports nutrition and training or competition routines lose credibility with athletes by making statements that seem irrelevant and uninformed.

Being knowledgeable is essential to building credibility. Using your knowledge to say things that make good sense is a critical part of the perception of credibility.

CREDIBILITY SHOULD NOT BE CONFUSED (3)

Since having credibility engenders many deep emotions it is often confused with other feelings that people have for one another.

Credibility Is Not Rapport

Many people confuse credibility with being personable, well-liked, or sociable. It is possible to have excellent rapport with someone and yet fail to have any credibility with them at all.

Credibility never covers all areas, issues, and topics. You may have credibility as a clinical renal dietitian but totally lack credibility as a diabetes dietitian. If you have no wish to establish your credibility as a diabetes dietitian, there is no problem.

The credibility issue arises only in those areas in which you want to build or maintain credibility. If you want to be credible as a renal dietitian, and you are not, you have a problem. Others may think you are a wonderful person, even want to spend their vacation with you, but you may still lack credibility as a renal dietitian. The rapport is no substitute.

In addition, the credibility issue arises only with those persons with whom you want to establish credibility. You may want credibility with your clients as a food service director, but have no wish to establish credibility as a dietitian with your preacher. You may want to establish credibility with your preacher as a choir leader.

So, you may have rapport with someone at all times, but you cannot possibly have credibility with someone in all areas, nor with all people in any one area.

While rapport is useful and positive in a relationship, it is not essential to credibility. You can have very strong credibility with someone who would not spend one more minute than necessary with you.

Confusing credibility with rapport can cause anxiety and hurt feelings. For example, as a consultant, you may fail to sell your program to a client whom you know very well. The client may not believe your argument that you are best qualified for the job.

Credibility Is Not Authority

Managers often confuse their organizational power or authority with credibility. He is wearing the badge and giving the orders so he feels he has credibility with his people.

Credibility is built between one person and another. It is intrinsic to the relationship between the two people. If you have credibility with other people, they believe certain things about your character, competence, experience, and knowledge. They learn these things about you as you relate to one another. Your authority is not something they learn; it goes with your position within that organization.

You may be obeyed because you have authority. Others may show you respect because you have authority. But you will never have credibility with them simply because you have authority.

Interestingly, credibility can give you a kind of authority. If you are credible on an issue, you are perceived as "authoritative," having sound knowledge and competence in that area. This quality can cause people to follow you even when you have no formal authority at all!

Consultants or salespeople get prospects to become customers usually with no formal authority over them. On the other hand, subordinates have been known to abandon ship on a manager with all the authority in the world--the manager lost credibility!

Credibility Is Not Fear

You may have power over other people, either organizational or brute power. Others may do your bidding, but you will not necessarily have a shred of credibility with them. In fact, people who use intimidation frequently damage their credibility in the very act of intimidation. If others perceive that you need to intimidate them, they might logically wonder why. If you have credibility with other people, intimidation is superfluous in most cases.

Credibility Is Not Submissiveness

All three of the above, rapport, the use of authority, and intimidation, can bring about submissiveness, even if they do not engender credibility.

Because you are personable and popular, you may cause someone to acquiesce to your wishes, perhaps because he does not perceive himself as very personable or popular.

You might submit to someone because he has authority---maybe you have been brought up that way. You might yield to someone's snarls and roars because you are scared stiff. Credibility never engenders submissiveness. If you are submissive, there is an undertone of coercion. You are acting against your will. If you go in someone's direction because of his credibility, there is never coercion, or the feeling of coercion. You go because you believe in him or her.

Credibility Is Not Awe

Finally, someone may be awe struck, enraptured, transported by you and your charisma, but you may fail to have a shred of credibility with him or her. If you perform some spectacular stunt or feat, you might well engender a feeling of awe and wonder, but you will have no more credibility than a beautiful rainbow. Except in one area: you will have credibility as someone who can engender awe and wonder in others.

Credibility is always built over time, as a result of sustained contact between two people. Awe comes in a sudden flash and can leave just as suddenly. Credibility, once built, never leaves suddenly, except through some calamitous event.

Because of the wonderful feeling associated with awe, it is easy to confuse with credibility. Remember: credibility always has a basis in reason and logic. It is always built over time, and brings about a feeling often quite different from awe.

PROXY CREDIBILITY (3)

Proxy credibility is any perception that eases or shortens the process of building credibility with you. Examples are reputation, rumor, rapport and several other personal promotional tools.

Reputation

If you are well-regarded, well-credentialed, or have a good record of performance, your reputation is enhanced, creating a favorable climate for building credibility for yourself, your company, your profession.

Rumor

Like good reputation, good rumors about you can cause other people to be favorable disposed toward you as you begin establishing credibility with them.

Rapport

If someone likes you, enjoys your company, shares common interests, and feels comfortable with you, the path to credibility is smoothed.

Proxy Credibility Tools

These tools can be used to help build your proxy credibility:

- Informal socializing activities

- Advertising (formal spreading of rumors)

- A good business record

- Successful experience with satisfied buyers

- A confident professional image

- Friendly manner and demeanor

- Positive personal and employer recognition

CONCLUSION

Credibility is essential for a long, sustained career in any field. It makes day to day dealings with people more productive and pleasant. Credibility opens doors of opportunity to you and lowers resistance to ideas you want to develop. Credibility is built day by day as you work and interrelate with other people. High achievers place attaining credibility as a top priority.

REFERENCES

1. Edwards, Paul and Sarah Edwards: "How to Win Credibility and Respect," *Home Office Computing,* May 1991.
2. Berne, Eric, Ph.D.: *Games People Play,* Ballentine Books, 1985.
3. Adapted from a presentation by Orlando Barone, "Credibility," used by permission, Copyright 1986.

section 4

Starting Your Business Venture

Words of Wisdom:

"Failure is not the worst thing in the world.
The very worst is not to try."

Chapter 11

Executive Summary and Business Plan

Successful dietetic business ventures are started in many different ways and under a variety of circumstances. Some are handed to the nutritionist by a physician, clinic, or client, while others are outgrowths of jobs, and still others start without contacts or encouragement from anyone.

There are some basic stages and decisions that are common to most business ventures. Those include: conducting market research, developing the scope of the business, determining resources, and establishing an office and client policies. The following chapters will discuss the topics in detail.

DEVELOPING THE VENTURE ON PAPER

Business consultants agree that a potential business owner should first put his plans in writing. Then do some research on the feasibility of his future venture. These tools are called the executive summary or business concept and the business plan, respectively. Their purposes are to share information, find problems, organize the business development, and raise capital.

Unfortunately, it is not rare for a future entrepreneur to be so sold on an idea for a new business that he is totally blind to obvious reasons why the idea will have a poor chance at success. Some examples are locating the business too close to the strongest competition---a nationally know hospital with a free clinic---or wanting to become a nutrition consultant to only Greek restaurants. Although these ideas have a chance of working, it may take too long before you generate adequate income.

An experienced business person or professional advisor could look over the executive summary and plan and perhaps find overlooked problems. Having your ideas clearly stated will help reduce the amount of time needed by paid advisors to assess your business needs. Many banks and all potential venture capital investors will request this information when considering a loan. Business people take the time to prepare these documents because they are useful, provide insight, and give the appearance of having one's act together.

EXECUTIVE SUMMARY OR BUSINESS CONCEPT

61

If you had to rank all of the components of the business plan, the executive summary will float to the top. Why? The executive summary captures in less than one typed page the general excitement, potential success, and resources required for a new product line for an employee or for a new business venture. The proposed scope of a new business---what you will sell, to whom, where, how, when---can all be stated briefly in the executive summary. It introduces the concept to the decision maker. It must stimulate them to read on, to analyze, and to buy into the idea. Without that stimulation, without that decision maker beginning to grasp the concept and share its excitement, the chances are more remote for full consideration of the business plan (1) (see Figure 11.1).

Jim Rose, R.D., food service director and entrepreneur stated in *Hospital Food and Nutrition Focus,* "Write your executive summary in present tense, active voice. Avoid the 'shall's' and 'will's'. Use verbs that show action and presume existence of the project. Make sentences short. Make paragraphs short. Use some bold or highlighted text---sparingly. But don't be too dramatic or trite, either. Include all the essential information. The executive summary must be possible to read in less than one minute. The first fifteen seconds of reading are critical; during that period the decision maker determines whether to 'put it aside,' trash it, or continue reading" (1).

When writing the executive summary, think of it as a promotional description of your venture. Avoid unnecessary details and concentrate on the strong, salable points.

An executive summary is used for a new business and for new projects, for example, a proposed eating disorder class, a new food service concept, or whatever.

Figure 11.1 Example of Executive Summary (1)

The lines in our hospital cafeteria are getting longer, especially at lunch. Why? Our reputation for good food has spread. The local business community is routinely dining here---paying premium prices, providing us with excellent profits. However, seating is at a premium, serving areas are congested, and customers are turning away.

Creating a deli operation in the vending area (now rarely used except during off-hours) that is contiguous to the cafeteria opens up opportunities for take-out services, tapping into new target markets and improving returns on profits.

A 50-seat deli operation faces no real competition within six city blocks. Only five percent of the potential population is now dining with us; both the percentage dining with us and the total population is growing---due to office building expansions with no food service operations included. Deli sales are growing in this region by twelve percent per year.

A capital investment of ____ provides a net return on investment of ____ on annual operations. Breakeven is at month ____. Operating breakeven is at ____ in annual sales. All gross revenues are based on an aggregate ____ cost of goods sold.

62

Renovation of the vending area requires $_____.   The current vending activities are incorporated into the deli operations scheme, offering expanded selections during off-hours.

Adequate labor pools exist, with recruitment simplified by our current food service recruitment programming. Management talent is already on staff.

BUSINESS PLAN

A business plan is a detailed document that evaluates the business potential and is used to interest lenders (1). By the time the plan is researched and written, you should have enough information to evaluate whether your business concept is viable. You can estimate how much the venture will cost. Like the executive summary, the plan can be used not only for new businesses but also for established ones and for new projects. The marketing survey (Chapter 12) will be needed to fill out the plan and to make an accurate assessment of what will "sell."

Business consultants will charge from $3,500 to $15,000 or more to research and fill out a business plan, but you can do it yourself. An accountant can be very helpful with much of the information.   Typically, a plan will be five to thirty pages long, but consultants report that they have seen ones with hundreds of pages when the project necessitated it. The larger size in no way improves the plan's acceptance; it may turn many readers away completely. The important point is to cover the subjects well with pertinent information. The plan should be updated and changed as needed.

A banker or venture capitalist uses a plan to evaluate whether he wants to invest in your business. Your plan can help you organize your venture and set priorities for better time and resource management.

In his book *How to Start, Finance and Manage Your Own Small Business,* Joseph Mancuso, goes into great detail about what a plan should include and highlight (2). He also shares results of his research on what items "sell" a venture capitalist or banker on a plan.

How a Business Plan Is Read

Although a business plan needs to be complete and thorough, the average investor only spends five minutes looking it over. Therefore the plan's layout and highlighted information are extremely   important.   In his research Mancuso found that there are typical steps in that five minutes of reading (1,2).

Step 1. Determine the characteristics of the project, industry and company. Is this a growing market of interest to the public? Is competition doing well? Is anyone making much money in this field? Could this company or project do well?

Step 2. Determine the terms of the deal. What is being offered in return for the money? How much is needed, and how will it be used?

Step 3. Read the latest balance sheet. Is the company making a profit or just scraping by? Are the income projections reasonable considering the balance sheet? Do the managers plan to pay themselves salaries that are reasonable?

Step 4. Determine the caliber of the people in the deal. This step, most venture capitalists claim, is the single most important aspect of the business plan. The employees' names, or founders, board of directors, current investors, and professional advisors' names are scanned in hopes of finding a familiar name. The reputation and quality of the team are important.

Step 5. Determine what is different about this deal. This difference is the eventual pivotal issue for whether an investor chooses to back a business venture. Is there an unusual feature in the service or product? Nutrition is "hot" but are your programs designed to take advantage of it, are they exciting? Does the company have a patent or a significant lead over competition? Does the company's strength match the skills needed to succeed in this industry? Does the inexperienced owner recognize his limitations and have good advisors? Or is there an imbalance? An investor is seldom intrigued with companies that hold a marginal advantage over competing firms or products. Good ideas or products that are better than others will attract capital.

Step 6. Give the plan a once-over lightly. After the above analysis, the final minute is usually spent thumbing through the business plan. A casual look at product literature, graphs, unusual exhibits, published articles, resumes, and letters of agreement or recommendation support the argument for unusual enclosures. Although additional items seldom make a difference to the outcome, they can extend the readership.

If the plan is rejected, it is customarily returned to you. When trying to interest a banker in your venture, it is not out of line to ask why it was rejected. If the banker wants to work with you, he or she may suggest ways to improve the plan, or offer a smaller loan, or ask for more collateral to secure the loan.

When an investor looks at business plans, Mancuso found that four elements determine which one is the chosen first: (1) company, department, or person's name submitting the plan, (2) its geographic location, (3) length of business plan--shorter ones are read first--and, (4) quality of cover--interesting but not necessarily expensive (2).

Writing a Business Plan

A business plan is a personal document. Yet there are some common ideas that should be considered when writing a plan. The different segments of the plan can be written in narrative form, as an outline, or in numbered, highlighted points. The easier it is to read and grasp the significant numbers or unique features, the better.

The order of the business plan is not so important as what information is included and how the information is highlighted. Adding too much detail can be a mistake. All of the following points of explanation do not have to be included; choose those that fit your needs.

Possible Components of a Business Plan (1,2)

I.   Introduction (a paragraph or two)
    A. In a sentence, what is this business venture?
    B. What is the public's probable interest in this idea? How big is the market?
    C. What is unique about your idea?
II. Goals and objectives of your venture. What are your professional and financial reasons for starting this business? What accomplishments do you want to strive for? What objectives will help you reach your goals?
III. Action strategies. List the stages of growth and development needed first to open the business and then lead it toward achievement of its objectives and goals. What should be accomplished or completed by the first month, third month, and so on?
IV. Business Summary
    A. Principal products or services. What are you going to sell? List your areas of strengths well as potential fields from the market survey that you would consider entering because they will sell.
    B. Describe the unique features of the business and its services.
    C. Describe patents, trademarks, copyrights, or other trade advantages.
    D. Describe any trends within the business environment that might be favorable or unfavorable to the company.
V.   Marketing and Sales
    A. Describe the market. History, size, trends, and your service's or product's position in the market. Identify sources of estimates and assumptions.
    B. Who is the end user of your services? Describe demographically. How will they be reached?
    C. Who are intermediate referral agents (physicians, clinics, corporations, hospitals, etc.)? How will they be reached?
    D. Advertising: annual budget and media used.
    E. Is business seasonal?
    F. Customers' primary motivation to purchase your services: price, performance, health reasons, and so on.
    G. Are any proposed government regulations expected to affect your market (DRGs, third party payment, etc)?
VI. Competition
    A. List major competition: their location, probable percent of the market, and strength and weaknesses. (It can be more

impressive that other businesses are doing well. Your challenge is to do it differently and better.)
   B. Is new competition entering the field?
   C. Compare your prices with those of the competition.
VII. Research and Development
   A. State any new field your firm contemplates entering. Is it complementary to what you presently offer? Are you planning to expand to health clubs or offer computer analysis of menus?
   B. Are you developing any new booklets, programs, or food items for sale?
VIII. Management
   A. Are resumes included?
   B. Are references included?
IX. Financial Reports (Ask a banker which reports he needs.)
   A. List projected start-up costs.
   B. Present pro forma balance sheets giving the effect of the proposed financing. What is your repayment plan?
   C. Show present and past balance sheets, tax returns, and profit and loss statements, if already in business or purchasing an ongoing practice.
   D. Yearly projections of revenues and earnings for five years.

This business plan should be considered a working tool, one that is just as valuable for internal audit as external promotion or fund raising. A well-thought-out executive summary outlining your expectations for your business venture and a plan to carry out those concepts are invaluable in translating your ideas into a successful business.

REFERENCES

1. Rose, James C.: "Business Plan," *Hospital Food and Nutrition Focus*, Aspen Pub., MD, vol.4, no. 10, p.3, 1989.
2. Mancuso, Joseph: *How to Start, Finance and Manage Your Own Small Business*, Prentice-Hall, New Jersey, 1978.
3. *Guidelines for Raising Venture Capital* from Corporate Financial Counseling Department of Irving Trust Company, 1976.

Chapter 12

Marketing

Kathy King Helm, R.D. and Marianne Franz, MBA, R.D.

In the last ten years, the need for marketing became obvious to dietitians and the dietetic profession. We know now that having educational credentials, good programming, and licensure will not make clients flock to our doors. It takes more. Clients must need or want *what we have to sell.* They must perceive that the value of our products or services is better than the competition's.

How will people know what we sell? *Eventually,* they will know it by word of mouth. However, in today's competitive markets, with limited budgets and shortened timelines, most businesspeople find that *organized, aggressive marketing is essential.*

Marketing's goal is consumer satisfaction. Too often in the past, we only offered what we felt our target markets *should* have. We gave out information, but seldom set up a program to assure behavior change. Because our clients were either too ill to walk away, or restricted to campus during mealtimes, we had consistent business. That has changed. Good, nutritious food and information on nutrition are "big business" now, attracting many people into the field that was once our's by default.

Marketing yourself and your business successfully is one of the hardest things an entrepreneur has to do. Why? Because you not only have to target your consumers, but you must continuously remind them of the benefits they can get from your service or product. Even public relations experts who have made it happen for their clients, do not find it so easy to promote themselves when they become entrepreneurs (1).

MARKETING IS NOT NEW TO SOME

Marketing is not a new philosophy. Basic ideology stems from the mid-1600s, when a Tokyo merchant named Mitsui opened what might be called the first department store. His intent was to serve his customers by offering a selection of products that were designed to meet their needs and backed by a money-back guarantee (2).

In the mid-19th century Cyrus McCormick invented more than just a mechanical harvester. Mr. McCormick invented basic tools of marketing; namely, market research, customer service and installment credit. He also introduced the idea that marketing should be a central function of doing business (2).

Marketing spread rapidly among firms that produced tangible products, such as industrial and consumer goods. Marketing intangible services caught on more slowly (2).

The American health sector tried hard to resist the encroachment of marketing philosophy. Marketing activities, such as sales and advertising, were not viewed favorably in an industry traditionally grounded in helping and caring. Because medical care was a God-given right, marketing seemed in opposition or at least "commercial" and nonprofessional. Yet, when the costs of health care began to spiral upward, and the number of patients began to decline, a few innovative hospitals hired marketing professionals. Competitive change was launched. Today, billions of budget dollars are dedicated to consumer health care marketing activities.

Sue Calvert Finn, Ph.D., R.D., marketing expert with Ross Laboratories, Columbus, Ohio, states that "a major reason dietitians seem to delay marketing is because we keep trying to refine or improve our product (our education and expertise) instead of using what we have while it's still useful and ahead of the field." Ms. Finn also adds, "Don't just create the opportunity and awareness for nutrition. Go after or create the paying job to use the information "(3).

MARKETING VISIONS

To encapsulate the many formal definitions that have evolved to describe the function of marketing, it simply means: Doing what you do best, in a way that solves a problem for your customer group. This basic definition requires two visions.

First, the marketing function involves an ongoing process of anticipating problems and opportunities through regularly analyzing the trends in the marketplace. You then develop *strategic assumptions* on what you expect the market to do. These assumptions could be as simple as, "The population base in my Phoenix area will continue to grow older, faster than the U.S. population," or "As long as this region is in a deep recession, wellness is not a high priority for most corporations, except as a health care cost-cutting tool." By deciding what the strategic assumptions are for your business area, you can better anticipate what will sell and how to sell it.

Next, you base your short- and longterm marketing decisions on your assumptions, and alter them as your assumptions change. Continuing with the examples, during the recession, you know in the shortterm you should immediately change the marketing focus for your corporate weight loss program. It should go from highlighting the satisfied participants and pounds lost, to how much less the participants spent on health care during the year following the program. Longterm, if you live in Phoenix, you may decide that over the next three years your services or products will be changed to satisfy the needs of people over sixty years old.

A second vision associated with marketing is your business *mission*. A mission is the "higher purpose" why your business exists. It could be "To provide high quality, healthy gourmet entrees and low fat desserts to the city of Midland through our catering business "The Natural Gourmet." Or, "My mission is to become a consumer-educator through the broadcast and newspaper media with special emphasis on nutrition and disease prevention, and vegetarianism." The mission statement sets your course. It helps you decide what your goals should be in order to keep your allocation of resources focused. You may have many different opportunities that present themselves during the course of the day or year. Underlying your decisions on which ones to take should be your ultimate dedication to your mission.

MARKETING STRATEGIES

Entrepreneurs soon learn that it is easier to sell something else to a satisfied customer than it is to find another customer. Some marketing experts estimate that businesses spend six times more to attract new customers than they do to keep old ones. If a patient is referred to you for a lower calorie diabetic diet, what else could you sell that person? What about a group weight loss class with an exercise component, or grocery store tour, or low fat cooking classes, or cookbooks discounted ten percent from bookstore prices? By having a line of products or services, you can satisfy your patients' needs better and generate more revenue.

If you have a catering business and someone comes to you wanting food, what else could you provide that person? What about flowers, table decorations, musicians, linens, theme parties, or photography? You may only do the catering and managing, everything else could be subcontracted to others.

Another strategy is to repackage a proven product to fit the needs of new target markets. This could be as simple as adapting a group weight loss program to fit the needs of patients in cardiac rehabilitation. You could offer a "senior meal" selection in your cafeteria at a lower price to attract a new target market.

Keep good records on your clients or patients. Try to identify who are your best buying customers and keep in touch with them through a newsletter, quarterly nutrition update, or year-end thank you note. The goal is to develop ongoing relationships that don't end when a consultation session or catered event is over. Every client has a sphere of influence that could mean increased business for you.

An OB/GYN physician in Lewisville, Texas, sends a year-end, personally addressed and signed letter to each of his patients thanking them for their business and discussing what new benefits he offers. His office also sends very attractive thank you cards for patient referrals and reminders for yearly pap smears. He keeps two large scrapbooks of baby pictures and thank yous from happy parents on the lobby coffeetable that help establish his credibility with expectant mothers. After delivery of a baby, he brings new mothers a baby picture frame and a newborn tee-shirt that says, "Hand Delivered by Dr. Franklin." He happens to be popular with the nurses, not because he is easy to work with, but because he has empathy for his patients and gives good medical care. He isn't a tall, fatherly figure like Dr. Marcus Welby. This marketing expert and great physician is under 5'2" and in his late-30s. He is an example of the kind of health care specialist who will succeed in the future--- patient-oriented and skilled in marketing as well as his specialty.

Market research and your own creativity and ingenuity can help you find niches in the marketplace where your products or services can flourish without heavy competition . . . at least initially (4). You will make better marketing decisions if you use the product life cycle model described in Chapter 8. Choosing the right point on the curve to enter the market is an art as well as a science.

SOCIAL MARKETING

Social marketing is defined as "the design, implementation, and control of programs calculated to influence the acceptability of social ideas and involving considerations of product planning, pricing, communication, distribution, and market research"(5). Social marketing focuses on changing personal or social behavior for the benefit of the public (6). It is used to accomplish three objectives (6,7):

- Disseminate new data and information on practices to individuals, like why to reduce their intake of high cholesterol and saturated fat foods.

- Offset the negative effects of a practice or promotional effort by another group or organization, like warning the public about megadoses of supplements.

- Motivate people to move from intention to action, like motivating clients to take control of their weight.

For a program to succeed it must have the following conditions (8):

- Adequate resources

- Strong support from agency administrators and community leaders

- Marketing skills and savvy

- Clear authority to make the necessary marketing decisions and implement them in a timely fashion

SELLING YOURSELF

While credibility and visibility are necessary to successful marketing, they are not sufficient (1). You must also know specifically what *message* you want to communicate. What benefits does your business provide? Key words can form your message. For example, "I'm a registered dietitian who has counseled over 6,000 patients in the past 20 years. My business provides the public with easy to understand, state of the art nutrition presentations and personal consultations."

In addition to credibility, visibility, and a message, you need to create an image. Image determines how people view you, how much they value you and whether they are attracted to you. Social and psychological research has found that the more similar you are to your audience in terms of attitude, values, interests and background, the more attractive you will be to them (1). By coming across as an all-business dietitian, we lose people before we have a chance to help them.

Your image is the first impression potential customers get of you. It must convey your expertise, professionalism, responsiveness and reliability, as well as creating warm, positive expectations.

A recent survey on marketing techniques by small-business owners found that informal speaking was the most effective means of promotion. You can talk to colleagues, the media, local business and professional groups, and work as a volunteer. **Six marketing rules that can help you get your message across in any kind of informal speech (1):**

1. **Appearance.** Use your attire and posture to project confidence, competence and status. Strive for a look that emphasizes quality and conservatism in both dress and gestures.

2. **Nonverbal behavior.** Make direct eye contact. Combined with smiling and nodding, eye contact helps create an image of social attraction, power and credibility.

3. **Verbal behavior.** Use simple, direct language without jargon; speak clearly and concisely.

4. **Involvement.** Listen carefully; tailor your message.

5. **Illustration.** Your words should paint pictures in the minds of your audience. Support important points with examples (and references if necessary).

6. **Control.** Stay in control of your image, your message, and your audience's response by deciding ahead of time exactly what you're going to say and how you're going to say it.

MARKETING AN INTANGIBLE---SERVICE

In most cases, dietitians deliver intangible services, instead of tangible products. Service marketing has some unique concerns. First, the service provider is selling something the potential customer cannot see, feel or evaluate before he buys it. He can hold an attractive brochure, or see quality in the business card and other surrogates that represent the service. Secondly, the production, delivery and customer evaluation of the service occur at the same moment in time. If the customer does not like the quality of the service, it can make things very awkward. The buyer places a high degree of confidence in the abilities of the service provider. In return, the provider must be sensitive to the needs of the buyer and adapt the service, as it is happening, to fit those needs.

It is your job, as the provider, to create perceived value by clearly letting the buyer know about the unique customer benefits that you offer (9). Because advertising and other forms of promotion are effective means to define and communicate benefits, they are vital parts of the marketing function. Use a distinctive "trade dress," or unique visual appearance to all of your promotion materials that is carried out in your logo, and business name on your business cards, brochure, letterhead, advertisements and so on. This makes you appear more successful and organized.

THE MARKETING PLAN

For many projects, the marketing plan serves as the sales tool. Along with a business plan, a marketing plan is essential when you start a business. For a more detailed discussion of marketing for the dietitian, refer to ADA's *The Competitive Edge: Marketing Strategies for the Registered Dietitian* manual (10).

Once you have identified one or more "big ideas" in Chapter 8, work through the following eight steps and evaluate the market potential for your concept(s). The trick is to adopt an objective approach and thoroughly analyze as you go (10):

Step One: Identify the Product Line and Target Market There are three basic parts to this step: identify the major product, narrow down the possibilities, and identify other opportunities.

- **Identify the major product and target market:** What is the "big idea?" What are the services or products you could sell? Who will buy it? Too many people wrongly believe they have universal products or services that *everyone* needs. They are surprised when only a few want them. The target market is the market segment that you intend to satisfy with your product or service. Therefore, it should fit their needs best, and be packaged to attract that group. Traditionally, markets were subdivided by geographic area. Today, customers are more likely to be differentiated by sex, age, income, educational level, profession, and other measurable personal characteristics. The newest market segmentation schemes are based on particular lifestyles that predict customer purchase decisions (11).

- **Narrow the possibilities:** Ask yourself questions that will define areas of concentration. Think in terms of three- to five-years period. The purpose of this section is to make your target market as specific as possible. Who do you like working with the most? What client ages and settings do you enjoy the most? Who will buy your product or service the most? Describe the characteristics of your target market.

- **Identify other opportunities:** During your evaluation phase you may have thought of secondary target markets who could use your product or service. Identify them, but concentrate on your primary market first.

Step Two: Conduct Market Research Here you will begin to find out if your assumptions about your "big idea" and its target market will work. Without knowing it, you probably have started your market research already. Have you started talking to people about the possibility of your venture? Have you started attending seminars or reading about ventures similar to the one you want to start? If so, you have started to test the waters.

- **General Situational Analysis:** What are the general characteristics of the market where you want to sell your product or service? What are the trends? Is the marketplace expanding? Shrinking? Is technology coming in rapidly? Are your current skills capable to meet the needs? What does your target market spend its money on? Primary market research is the research you conduct yourself. Secondary research involves statistics and information collected by someone else, such as business, trade, government, university, and professional groups. Use both sources to be assured that you have thoroughly researched the concept.

  Talk discretely to potential customers and trusted referral agents or business associates about your plans. Ask open-ended questions and get them to give you feedback on the concepts.

  Mailed surveys today must compete with mounds of junk mail and solicitations. If you decide to mail a survey, call ahead of time to identify to whom it should go. Try to give some incentive (a silver dollar, a cover letter from a respected expert in the area, or whatever) along with the survey to improve its chances of being filled out. Make a follow-up call within a few days of when the person should receive it to remind him or her to fill it out. You may find that a few minutes on the phone with someone could give you all the information you need in a fraction of the time and effort. Write out questions and have them ready when you call.

- **SWOT (Strengths, Weaknesses, Opportunities, Threats) Analysis:** The strengths and weaknesses are internal characteristics. In other words, what do you (or your department) do well that could make this project a success? What are your weaknesses that must be delegated, retrained or compensated for to make this project work? Opportunities and threats are in your environment or marketplace. The opening of a new fitness center or research unit could offer you an opportunity to use your new product or service. What things could threaten the success of your project like an oversupply of dietitians, or new competition, or other departments vying for the same tight start-up money?

- **Analysis of the competition:** Go deeper in your analysis. Identify your competition, its locations, its products or services, and any advantages or disadvantages it may have. The purpose is to find niches or weaknesses that the competition has in order for you to position your services or products as "different or better." When entering the marketplace, it's important to determine if you are a leader or a follower. A leader sets the pace and usually has the largest market share, such as Quaker Oats in the oat cereal market. A follower like Total oatmeal marketed itself as being different and better in the one area in which Quaker Oats was weak: fortification. Without an advantage over its competition, a product or service must either compete on price or spend lots of money on advertising to make a niche for itself.

Step Three: Setting Goals and Objectives Define what you want to achieve, given the mission you have chosen. Make *goals* as succinct and measurable as possible. Identify shortterm goals that can be accomplished in several months to a year and longterm goals that will take three- to five-years. Reevaluation of the marketplace through trends and strategic assumptions is a continuous process that will help keep the business operating and marketing goals on target. Think about the *driving force* of your project or career---the ultimate goals that will make you feel you have succeeded professionally. Write down specific profit and marketing *objectives* that will help you reach your goals. Also, write down bail-out signals that, if they occur or do not occur, would mean it is time to change direction or abandon the project.

Step Four: Determine Major Strategies Now is the place to determine your marketing mix, or the 4-Ps of marketing for your product or service. **Product, Price, Place and Promotion.** What you decide can determine the success of your venture. You know your *product or service* you want to sell, but take a few minutes to describe its "positioning" in the marketplace---what is its market "niche," what benefits will the consumer get, how is it unique, who is its target market? What are your *pricing* strategies (see Chapter 16)? *Place* refers to the location or distribution system where the customer buys your product or service. Is it convenient? If it is a product for the grocery shelf, where will it be sold? The key is to make your products or services as available and convenient as possible. What means of *promotion* do you plan to use (see Chapter 20)? Specifically explain your promotion plans.

Step Five: Develop Action Plans and Assign Responsibilities Take the strategies in Step Four and break them down into specific activities on a timetable with dates, resources required, budget allocation, deadlines, etc. Assign responsibilities if there is someone other than you also working on the project, such as a printer, graphic artist, publicist, and so on. Don't assume anything. Stay on top of the project.

Step Six: Establish a Financial Reporting System What kind of resources will it take to complete your project and market it? What kind of return on investment do you expect? How much do you have to sell to breakeven? Is the return worth the effort and investment? Look at the project over a three- to five-year span, not just start-up costs.

Step Seven: Measure and Evaluate Results If so far, your research and estimates are favorable, what criteria will you use along the way to show that you are on the right track to your goals?

Step Eight: Enlist Support If you have an employer, supervisor, consultant account, or family who will be affected by this plan, how do you intend to approach them? What points can you offer that will sell this concept? Will this plan need to be formally packaged and presented? If so, to whom and when?

When you produce this tangible report of your best research on the feasibility and costs involved in producing your product or service, you, better than anyone, will have a feel for whether the project should go forward.

USING THE MARKETING CAPABILITIES OF ADA

The American Dietetic Association has an extremely capable staff of professionals at headquarters who, along with volunteers, produce a terrific number of marketing opportunities for members with services or products to sell, or for you to gain exposure. For a few chosen members there are the Ambassador and state-sponsored Media Representative programs. You can be on the national resource list of experts who are called at times by the media, professional groups and ADA leaders to offer your expertise.

If you have an idea for a study kit, audio tape program, book, or other publication, you can submit a proposal to ADA's Publication Department for consideration by the Publication Committee. If you have a study or project that is unique, consider writing an article for the ADA Journal. Your idea could be a presentation or a poster display at ADA's Annual Meeting. If you belong to a dietetic practice group, you could present the idea at a meeting or write about it in a newsletter.

CHANGE IS NORMAL

The marketplace is always changing, and what sells today, may not next year. Be watchful of business trends, changes in the public buying habits, stories that make the news, and the economy, as well as feedback from your clients. Ask each client how he or she heard about your service or product, and then use that market research in the future.

REFERENCES

1. Dayhoff, Signe: Hype Yourself, *Entrepreneurial Woman,* May/June 1990.
2. Kotler, Phillip: *Marketing Management, Analysis, Planning and Control,* Prentice-Hall, Englewood Cliffs, NJ, 5th ed., 1984.
3. Finn, Sue Calvert: Marketing presentation at the Alabama Dietetic Association, May 1985.
4. Helm, Kathy King: *Becoming An Entrepreneur In Your Own Setting,* Study Kit, American Dietetic Association, 1991.
5. Kotler, Philip and Gerald Zaltman: Social Marketing: An approach to Planned Social Change, *Journal of Marketing,* 35:5, 1971.
6. Kerwin, Diane, Chapter 15 "Marketing Nutrition Programs and Services," in *Nutrition in Public Health* by Mildred Kaufman, Aspen Pub., Rockville, MD, 1990.
7. Fox, Karen and P. Kotler: The Marketing of Social Causes: The First 10 Years, *Journal of Marketing,* 44: 26-27, 1980.
8. Population Information Program: Social Marketing: Does it Work,? *Population Reports,* Series J, no.21 (January 1980): J394.
9. Ward, Marcia: *Marketing Strategies, A Resource for Registered Dietitians,* New York, 1984.
10. *The Competitive Edge:* American Dietetic Association, Chicago, IL, 1986.
11. Bagozzi, R.: *Principles of Marketing Management,* Science Res. Assoc., Chicago, 1986

Chapter 13

Legal Forms of Business Ownership

When starting your business, there are three basic business structures from which to choose. You can go into business as a sole proprietor, a partnership, or as a C (full) or S Corporation.

The type of structure is often vital to the success of a business. It can affect your ability to attract financial backing, what you pay in taxes, and the extent that your personal belongings are at risk if the business gets into trouble. The structure also affects the amount of control you will have in running the business and the amount of bookkeeping you must do. The more partners or investors you have, the more bookkeeping required [1,2].

No business form is best for all purposes. A sole proprietorship offers freedom, but if a person needs money, it may be useful to find a willing partner with capital. At the same time, disagreement between partners on something so simple as how to spend the profit has undermined many new ventures. A corporation may require too much money and bookkeeping time to make it feasible for a very small operation. (See Figure 13.1.)

To organize your business in the most advantageous way, talk with a good small business lawyer at the outset. Because tax laws are in a state of flux, consult with a tax or accounting specialist. You will feel more comfortable with business, if you become familiar with the types of ownership.

To be recognized for tax purposes, whatever form you choose must be a genuine business---in other words, started and pursued in good faith to make a "profit." This makes it different from a hobby or philanthropic work. Your work will be classed as a business if it produces a profit in any two out of five consecutive years. It is the Internal Revenue Service, not local or state laws, that decides your federal tax and business status [1].

FEDERAL IDENTIFICATION NUMBER

To be registered as a business with the Internal Revenue Service, a Form SS-4 (see Figure 13.2) should be submitted. This form requests a Federal Identification number and should be used when filing your taxes and when you are paid by a client, instead of your Social Security number. Local IRS offices can give or mail you the form or your accountant will have it.

Figure 13.1

Forms of Business Organization
(*Source:* Reprinted by permission of the U.S. Small Business Administration from *Starting and Managing a Small Business of Your Own.*)

WHAT FORM OF BUSINESS ORGANIZATION?

SOLE PROPRIETORSHIP

Advantages

1. Low start-up costs
2. Greatest freedom from regulation
3. Owner in direct control
4. Minimal working capital requirements
5. Tax advantage to small owner
6. All profits to owner

Disadvantages

1. Unlimited liability
2. Lack of continuity
3. Difficult to raise capital

PARTNERSHIP

Advantages

1. Ease of formation
2. Low start-up costs
3. Additional sources of venture capital
4. Broader management base
5. Possible tax advantage
6. Limited outside regulation

Disadvantages

1. Unlimited liability
2. Lack of continuity
3. Divided authority
4. Difficulty in raising additional capital
5. Hard to find suitable partners

CORPORATION (FULL)

Advantages

1. Limited liability
2. Specialized management
3. Ownership is transferable
4. Continuous existence
5. Legal entity
6. Possible tax advantages
7. Easier to raise capital

Disadvantages

1. Closely regulated
2. Most expensive form to organize
3. Charter restrictions
4. Extensive record keeping necessary
5. Double taxation

PERMITS, LICENSES, AND DBA TRADE NAME FORMS

In many localities, a person can do business under his or her own name without registering it with anyone. In different locations, certain types of businesses need a permit, a small business license, a sales tax license, or various other documents that someone at the State Taxation Department,

Application for Employer Identification Number

Figure 13.2 (*Source:* U.S. Department of the Treasury, Internal Revenue Service, 1983.)

Form **SS-4** (Rev. 9-82) Department of the Treasury Internal Revenue Service	**Application for Employer Identification Number** (For use by employers and others as explained in the instructions. Please read the instructions before completing this form.) For Paperwork Reduction Act Notice, see page 2.	OMB No. 1545-0003 Expires 9-30-85

1 Name (True name and not trade name. If partnership, see page 4.)	2 Social security no., if sole proprietor	3 Ending month of accounting year

4 Trade name, if any, of business (if different from item 1)	5 General partner's name, if partnership; principal officer's name, if corporation; or grantor's name, if trust

6 Address of principal place of business (Number and street)	7 Mailing address, if different

8 City, State, and ZIP code	9 County of principal business location

10 Type of organization ☐ Individual ☐ Trust ☐ Partnership ☐ Other (specify) ☐ Governmental ☐ Nonprofit organization ☐ Corporation	11 Date you acquired or started this business (Mo., day, year)

12 Reason for applying ☐ Started new business ☐ Purchased going business ☐ Other (specify)	13 First date you paid or will pay wages for this business (Mo., day, year)

14 Nature of principal business activity (See instructions on page 4.)	15 Do you operate more than one place of business? ☐ Yes ☐ No

16 Peak number of employees expected in next 12 months (If none, enter "0") ►	Nonagricultural	Agricultural	Household	17 If nature of business is manufacturing, state principal product and raw material used.

18 To whom do you sell most of your products or services? ☐ Business establishments (wholesale) ☐ General public (retail) ☐ Other (specify)

19 Have you ever applied for an identification number for this or any other business? ☐ Yes ☐ No If "Yes," enter name and trade name. Also enter approx. date, ► city, and State where you applied and previous number if known.

Under penalties of perjury, I declare that I have examined this application, and to the best of my knowledge and belief it is true, correct, and complete. Signature and Title ► Date ►	Telephone number (include area code)

Please leave blank ►	Geo.	Ind.	Class	Size	Reas. for appl.	**Part I**

City Hall, and the County Court House can advise you about. Some states tax professional services.

If you want to use a trade name or fictitious business name other than your own, a sole proprietor or partnership probably will need to check county files to see if the name is available. If so, then register it at the county clerk's office or some similar place as a "fictitious" or Trade or DBA (Doing Business As) Name. This form lets people know that "Seattle Nutrition Consultants" is Jane Jones' business. This form may be necessary to obtain bank accounts in the business name or to bill clients in your county. Some states also have a registration fee for small businesses of $10-20.

PROPRIETORSHIPS

If you plan a small, low risk private practice, or you do not own many assets, a sole proprietorship may be your best bet. It means a one owner (or two spouses) operation. Although there are no studies to support it, this is probably the business form chosen most often by new private practitioners. The owner is responsible for all debts of the business, and he reaps all its profits. Other than for initial questions and occasional problems, a lawyer is seldom needed. It is the least involved of the business structures under the least government control (3).

Starting a Proprietorship

Anyone can start a proprietorship by simply stating that you are "open for business." Fill out a Form SS-4 to receive a Federal I.D. number. Legally, to conduct business in your area, you may need a local license, permit, or Trade Name form filed. Otherwise, very little is required of you (1). You should keep business records and bank accounts separate from personal records for tax purposes.

Taxes

At the end of the year your tax advisor can help you fill out and file the appropriate forms that briefly list your income and expenses and arrive at a net profit or loss. The IRS will look closely at your deductions, and whether it appears you are actively pursuing your business or just trying to write off your purchases and travel.

As a sole owner, your profits are only taxed once, as your personal income. The business profit is not taxed separately. A business loss can be deducted from any other income for that year. You will pay self-employment social security taxes (15.3% in 1991 on net income up to $53,400). If you have employees, you also will pay payroll taxes, worker's compensation, unemployment tax, fringe benefits, and so on (1). A proprietor may invest in an IRA (Individual Retirement Account), KEOGH (HR-10 Pension Benefit Plan) or SEP (Simplified Employee Pension) to help reduce his taxable income.

Advantages

Many practitioners choose the sole proprietor route in business because they like to have as much control as possible and have the option of making all the decisions. There are no partners or stockholders trying to lobby you, usurp your power, or change the quality of service. If you do not like the way the secretarial service answers the phone or how your lawyer works with you--you make a change. This way of doing business can be very efficient and fast, with only one person making the final decisions.

A sole proprietorship can offer a business owner the opportunity to have the freedom to act out his dreams or wishes with only the obvious limitations of time, effort, and money. At least no person is in the position of changing your company name or the way you counsel patients unless you allow him to do it.

Many consulting nutritionists choose this type of business structure or an S Corporation because it is less cumbersome and less expensive to manage. Lawsuits can be minimized by being very careful and clear about all business agreements and by having them in writing. Also, by carrying malpractice and other liability insurance, litigation expenses and losses can be kept to a minimum. However, if a practitioner plans to have a business that publishes controversial expose's, manufactures a food or beverage, pursues large contracts with other businesses, or in other ways handles large sums of money, or if he or she personally owns many assets, for peace of mind, the corporate structure that limits the owner's liability may be more in order.

Disadvantages

The most obvious disadvantage to a sole proprietorship is the unlimited liability the owner must assume. An owner is personally liable for all the business' debts, its obligations, and suits against it. Your house, car, savings, and other possessions may be claimed by people who have won a suit against you. Additionally, your business assets are potentially at risk if you have personal debts that are unpaid. Malpractice insurance will cover you in a lawsuit against your professional abilities, but not for your business ventures, financial responsibilities, and unpaid bills.

Another disadvantage that many sole proprietors, especially women, experience is lack of credit. Credit is difficult to attract, both personal, from lack of assets, and business, due to lack of track record and business experience. Limited credit makes it hard when an owner needs extra money to expand into a new office, publish a booklet, or cover the cash flow when a big creditor does not pay on time (1).

A sole proprietorship's success is very dependent upon the abilities, energy, and output of the owner. We are not all good at all business functions, so we must be willing to delegate. Also, if the owner gets sick or has personal problems that affect his work, the business usually suffers. Should the owner die, the enthusiasm and knowledge of conducting the enterprise usually goes with him.

All fringe benefits are at the owner's expense, but at this time half the amount paid to social security and one quarter of the cost of your health insurance are deductible.

PARTNERSHIPS

Two or more people may begin business as partners. The advantage of this type of arrangement is that one partner may complement the talents or resources of another. Another alternative could be for one person to hire the other as a consultant or employee.

Often money, a broader base of expertise, or influential personal contacts is the ingredient needed. A partner may be a well-known person who will attract business. Legally, a partnership is a group of persons having a common business interest, each doing something to make the business succeed (2). However, because of internal problems, our mobile society, and changing partner priorities, the average partnership only lasts eighteen months to two years (3).

Partners must get along well. They should be clearly able to do better as a team than they could separately. Partnerships take special understanding and a definite amount of patience. The biggest hurdles to work out are differences in value systems and expectations, lack of delineation of roles (partners step into each other's territory), and unequal contributions of start-up money (the major contributor may expect final say on all decisions) (2).

Successful partners often attribute their working relationships to the fact that they had talked about exactly how the business would run and what would be done "in case this happens" before the partnership was formed. Also, they had to accept that in many instances the "good of the business" had to prevail over their own opinions.

A partnership agreement should always be put in writing with the aid of your lawyer. The agreement should describe the proposed business in detail, and state the business name. It should tell (1,2,3):

- What each partner's initial investment will be, either in money or in other valuable consideration

- The percentage ownership of each partner, and how profits and losses will be divided

- How much time each partner will give to the business

- Who can sign the checks or if two signatures are required

- Who can sign contracts, incur liabilities, and sell assets

- What each partner's functions, duties, and powers are

- How the business will be managed

- What happens if a partner wants to get out

- How a new partner can be admitted

- Who will arbitrate if partners disagree

- How the partnership can be dissolved

- How the value of any partner's interest will be computed

- What happens when a partner dies, divorces, goes bankrupt, or becomes unable to function

- The size and nature of "key person insurance policies" to be carried

Financially, a partnership may be able to get bank loans more easily than a sole owner. Many times this is true just because the assets of two people instead of one are used to secure the loan.

The partnership must file a year-end tax return, but it does not pay taxes. The return is for information only, identifying each partner and showing her or his income and deductions from the partnership. The profit (or loss) is divided among the owners using preagreed-upon percentages. Each partner must attach a copy of the partnership's tax return to his or her personal one.

Partnership Pitfalls (1,2)

1. To be recognized as a partner for tax purposes, a person must actually contribute either money, time, reputation, or something else of value. A joint venture merely to share an office or other expenses is not a partnership to the IRS.

2. Conversely, people may sometimes be liable as partners even though no partnership agreement was drawn up.

3. Bookkeeping for a partnership can become complicated if the partners own different percentages or draw unequally for expenses.

4. Partnership income is taxed to each partner each year, even when the partnership decides to retain the profit for future expansion. Taxes may be owed on money that is never actually received.

5. A partnership is only as stable as its weakest member. Usually it dissolves if a partner dies or withdraws, becomes insane or incompetent, or goes bankrupt.

6. The riskiest drawback is that every partner can be held liable for what the other partners do. This means that one partner binds the other when she or he signs a contract or check. If an accident is caused by one partner, all can be sued. If one partner is dishonest, all may be prosecuted.

Partnership Buy-Sell Agreement (2)

In case a partner wants to leave the business, a preagreed-upon Buy-Sell Agreement could help make the dissolution easier. The agreement should include the following points:

* A formula to determine the value of the business at the time of a sellout, taking into account initial contributions by each partner, assets, debts, and goodwill generated since the business start up.

* Terms governing the sale--for example, monthly payments over a 5-year period at ten percent interest.

* Provisions in the event of death of a partner to protect the survivors against the estate of the deceased. To cope with the added expense of one less person running the business, partners should consider carrying insurance on each other.

* An agreement should be made up front before it ever becomes necessary to determine; how deadlocked negotiations can be resolved-- probably through arbitration.

Limited Partnerships

If a limited partnership is formed, the "limited partners" will have no personal liability for business indebtedness or the acts of their partners. To have a limited partnership there must be at least one "general" partner who is legally responsible for all business indebtedness and the acts of all general partners. A primary drawback to using a limited partnership, depending upon how you look at it, is the requirement that limited partners cannot play an active role in the management of the business or the partnership affairs. Limited partnerships are used most often when the partners want to have some of the advantages of a corporation (limited liability) but pay income taxes as a partnership (1).

CORPORATIONS

A corporation is a legal form of business granted by states. A corporation can be created from a new business or an already existing one (a sole proprietorship or partnership). The corporate structure (C or "full" and S forms) is the second most common business form in America, but incorporated businesses generate over eighty-eight percent of total profits (4).

A corporation is a legal entity separate from its owners with its own property, debts, and responsibilities. Even though shareholders may own the corporate stock, they do not owe the bills, unless they helped secure the loans in their own names. As a shareholder, your personal property is not at risk for your business debts (1).

State laws differ on the specifics of a corporation, but generally a corporation is formed by filing articles of incorporation along with paying a fee to the Secretary of State of any state in the United States (see Figure 13.3 and 13.4). The records are checked to make sure that no one else is using your proposed business name, and the forms are checked for completeness. If all is well, you will automatically be sent a charter.

The new corporation then issues shares of its total issue of stock (3). In a closely held corporation only the owner(s), family, and friends own shares. No shares are sold to others so that control of the business is maintained. Selling shares is one way to generate capital to run the business, but because it dilutes control and can complicate business as you grow, many advisors recommend trying to borrow the money first. People who buy your stock take a chance that the corporation will be successful: they do not have to be paid back if it is a failure.

The corporation name must include one of the three following words: "Inc.," "Corp.," or "Ltd." It is required so that others will know they are doing business with a corporation (1).

It is important that a business owner seek legal advice when planning to incorporate. It is possible to incorporate your business yourself. However, if you are sued or audited and the appropriate records and forms have not been filed or filled out, it could be far more costly to remedy. Fees charged by lawyers to incorporate a business can vary from $800 to $3500; check around to find the best fee for service. The more you know about incorporation, the more you can do for yourself; seek out information.

Some of the advantages of a closely held C or "full" corporation (1,3):

- Owners risk only the money they put into their corporation. It can go broke, and the owners can stay solvent.

- The corporation generally has greater borrowing power than other business structures.

- A shareholder can transfer his part ownership to someone else instantly by selling it, giving, or bequeathing his stock certificates.

- Corporate executive can deduct many expenses from his gross income that he probably could not deduct as a sole proprietor, for example, the

Figure 13.3

Sample Articles of Incorporation (Colorado)

ARTICLES OF INCORPORATION
OF
DIET CONTROL, INC.

The undersigned natural persons, each more than twenty-one years of age, hereby establish a corporation pursuant to the statutes of Colorado and adopt the following articles of incorporation:

FIRST:　　The name of this corporation shall be Diet Control, Inc.

SECOND:　This corporation shall have perpetual existence.

THIRD:　　The business and purpose of the corporation is to engage in and carry on the general business of nutrition consultation, public speaking, publishing and menu development. In furtherance of the foregoing purposes the corporation shall have and may exercise all of the rights, powers and privileges now or hereafter conferred upon corporations organized under the laws of Colorado. In addition, it may do everything necessary, suitable and lawful for the accomplishment of any of its corporate purposes.

FOURTH:　1. The aggregate number of shares which the corporation shall have to issue is 50,000 shares of common stock, each having no par value.

　　　　　　2. Each shareholder of record shall have one vote for each share of stock standing in his name on the books of the corporation and entitled to vote, except that in the election of directors he shall have the right to vote such number of shares for as many persons as there are directors to be elected. Cumulative voting shall not be allowed in the election of directors or for any other purposes.

　　　　　　3. At all meetings of shareholders, a majority of the shares entitled to vote at such meeting, represented in person or by proxy, shall constitute a quorum.

　　　　　　4. All shareholders of the corporation shall have preemptive right to subscribe for any additional shares of stock, or for other securities of any class, or for rights, warrants or options to purchase stock or for script, or for securities of any kind convertible into stock or carrying stock purchase warrants or privileges.

　　　　　　5. The Board of Directors may from time to time distribute to the shareholders out of its assets, in cash or property, subject to the limitations contained in the statutes of Colorado.

FIFTH:　　Three Directors shall constitute the initial Board, their names and addresses being as follows:

　　　　　　a. Jane Smith　　8403 Bryant, Westminster, CO 80030
　　　　　　b. Reed Jones　　1414 Grant, Denver, CO 80218
　　　　　　c. John Doe　　　2034 Sage Circle, Golden, CO 80401

Thereafter, the number of Directors constituting the Board of Directors shall be not less than the minimum number of Directors permitted by the statutes of Colorado, nor more than five, the exact number thereof to be fixed from time to time by the By-Laws of the Corporation. Directors need not be shareholders of the corporation.

84

Figure 13.3 (Continued)

5 / LEGAL FORMS OF BUSINESS OWNERSHIP   **61**

most often when the partners want to have some of the advantages of a corporation (limited liability) but pay income taxes as a partnership (1).

CORPORATIONS

A corporation is a legal form of business granted by states. A corporation can be created from a new business or an already existing one (a sole proprietorship or partnership). The corporate structure is the second most common business form in America, but incorporated businesses generate over 88 percent of total profits (see Table 5.1).

A corporation is a legal entity separate from its owners with its own property, debts, and responsibilities. Even though shareholders may own the corporate stock, they do not owe the bills. As a shareholder, your personal property is not at risk for your business debts (1).

State laws differ on the specifics of a corporation, but generally a corporation is formed by filing articles of incorporation along with paying a fee to the Secretary of State of any state in the United States (see Figures 5.4 and 5.5). The records are checked to make sure that no one else is using your proposed business name, and the forms are checked for completeness. If all is well, you will automatically be sent a charter (see Figure 5.6, p. 65).

The new corporation then issues *shares* of its total issue of *stock* (3). In a closely held corporation only the owner(s), family, and friends own shares. No shares are sold to others so that control of the business is maintained. Selling shares is one way to generate capital to run the business, but because it dilutes control and can complicate business as you grow, many advisors recommend trying to borrow the money first. People who buy your stock take a chance that the corporation will be successful; they do not have to be paid back if it is a failure.

The corporation name must include one of the three following words: "Inc.," "Corp.," or "Ltd." It is required so that others will know they are doing business with a corporation (1).

It is important that a business owner seek legal advice when planning to incorporate. It is possible to incorporate your business yourself. However, if you are sued or audited and the appropriate records and forms have not been filed or filled out, it could be far more costly to remedy. Fees charged by lawyers to incorporate a business can vary from $400 to $3500; check around to find the best fee for service. The more you know about incorporation, the more you can do for yourself; seek out information.

Some of the advantages of a closely held corporation (1,3):

- Owners risk only the money they put into their corporation. It can go broke, and the owners can stay solvent.
- The corporation generally has greater borrowing power than other business structures.
- A shareholder can transfer his part ownership to someone else instantly by selling it, giving, or bequeathing his stock certificates.
- Corporate federal income tax rates are below the top brackets for individuals.

85

Figure 13.4   Sample Articles of Incorporation

(*Source:* State of Colorado.)

SS Form DI (Rev. 1/86)

MAIL TO:
Colorado Secretary of State
Corporations Office
1560 Broadway, Suite 200
Denver, CO 80202
(303) 866-2361

TOTAL OF FEES: $11.00
MUST BE TYPEWRITTEN (BLACK)
SUBMIT ORIGINAL AND ONE COPY

FOR OFFICE USE ONLY

ARTICLES OF INCORPORATION

I/We the undersigned natural person(s) of the age of eighteen years or more, acting as incorporator(s) of a corporation under the Colorado Corporation Code, adopt the following Articles of Incorporation for such corporation:

FIRST: The name of the corporation is _____

SECOND: The period of duration if other than perpetual: _____

THIRD: The purpose or purposes for which the corporation is organized if other than Any Legal and Lawful Purpose Pursuant to the Colorado Corporation Code. _____
_____
_____

FOURTH: The aggregate number of shares which the corporation shall have the authority to issue is _____ and the par value of each share shall be _____
(dollar amount or "no par value")

FIFTH: Cumulative voting shares of stock is _____ authorized.
(not)

SIXTH: Provisions limiting or denying to shareholders the preemptive right to acquire additional or treasury shares of the corporation, if any, are:

SEVENTH: The address of the initial registered office of the corporation is _____
(Address must include Building number, Street (or rural route number), Town or City, County and ZIP CODE.)

and the name of its initial registered agent at such address is _____

EIGHTH: Address of the place of business: _____
_____
(If different from registered office)

NINTH: The number of directors constituting the initial board of directors of the corporation is _____, and the names and addresses of the persons who are to serve as directors until the first annual meeting of shareholders or until their successors are elected and shall qualify are:

The number of directors of a corporation shall be not less than three; except that there need be only as many directors as there are, or initially will be, shareholders in the event that the outstanding shares are, or initially will be, held of record by fewer than three shareholders.

NAME	ADDRESS (include zip code)

TENTH: The name and address of each incorporator is:

NAME	ADDRESS (include zip code)

Signed _____

Signed _____

Signed _____
Incorporators

DC-28-1602a-84

86

- Costs of health insurance can be deducted as legitimate business expenses if the insurance is offered to all employees, and only half the deduction for social security is taken out of the executive's pay.

- If an executive or any employee lives on company premises "for the convenience of the corporation," he need not pay anything for it, as well as company-supplied food, and so on.

- Fringe benefits can be better in terms of pension plans, profit sharing and stock purchase plans.

Corporate Disadvantages (1,3)

- Incorporation is more costly--both to begin and maintain (added state fees, bookkeeping, records, holding meetings, and electing officers and directors).

- Corporate income taxed twice--first on its profits, then shareholders pay tax on the distributed dividends.

- Corporate federal income tax rates have recently been increased by Congress.

- Owners cannot write off the loss from their personal income if the corporation loses money, nor deduct personal loans or expansion money given to the corporation when it is short of cash.

- Many banks and businesses will not accept a corporate signature without a personal guarantee by one or more of the executives.

- An executive's salary must be "reasonable" in IRS's eyes, or it may be disallowed as a business expense.

- Shareholders may sue a director if his incompetence or misdeeds causes the corporation to lose money.

- Some states tax corporations more heavily than individuals.

- If corporate stock is offered to the public, the corporations must conform to the complicated rules of the Securities and Exchange Commission (SEC).

S Corporation Election

If a business has fewer than thirty-five shareholders and meets other specifications, an "S Corporation" offered by the federal government for small businesses should be considered. It offers the same limitation on liability as a "full" corporation, but like the sole proprietorship and partnership, the business itself pays no income tax. All profits or losses become part of the individual's personal income tax responsibility. Benefits are also slightly different from a full corporation, so talk to your attorney and accountant about the pros and cons for you. Many private practitioners have been advised to choose this business form for the above reasons.

Final Words on Corporations

Dietitians, as members of the health care professions, are being advised to think seriously about some form of incorporation for their businesses because of the interest in suing health care professionals. If a practitioner chooses this route, it is important to emphasize that all business and contracts should be done in the corporate name, using its Federal Identification Number instead of her or his own Social Security Number to establish that it is the corporation doing the work.

CONCLUSION

It is not necessary to become overly concerned about areas of business that are completely unfamiliar to you. There are many resources and advisors to offer help. You will know more with every discussion and decision you make. Rest assured also, once a decision has been made on the business structure, it can be changed if it needs to be with some additional effort and money. Nothing is forever "cast in stone."

REFERENCES

1. Lowry, Albert: *How To Become Financially Successful by Owning Your Own Business,* Simon and Schuster, New York 1981.
2. Shyne, Devin: In Business: From Friendship to Partnership, *Working Woman,* August 1983, pp. 48-49.
3. Curtin, Richard T.: *Running Your Own Show,* New American Library, New York, 1982.
4. *Statistical Abstract of the United States, 1990*

Chapter 14

Developing Your Business Management Team

Olga Satterwhite, R.D.

Now that your business venture is developed on paper, you need to evaluate who will make up your team of mentors and professional advisors. You could go it alone. To give yourself a better shot at success, create an informal network you can turn to when you need them. You may be surprised to discover how many people are willing to help you--if you seek them out.

Business authors Sarah and Paul Edwards tell of a sales trainer who needed more information to develop her business and she noticed a course available at UCLA. She did not have time to take the course, so she hired the instructor to give her a series of private instructions. The instructor became an important mentor and introduced her to many business prospects (1).

A team of advisors could include a lawyer, accountant, banker, insurance agent, business consultant, and a marketing, advertising, or public relations consultant. You will benefit from each profession's expertise and learn different perspectives on the same issues. These advisors will evaluate your business, its liability, marketability, and legalities.

In their column "Working Smarter" in *Home Office Computing* magazine, the Edwards give a few steps to attract benefactors (1):

1. **Go to the source.** Go to the best. Go to the people who are clearly authorities, if they can't help you, they may know people who are even better for you to know.

2. **Ask specific questions.** Many mentors and advisors will want to help, but only if it appears you have done your homework first.

3. **Be willing to pay.** Most people take it as a compliment when you ask for their help. But, if what you need requires more than a short phone conversation or taking them to lunch, offer to pay for their expertise. Certainly, asking lawyers and accountants for advice on your business will cost you when they work on your business. A private consultation with an expert shouldn't cost more than $50 to $150. With the right expert, it will pay for itself many times.

4. **Accept and try their advice.** Of course evaluate whether it fits your needs, but if it fits, put in enough effort to see if the idea works, or being willing to explain why you didn't try it.

5. **Express appreciation.** Most people like being appreciated, that's one of the reasons they help each other. A phone call, note or thoughtful gift can go a long way in building a relationship. Also, let your benefactors know they can call on you if they need to.

6. **Pass on good advice.** Establish yourself as a resource for others, someone others can turn to. You'll be amazed at the doors it will open for you.

LOCATING PROFESSIONAL ADVISORS

When seeking good professional guidance obtain several different names of highly recommended specialists. Ask for referrals from your friends, other small business owners, and the Small Business Administration. Look for professional consultants who have experience setting up and working with small businesses. Be specific in what you are looking for. Remember too that *you* interview the consultant. They work for you, so do not be intimidated and feel you must hire the first person. Consider the following questions as guidelines when discussing a business consultant's services and her or his suitability for your practice:

1. What is the consultant's experience in your area of business--a divorce lawyer or large corporate banker or accountant will probably not fit your needs.

2. What specific services does the consultant propose for your practice?

3. Approximately how much will you be charged? If it will be on an hourly basis, obtain an estimate of how many hours the consultant feels your practice will take.

4. Will phone calls be charged? Although fees are important, be aware that bargain rates sometimes get you bargain services.

5. Does the professional advisor have the time to take on your practice? Will you get both adequate advice and reasonable turn-around times on contracted work?

The better you know your needs, the more work you can do for yourself, and the less you have to pay someone else. Before you commit yourself to a specific consultant, ask yourself: Was I comfortable with him or her? Did she or he seem interested in me and my practice? Keep records of all correspondence with a contract consultant. Follow up any telephone conversations with a letter reiterating any points you feel uneasy about or that you feel were important. Keep a copy of the letter for yourself.

Do not assume anything about an agreement, always ask! Change to another consultant and transfer your records if you are unhappy with the work you receive. As a rule, don't hire family and professional friends to do your work because it is so hard to fire them when the job isn't done right.

Learn how to use each consultant's expertise to your best advantage. Talking with other business owners and professionals will help supplement the research and reading you must do before going into private practice.

ATTORNEY

Look for an attorney with reasonable fees you can trust. Trust is believing that the attorney can do the job, is competent, and cares about helping you (2).

The legal fee you will be paying is important. Often the lowest hourly rate is not always the lowest total bill, especially if the attorney is not familiar with the legal problems of your type of business. An attorney may spend a lot of time at your expense learning what to do. Legal services are the last of the "cottage industries," meaning that each item is custom made (2). There is a great deal of discretion involved as an attorney does his or her job, so take the time to find a good one.

On matters such as suing or countersuing, obtain a second (independent) decision before pursuing it. Make sure that you agree with the language and possible consequences of any legal action before you let your lawyer take action in your name. You have to live with the results.

Good legal advice at the beginning of your practice can prevent problems in years to come. A lawyer will help you understand regulations and licenses. He or she can help with copyrighting materials, trademarking your business logo, and patenting a product. He or she can write or look over all your contracts or letters of agreement. Most importantly, a lawyer will help you develop the appropriate structure for your practice--sole proprietorship, partnership, or full or S corporation. Attorney fees range from $65 per hour in smaller communities up to $200 per hour or more for specialized work. They usually charge for phone calls.

ACCOUNTANT

Accountants are divided into two groups: those who are Certified Public Accountants (CPAs) and those who are not certified. States award certification and verify that the recipient has completed a two-year apprenticeship under a CPA. The person must pass a series of difficult tests in the areas of auditing, accounting, theory, and business law. CPAs are accountants with an assured high level of skill; however, other accountants may be highly qualified, but not certified. In most states a bookkeeper is not required to meet any standards to use the title, but he or she may be knowledgeable.

As you look for an accountant or bookkeeper, ask other business people whom they use. Your best source of information is a satisfied customer.

Your accountant should help structure your practice to your best tax advantage. He or she will be valuable in helping choose a bookkeeping or record system that will fit your needs. If the system is set up correctly and simply, you should be able to do the bookkeeping yourself, aided by year-end income tax assistance. An accountant can prepare financial reports that help determine business strategies, or marketing and tax analysis, or help obtain financial backing. Some accountants also give advice on how a business should be operated, called management services.

The hourly fee for an accountant or CPA usually ranges from $60 to $175 per hour or more. A bookkeeper may charge $30 to $60 per hour. Always ask for an estimate of time and fees before the work begins. Inform your financial advisor of any time limitations you have and request that the work be completed by that date. Beware of fancy "Cadillacs" that you don't need and "bargains," such as new people on staff for "special" rates. They may take twice as long, and a supervisor may charge full price to look over their work. Even more crucial, the person may not have any business experience, and an accountant should be a valuable business resource.

BANKER

Get to know your area banks and the services they offer. Even if you do not intend to borrow working capital from a bank, your business accounts will make you a welcome customer. Get to know a bank officer. A friendly banker is more important than which bank you use. Discuss your plans for your practice with him or her. An experienced banker can give you a wealth of valuable business information not only on financial matters, interest rates, and so on, but on trends in the community.

Ask for a loan officer or vice president of the bank when you want to talk about a business loan. Try to use the same personnel when doing your banking and speak up if you are always directed to new inexperienced ones. Banking personnel never charge for their services and can be good advisors.

BUSINESS CONSULTANT

A business consultant will advise you on major decisions such as your central business concept, location, image development, fees, marketing, new market areas, and so on. Good, affordable consultants for small businesses are hard to find, but well worth the research time. Their fees range from $50 per hour on up.

Very good free services available in larger cities are the SCORE (Service Corps of Retired Executives) and ACE (Active Corps Executives) programs of the Small Business Administration. These two programs will work to match you with a retired or active business person who answers your business questions. Their knowledge and experience can be valued resources. Many local banks, Chambers of Commerce, YMCAs or YWCAs, universities, and adult education courses offer programs to help the beginning and expanding business owner.

92

PUBLIC RELATIONS/ MARKETING/ ADVERTISING CONSULTANT

The services of these three specialists often overlap, depending upon the consultant and her or his business knowledge and skills. Public relations experts specialize in letting the world know you have arrived. They use their contacts and expertise to put you and your business venture in front of the public. That may sound intimidating, but it may be as simple as being interviewed by a local newspaper or radio station. Many business people credit their success to having a public relations firm working for them at a crucial stage in their business. As nutrition practice becomes more sophisticated, public imaging will, no doubt, be more important.

Figure 14.1 Business Management Team

Attorney	Form of business structure
	Contracts and letters of agreement
	Office leases
	Copyrights, trademarks, patents
	Lawsuits
Accountant	Bookkeeping systems
	Financial statements/Audits
	Income tax records and reports
Banker	Loan
	Credit information
	IRA, Keogh , and SEP accounts
	Business checking and savings
	Community trends
Business Consultant	Image development
	Networking and contacts
	Setting priorities
	Management
	Marketing
	Business agreements
Public Relations/ Advertising	Image development
	Business cards/ brochure
	Market research
	Promotion ideas
	Advertising layouts
	Media contacts
	Logo design

Hiring a public relations firm is expensive (ranging from $500 to $2500 or more per month often for a minimum of six to twelve months). Be careful and specific in your negotiations on prices and services. To assure that you like what is produced, ask to be involved in all stages of development.

A marketing or advertising firm usually can offer logo development, business card and brochure design, market research, and advertising savvy. All avenues that get your message to your target markets. Again, fees can vary greatly from a few hundred dollars to many thousands. Advertising fees can be a percentage of the cost of the ad campaign, or it can be a project fee. Most firms can create the artwork and broadcast ads.

Get quotes from several firms and be honest about what you can afford to pay. Often, if they need the business or they especially want to work with you, they will negotiate a fair price for your needs. All of the options are independent of one another , so don't feel you have to buy a full package. Buy what will work best. To determine that, you can talk to people who have marketed other services in your area and to several marketing firms until you feel comfortable with the answers.

If you want to do your own marketing and feel confident that you can generate the artwork or wording, look into using a local university art department or freelance artist. All newspapers, magazines, radio, and television stations offer free advice through their sales consultants. Not only can they assist with simple suggestions, but they can advise you on the best time to run your ad, e.g., morning spots on radio or Sunday newspapers, and so on. Use the experts to help sell your products or services, or to improve your image.

FINAL WORD

The wise use of professional advisors will save you time, energy, and money. Their combined expertise will enable you to enter into your business venture confident that your organization will run at its optimum. (See Figure 14.1.)

REFERENCE

1. Edwards, Paul and Sarah Edwards, Working Smarter, *Home Office Computing,* July 1991.
2. Curtin, Richard, *Running Your Own Show*, New American Library, New York, 1982.

Chapter 15

Money, and Bookkeeping

Jan Thayer, R.D. and Kathy King Helm, R.D.

The measure of success in business is to make money. The more socially aware would say, "a successful business is one that can pay its bills while it satisfies its clients." A business venture that does not make enough money is either a hobby or one that has a limited lifespan. Entrepreneurs and employees must appreciate the importance that generating revenue means to the success of businesses.

A hospital wellness program may advertise that it's for the enjoyment and health benefit of the employees, but cutting medical insurance costs is usually the underlying reason for in-house programs. From the beginning, the nutritionist and other wellness staff should establish the attendee and financial record keeping that will show the programs are successful *and* cost effective. Anecdotes from successful clients can be used in marketing, but the management will want good numbers along with successful programs.

A financially successful business usually starts with sufficient capital investment, followed by fair prices, good collection of revenue, timely payment of bills, and appropriate record keeping for yourself, the IRS, and any lender or employer. Managing money and keeping records should not be difficult tasks. The challenge is to know what needs to be done.

Before anyone will be able to help you secure a loan or set up your books, he or she will need to know what you plan to do. The information generated in the business concept and plan will be beneficial, also knowing the type of business structure you will use and an estimation of your start-up costs (see Chapter 18).

INITIAL INVESTMENT

Good financing offers peace of mind, the option of changing your mind, and freedom to create without survival being in peril. When asked, successful private practitioners estimate that years ago they invested $5,000 to $20,000 or more their first year in business (1). With so much sophisticated competition today, plus inflation, start-up costs may be two to three times that needed ten years ago. The money usually comes from savings, loans, and reinvestment of profits throughout the year.

Practitioners with well-equiped, well-staffed offices in their own rented space pay the higher fees. They usually develop the appearance of stability and success much sooner than poorly financed, small ventures. Investing more money into a business will not necessarily make it more successful. However, an adequately financed venture has a better chance of becoming a lucrative business faster.

Practitioners who either have more time than money or those who want to keep the risk and investment low, make smaller investments. By sharing office space in a physician's office, or health club, or by working from home, this is possible.

SOURCES OF FINANCING

One reality to face in developing a business venture is the money commitment. As an employee, this might be accomplished by changing a budgeted item, or as involved as preparing a business plan and financial pro formas. Financial experts encourage new business owners to try to use someone else's money for part of the capital instead of exhausting personal assets. This maintains the owner's financial strength. The owner may need to contribute later during financial emergencies or expansion projects.

There are several options for obtaining money. Your success depends upon your assets, business expertise, connections, and in today's financial climate, the solvency of the lending institution.

Lending institutions are in business to make money by loaning money for an interest fee. Loaning money involves taking a risk that the new business will be successful, and the owner is honest and reliable. Risk taking is not a quality found in most lenders today. Many business owners are complaining that loans are very hard to find.

Your job is to convince the loan officer that you are committed, sincere, and qualified to establish this business. It is not unusual today for a lending institution to require you to invest a certain percentage of your own money. They may ask you to place your money in an account and borrow against It, or secure the loan with personal assets. If you are seeking an expansion or recapitalization loan, your financial records, ongoing business image, and reputation will be evaluated.

Commercial Banks

Commercial banks are the most common lending institutions. They offer many services beside checking and savings accounts. Banks offer basic financial counseling and credit analysis at no cost to regular customers. Most commercial banks make short, intermediate-term and long-term loans. You may be asked to put personal property, Certificates of Deposit, savings or other assets of value up as collateral. Occasionally where you have established credit, you may be asked only to sign for the loan. When you use assets to secure a loan, they are not to be sold, spent, or used without approval by the lending institution. Read your loan agreement carefully.

Industrial Banks

Industrial banks usually give loans by offering second mortgages on real property (home, building, or land). The interest rates are usually higher than those asked at commercial banks. Not all mortgage loans or states allow second mortgages on homes so be sure to check. Also, look to see if they ask for a substantial prepayment penalty.

Finance Companies

Finance companies offer credit on a variety of inventory, equipment and personal assets, but the rates, especially on short-term loans are usually much higher. Companies may charge thirty to thirty-five percent interest per year.

Savings and Loan Associations or Savings Banks

Savings and loan associations or savings banks usually offer long-term loans on real estate, for example, on land, buildings, and homes. For the practitioner considering purchasing a condo office or other office complex, this may fit your needs.

The Small Business Administration (SBA)

The SBA of the United States Government is another resource alternative for a new or established business loan. The law stipulates that SBA loans can be made only to businesses that are unable to get funds from banks or other private sources. This is usually because the personal assets or type of business will not qualify for a regular loan, not because the person is a poor risk. A commercial bank, however, will usually make the loan, guaranteed by the SBA up to as much as ninety percent. Especially with new businesses, the SBA may ask you to contribute fifteen to fifty percent of the initial investment. Occasionally, the SBA will make the loan itself, but this is rare. Only one-quarter of the total 30,000 or so loans that the SBA makes or guarantees each year goes to new businesses, so competition is tough. Less than ten percent of SBA loans go to women-owned businesses each year although the SBA reports that women are more successful in starting a small business (2). Interest rates on an SBA loan are attractive because they are lower than banks usually offer. As attitudes change in the federal government SBA money becomes more or less available.

The SBA requires extensive information about you and your business venture. An accountant or CPA can be hired to put the proposal together for you or to guide you in assembling and filling out the documentation required. When pursuing this type of loan, be sure to allow plenty of time because the approval process takes many months.

Outside Investors/ Venture Capital

Outside investors, friends, or relatives may have venture capital that they would like to invest in your company. Discuss what you can offer them in the way of interest, limited partnerships, or percentage of ownership with your professional advisors. Consult with your lawyer about drawing up any legal agreements. Most business advisors say that the ideal situation is getting a loan without giving up decision-making control of the business. Also, be aware that business and friendships or relatives do not always mix well.

Venture capitalists usually are looking for at least a 30 to 40 percent return on their investment, often calculated as part interest, say 15 percent with a 15 to 25 percent ownership of the business. Depending upon the interests of the venture capitalists, they also may want a major role in making decisions for the business (3).

LOAN PACKAGE

The loan package is the finalized presentation compiled to secure a loan from a bank, investor, venture capitalist, SBA, or a combination of these sources (4). It succinctly presents your basic idea through the executive summary and plan. In a nutshell it explains who you are, your financial status, and how the money will be used and repaid. Usually, having an accountant or CPA provide a review of the figures presented substantially improves the chances for getting a loan. A review is less involved and less expensive than an audit and only as accurate as the figures used, yet it often satisfies bankers because it offers some limited assurance about the reliability of the financial information (4).

Typically, bankers will request or appreciate having the following; ask what is necessary and then use your best judgement on the other items depending on your loan needs (4,5,6):

Loan Proposal Outline

1. Cover letter
2. Table of contents
3. Amount and uses of loan proceeds
4. A business executive summary and plan with its market analysis
5. Personal history of each owner (resume, business experience, letters of reference)
6. Product or service information
7. Company information: copies of contracts you already have signed, lease agreements, insurance carried, etc.
8. Personal balance sheet and your personal income tax returns for the past three years   (see Figure 15.1 Balance Sheet)
9. If already in business:
   - a. Company balance sheet and tax returns
   - b. Company profit and loss statement (see Figure 15.2)
   - c. Aging of accounts receivable and payable as of current date

98

10. Business cash flow projections for at least one year (see Figure 15.3)
11. Source of repayment
12. Duration of loan
13. Collateral to be offered to secure the loan (official appraisals of assets may necessary when the market value is not easily determined)

Figure 15.1

Sample Balance Sheet

BALANCE SHEET

Assets

Cash in checking account	$_____
Cash in savings account	_____
Credit union savings account	_____
Life insurance cash value	_____
House fair market value	_____
Car	_____
Furniture and personal effects	_____
Other	_____
	_____
Total assets	$_____

Liabilities

Department store account balance	$_____
Balance on car loan	_____
Home mortgage	_____
Other	_____
	_____
Total liabilities	$_____
Net worth (Assets minus liabilities)	$_____

Figure 15.2

Sample Profit and Loss Statement

PROFIT AND LOSS STATEMENT

Income

Nutrition counseling $ _____

Public speaking   _____

Nursing home consultation   _____

Book royalties   _____

Other   _____

   Total income
   (To date, monthly, yearly) $ _____

Losses (or Expenses)

Rent $ _____

Utilities   _____

Telephone and answering service   _____

Equipment   _____

Salaries or consultant fees   _____

Insurance   _____

Auto   _____

Benefits   _____

Supplies   _____

Other   _____

   Total expenses $ _____

   Net income $ _____

Other reductions

Taxes $ _____

Depreciation   _____

Other noncash reduction   _____

   Adjusted net income $ _____

Figure 15.3

Sample Cash Flow Planning Form

CASH FLOW IN

	Jan.	Feb.	Etc.
1. Beginning cash balance			
2. (Income sources)			
3.			
4.			
5.			
6.			
7.			
8.			
Total cash available			

CASH FLOW OUT

Operating Expenses

1.
2.
3.
4.
5.
6.
7.
8.

Capital Expense

1. Loan payments
2. Income tax and Social Security

Total cash required

Cash available less cash required

Money to be borrowed
(if negative total)

Debit payments (if positive)

Ending cash balance

Operating loan balance
(at end of period)

Before beginning to prepare all of these documents, ask your individual loan agent what forms he or she needs. Many business consultants suggest that the loan package be typed and bound in an attractive folder or notebook (6).

101

Numerous options exist on loans so work with your loan officer and financial counselor to choose one that fits your needs. Loans termed "line of credit" are very helpful for peace of mind and yet do not usually cost anything if you don't use the money. Loans may be set up so that during the first year, you only make interest payments. A bank may request that you submit semiannual, or yearly financial status reports, but occasionally, nothing may be needed.

A "no" answer should not be seen as a total defeat. Ask the banker what else he or she needs, and to go back several times to achieve your desired results or until an agreement will not work out.

BUYING/ SELLING AN ONGOING PRIVATE PRACTICE

Today more successful dietitians own their own businesses, but with our mobile society, their businesses might be for sale. After years of working on a private practice it is painful to think about giving it up, especially if the owner just lets it dissolve instead of selling it. However, determining the value of a service-type business whose success is closely associated with the personality of the owner is not easy.

Stuart Rosenblum, CPA with Wilkin and Guttenplan, made a nationwide study of how to set purchase values on various types of businesses (7). Although he did not identify a medical-related private practice, he did mention several service businesses. He estimated that an employment agency owner could ask .75 to 1.0 times the gross annual income, equipment included, for the business (the price varying with the business reputation, specialization and client relations). The owner of an insurance agency with its policies renewed each year could ask 1 to 2 times the amount of the annual renewal commissions. A travel agency owner with good contacts but no ongoing revenue from prior sales could only charge .04 to .1 times the annual gross revenue for his business. The major determining factor in valuing a business is how much ongoing worth can be transferred to the new owner.

A buyer should consider the following factors (8):

Profitability What is the future profit potential of the business? Start by analyzing balance sheets and profit and loss statements of the present owner for the past five years or however long the practice has existed. If these forms are not available, ask for copies of the income tax forms. Are the profits satisfactory? Have profits continued to grow? Ask the seller to prepare a projected statement of profit and loss for the next two months and compare it to your own estimations.

Tangible and Intangible Assets The most common are inventories, typewriter, computer, furniture, and teaching materials. Make sure that they are in working order and not outdated. Consider whether the items are something you can use. If the asking values seem too high call around to obtain estimates of similar equipment from dealers of new or secondhand items. Intangible assets would include the business name, any trademarks, copyrights, patents or similar items. Make sure the seller owns the assets

102

and can prove it. If a third party also has rights to the assets, a written consent assigning the rights to you must be obtained. The assets could be licensed to you for your unrestricted use as the buyer of the business. Also be sure that the seller is restricted from adapting the mark to use again (9).

Goodwill   This is the dollar amount that the owner is asking for the favorable public and professional attitudes toward her or his going concern. You should be realistic in determining how much you should pay for goodwill. Since it is payment for favorable public attitude, you should make some effort to check this attitude. Judge the value of this intangible asset by estimating how much more income you will make through buying the going business verses starting a new one. How much of the business will stay and how much will be lost because of the present owner leaving? Even with the owner's best marketing efforts, her or his client accounts at nursing homes, drug centers or physicians' offices may not choose to contract with you for nutrition services. If that is the case, the business owner can't include those contracts in her or his determination of the business' worth.

Liabilities   You should be sure that there are no outstanding debts or liens on the assets. The seller should pay off all accumulated debts before signing an agreement.

Business worth After you have researched the above variables there is still the question of worth. Determine this through negotiation and bargaining. Are you sure that local physicians and contracts will use your services? Do you have any verbal or letters of agreements to that effect? Have you carefully evaluated the lease agreement, zoning, the growing competition, and other possible factors that may affect your business? Will the seller train the buyer in running the business or offer any other intangible services?

Some business owners have sold out only to start a new business in competition with the buyer. Consider placing limitations upon the seller's right to compete with you for a specific period of time and within a specified area. As a safeguard against costly errors, get legal advice before signing any agreement.

Items typically covered in a contract selling a small business are (8):

1. Describe what is being sold

2. The purchase price

3. The method of payment

4. A statement of how adjustments will be handled at closing (prepaid insurance, rent, remaining inventory, etc.)

5. Buyer's assumption of contracts and liabilities

6. Seller's warranties (against false statements and inaccurate financial data)

7. Seller's obligation and assumption of risk pending closing

8. Covenant of seller not to compete

9. Time, place, and procedures of closing

The seller and buyer must comply with the bulk sales law of the state in which the transaction takes place. The purpose of such a law is to make certain the seller does not sell out, pocket the proceeds, and disappear, leaving creditors unpaid. The seller must furnish a sworn list of her or his creditors and you, as the buyer, must give notice to the creditors of the pending sale. Otherwise, the seller's creditors may be able to claim the personal property that you purchased (8).

Payment   There are several ways that practitioners have negotiated the payment for a practice. One is, of course, a lump sum of money up front. Another way is time payments with either a balloon note at the end of three to five years, or money up front followed by regular payments for several years. Another option is to pay an up-front amount followed by a percentage of the gross income for a period of one to five years.

When the buyer and seller cannot agree on the worth of the practice, the option several have used is the last one: up-front money followed by a percentage. To keep sales from dropping, it's advisable for the seller to train the buyer on how to run the business and market it.

MANAGING MONEY

Whether you decide to incorporate your business or not, when your business begins to make money, it has a life of its own. The money that is generated must be accounted for. Records on incoming revenue should match bank deposits into the business bank account. All business expenses, plus the owner's salary or consultant fee, should be paid by check from that account. Personal expenses for groceries or the house note should only be paid out of funds appropriately transferred to the owner's personal account. Banks usually charge   higher service charges on business accounts than on personal ones but the charges are deductible.

Large amounts of business money should not be left in a noninterest-bearing checking account when it will not be used immediately. A checking-with-interest, savings, money market, or other interest account should be used even for just a few weeks to generate interest.

A business check should be written and cashed when you need petty cash. Cash taken in as payment from clients should be recorded as income and deposited, not pocketed or used.

Good Banking Relationships

In his column in the *Dallas Business Journal,* bank executive Guy Bodine suggests that small business owners take the time to develop a relationship with their bankers before they need a loan. He gives the following eight points to help the relationship grow (10):

1. Keep your banker informed.

2. Educate your banker on the type of business you run, and make him or her come to *your* place of business.

3. Seek counsel from your banker.

4. Build credibility.

5. Limit surprises.

6. Do your homework: Develop a business plan.

7. Submit timely financial information to your banker---good and bad.

8. Keep your money deposited in the bank.

Cash Flow

Cash flow is just what the name states, the flow of money through the business. How much money is coming in regularly as compared to that needed to pay current bills. It could be compared to not having more monthly bills to pay than your paychecks can cover.

As a new business owner it should be assumed that it may take six months or more before enough money will come in to cover all expenses. When planning for working capital in your start-up costs, allow enough to keep cash flowing and bills paid. Limited cash flow is not only frustrating, but if it becomes serious, more money may have to be borrowed or supplied by the owner to keep the business open.

Suggestions for improving cash flow include (6):

- Request all payments at the time of the visit.

- Improve collection efforts on outstanding accounts, especially the larger ones.

- Lower inventories of purchased teaching materials, printed diets, and promotion tools.

- Avoid making new purchases that will increase the business overhead and either deplete savings or create additional time payments.

- Deposit temporary excess funds in a savings account or money market fund to draw interest.

- Evaluate when to take cash discounts and pay a bill quickly to save money, or when to delay paying bills until the end of the pay period to conserve cash outflow.

CREDIT CARDS

A number of consulting nutritionists offer the use of credit cards to their clients as a means of payment. Many patients like this convenience and the fact that they can then delay their payments. Credit cards help attract patients who would have delayed coming due to lack of ready cash. People who conduct group classes have found that there is less resistance to the up-front fee when credit cards can be used. According to a study of retail businesses by Arthur Anderson and Co. the average credit card purchase is $50, about twice the average cash purchase and only two percent charge their customers more for using credit (11).

A representative from your local bank can explain the service to you, but check around for the best services and prices. Today, it is very difficult to become a merchant who offers credit cards unless you have a place of business other than your home, you have a good financial relationship with the issuing bank, and good credit rating. Charge forms and a printer, or the more sophisticated automated equipment that makes an immediate charge to an account are available to buy or rent for anywhere from $125 to $450. Deposit the credit card forms into your bank account just like other checks, except for one item: a percentage is deducted for use of the card. The company charges usually vary between 2.5 to 8 percent per bill.

You can increase your fee slightly to cover the service charge cost but that would mean that all patients are subsidizing the credit card users. Some other types of businesses have tried to offer discounts for cash or extra fees for using credit and they have found it created a negative response. Actually, the increase in business may offset the added service charge so that no fee increase would be necessary.

COLLECTION

The older your accounts receivable grow, the more stale they become. In a service business such as nutrition counseling, since no inventory is lost, no write-off can be taken for bad debts (except for actual expenses such as teaching materials, computer printouts, etc.). Therefore, new practitioners must realize that the money must be collected or else the diet appointment did not have financial value. When you sell a product like catered food, the actual expenses can be deducted but not the lost profit.

A written contract or letter of agreement for a completed consultant job is very good proof that the other party should pay you. You may have to get a lawyer and go to court to get the money. You will be able to deduct your actual expenses for the job and the cost to recover the money. But the actual cost of time, aggravation, and legal fees may mean you are only breaking even or less. Timely collection of funds should be a business priority.

Precautionary action can often keep an entrepreneur from having to bill in the first place. The purpose of establishing credit policies and setting credit limits is not so much to assure collection of accounts, but to set limits on the risk of loss. Patients should be asked to pay at the time of the visit. Even if they know that their insurance company will cover your charges, ask patients to pay you and give them an itemized receipt.

Contracts or letters of agreement can be written for large consultant contracts so that your fee and expenses can be submitted bimonthly and paid in two weeks. Another option is to break the total expense for a project into thirds, for example, and have one portion paid when the proposal is finalized, another halfway through the project, and one at the end.

If billing becomes necessary, here are some hints. Date statements as of the last day of the preceding month rather than the first day of the current month. The customer will be inclined to pay sooner since the statement appears to be a month older. Quickly identify delinquent accounts and speed up the collection process by a more vigorous follow-up. Accounts delinquent over sixty days should receive a pleasant, tactful phone call from you or someone representing your business requesting that a payment be mailed by a deadline date. If you do not receive payment or a partial payment is not followed shortly by the balance, a second tactful call should be made. Request immediate payment before the account is turned over to collection.

Collection agencies state that small medical bills are one of the hardest types of bills to collect on. They state that any account over six months old, and often only two to three months, is usually uncollectible. Most agencies charge 50 percent of the bill as their fee if they collect it, and few will touch an account with under $100 outstanding.

Credit is costly if you can't collect. As an example, you provide $100 worth of services to a patient or other client, and your profit margin is 25 percent. If the patient never pays, you will have to collect $400 worth of fees just to recover the uncollected $100 (12). When you consider how much you have invested in your business, you can easily appreciate why business-people do not tolerate delinquent accounts.

BOOKKEEPING

Accounting keeps track of money you earn and spend, what you own and owe: i.e., your worth. Your income (revenue minus expenses) is recorded on an income (profit and loss) statement (see Figure 15.2). Your assets are capital worth minus liabilities and are recorded on the balance sheet (see Figure 15.1).

A good bookkeeping system is necessary to record all of your financial transactions, but it should be simple enough for you to use yourself. The larger and more complex the business is the more comprehensive, but not necessarily the more complicated, the bookkeeping system must be. The information generated will help you know your financial position, evaluate success, and pinpoint problems. These records can also help you make comparisons from year to year and help make more accurate projections for the future.

A good accountant or CPA will be able to help you choose the system that is most appropriate for your business. Office supply stores have a variety of simple bookkeeping record systems. One of the most popular is the Dome book entitled "Simplified Monthly Bookkeeping Record" (12). More elaborate "pegboard" systems are available from accounting supply companies. Pegboard systems use carbonless paper to make recording a patient bill receipt, bank deposit, appointment card, and patient ledger card a one-step process. This system can be imprinted with the business name, address, and phone. And it is becoming more reasonable in cost as competition between companies increases. You can usually see this system in physicians' offices and clinics.

Budget

In his book *Private Practice*, Jack D. McCue, M.D, says that "fewer than two percent of (medical) practices have a budget" (13). The number of self-employed dietitians using a budget is no doubt as small. Agreeing on a budget forces you to examine projected expenses and agree on the gross income, hours of work, and charges necessary to generate the projected net income. A monthly check of your records allows you to examine the actual figures and make adjustments if necessary.

Budget projections are very difficult to make during a year when a person's income is dependent upon inconsistent projects and short term consultant jobs. In those cases, a budget for each project and good fiscal management can help assure that the year is balanced financially.

Cash Versus Accrual Accounting

The IRS will ask that you indicate which form of accounting you use in your bookkeeping--cash or accrual. Cash accounting is when you record income as you receive it and expenses as you pay them. When you record income as it is earned, not necessarily collected, it is called accrual accounting. Accrual accounting is usually used in businesses that have large inventories of products where flexibility of figures and dates may be beneficial. Financial consultants usually suggest that service businesses such as consulting and private nutrition practices use cash accounting because it is simple and easy to use.

Recordkeeping

The following list shows the typical progression of recordkeeping for a physician-referred clinical patient visit.

1. Record patient's appointment.

2. Obtain medical diagnosis, written or verbal diet order from referring physician along with pertinent chemical scores.

3. Fill out initial interview sheet, assessment, history and food analysis.

4. Give patient written handouts.

5. Give the patient an itemized bill and request payment as he or she gets ready to leave.

6. Record the payment.

108

7. Mark the bill paid.

8. Give an appointment card to the patient if there is to be another visit and make an entry in the appointment book.

9. List the payment on the bank deposit slip.

10. Send a follow-up communique to the referring physician.

11. File the patient's interview sheet or folder.

If a payment is not made, give the unpaid statement to the patient, and make a note in the ledger. Ask patients to send in the payment as soon as possible. Some practitioners even put the statement in an addressed, stamped envelope to make the process easier.

Each day record all income (checks, credit card receipts, and cash) on the business bank deposit slip. List the total income under daily receipts. All bills should be listed as you pay them under expenses. The date, check number, amount, and deduction code if you use one should be listed also.

Monthly, all income and expenses should be tallied and totals to date brought forward. You should also know how much money is uncollected in accounts receivable and how old each account is. Bills may be sent out biweekly or monthly.

You may choose to do your own bookkeeping by hand or on software, or hire an experienced accountant, CPA, or bookkeeper. If you carry a heavy client load, you may not have the time or energy to complete your financial analysis as often as you should. Since computers are commonplace in dietitians' offices, their use in financial and patient/client recordkeeping has made them invaluable. Whatever mode you choose for bookkeeping, never lose sight of the fact that as the owner or project manager you will ultimately be held responsible for the accuracy of the reporting system and its figures.

Record Retention

Files need to be kept on your business for important documents and records of business transactions. There isn't total agreement among experts as to the actual length of time to hold records, so check with your own advisors. **Suggested record retention schedule:**

Permanent

- Audit reports of accountants, financial statements

- Capital stock and bond records

- Cash books and charts of accounts

- Cancelled checks for important payments

- Contracts and leases still in effect

- Correspondence (legal and important matters)

- Deeds, mortgages, bills of sale, appraisals
- Insurance records, claims, policies, etc.
- Patient files
- Corporate minute books of meetings
- Tax returns and worksheets
- Trademark registrations and copyright certificates

Seven years

- Accident reports and claims
- Accounts payable and receivable ledgers
- Cancelled business checks (see permanent listing)
- Contracts and leases (expired)
- Invoices
- Payroll records
- Purchase orders and sales records

Three years

- Correspondence (general)
- Employee applications and personnel records (terminated)
- Insurance policies (expired)

One year

- Bank reconciliations
- Correspondence (routine)

TAXES

Filing income tax and Social Security tax forms is made easier by working closely with an advisor. Learn which forms to file and how to fill them out, dates to file, and tips to minimize over- or underpayment. Even if your accountant or CPA fills out the forms, you should be familiar with what he or she is doing.

Who Must File

As of 1991, any single or widowed person who grossed more than $5,300, or a married couple filing jointly who grossed more than $9,550 must file a tax return. Partnerships must file returns and state specifically the items of their gross income and deductions. Corporations must file and pay taxes on any

110

profit. S Corporations do not pay taxes, but have their profit or loss reflected on the shareholders' tax returns.

Deductions

Self-employed practitioners usually deduct the following expenses (12, 14):

- Cost of office supplies, postage, teaching materials, etc.

- Rent paid for a commercial office or a home-office (if it meets IRS rules of used regularly and exclusively for your business) plus a percentage of the real estate taxes, mortgage interest, utilities, insurance, depreciation, repairs and cleaning costs, but not landscaping

- Cost of fuel, water, lights at a commercial place of business

- Advertising and promotion

- Telephone, answering service, fax, modem, computer, copy machine (present tax laws allow a $10,000 deduction in the year you buy it, without having to depreciate it)

- Hire of office assistants and subcontractors

- Dues to professional societies (social clubs, usually excluded)

- Cost of operating an automobile for business: $27.5 cents per mile in 1991

- Furniture purchased new; used furniture can be depreciate, but not deducted

- Professional books, newsletters, journals that help you run your business or keep you current

- Usually 80% of the cost for business-related meals and entertaining

- Job hunting expense, if not looking for first job or a position in an unrelated field

- Expenses incurred in attending business conventions; be careful if mixed with pleasure

- Gifts to clients up to $25.00 each

- Health insurance: C corporation--write off as a company benefit; all self-employed people can deduct 25 percent if no other policy was available

- Disability insurance if you have a C corporation as an employee benefit

- Contribution to retirement accounts

- Interest on loans and credit cards, if business-related

- Bank charges on business accounts

- Professional dues, licenses, fees

- Special uniforms

- Social security taxes: deduct half of your 15.3 percent payment

Any additional types of deductions should be discussed with your tax advisor. Personal, living, or family expenses are not deductible. These would be items such as:

- Withdrawals of money by owner

- Insurance paid on a dwelling house

- Life insurance premiums (except key person insurance for business owners)

- Payments made for house rent, food, clothing (except uniforms), servants, upkeep of pleasure auto, etc

Loans

Since money borrowed is not considered taxable income, repayment of the loan is not an allowable deduction. Interest paid on a business loan can be deducted.

Retirement Plans

IRA, KEOGH (HR- 10 pension benefit plan), SEP (Simplified Employee Pension) and profit sharing plans are forms of retirement plans. These plans allow an entrepreneur to invest in tax deductible accounts that accrue interest tax free until retirement. Each option has its advantages and limitations. Before choosing the program(s) you will use, talk to your banker, accountant, and insurance agencies to see what they offer.

A person self-employed even part-time can still set up a KEOGH by December 31st of each year and contribute as much as 20 percent of the net business income up to a maximum of $30,000 per year. A SEP can be started up until April 16th of the following year for contributions that are tax deductible for the present year (9).

WAYS TO IMPROVE YOUR BUSINESS

Regardless of the type of business you have and what you sell, there are common problems shared by most businesses. There are also common business practices that may improve a business or business venture:

- Use a budget and become involved in the regular evaluation of your business output and financial status.

- Keep accounting systems relevant and effective--revaluate regularly.

- Take calculated, well-thought-out risks.

- Use prosperous periods to reduce your firm's debts and strengthen its finances.

Many businesses and financial consultants encourage new business owners to use their first year in business to become established in the marketplace while keeping overhead minimized. The second year should be used for gaining stability and becoming financially secure. The third year and on could be used for expansion and calculated risks. To be rewarded with longevity, a business must first have a stable income generated from clientele support.

REFERENCES

1. Leonard, Rodney E.: " Private Practice: On Your Own," *The Community Nutritionist*, Washington, D.C., July-August, 1982.
2. SBA Conference: *"Finding Funding,"* Dallas, TX, 1990.
3. Roderick, Pamela: "Beyond Banks," *Entrepreneur*, June 1990.
4. Bel Air, Roger: "Finding Money," *Success*, May 1991.
5. Curtin, Richard T.: *Running Your Own Show*, New American Library, New York, 1982.
6. Wexler, Hildegarde: *A Businesswoman's Guide to Working with Professional Advisors*, Mid States Bank, Denver, CO, 1980.
7. Pollan, Stephen M. and Mark Levine: "Playing To Win," *The Atlantic Monthly*, Fall 1988.
8. *Starting and Managing a Small Business of Your Own*, U.S. SBA, 4th edition, U.S. Government Printing Office, Washington, D.C., 1982.
9. Maturi, Richard: "Hidden Assets," *Entrepreneur*, April 1991.
10. *Entrepreneur:* "It's In The Cards," April 1991.
11. "How To Collect Accounts Receivable" in *Business Perspectives*, United Bank of Denver, December, 1979.
12. Picchione, Nicholas: *Simplified Monthly Bookkeeping Record*, Dome Pub., RI, 1983.
13. McCue, Jack D.: *Private Practice*, The Collamore Press, Lexington, MA, 1982.

HERMAN

"You mean I've gotta pay tax on money I've
already spent?"

Chapter 16

Prices and Fees

VALUING YOUR TIME

An important element of managing money is knowing the value of your time and effort. Too often we spend countless hours doing $8 per hour secretarial work when we should be doing "boss work" like writing ads, making public appearances, or negotiating contracts. If you have something more important that you could be doing and you have the money to pay for it, don't sit around doing work that can be easily delegated.

PRICING STRATEGIES

One decision you must make about each service or product you offer is its price. There is an image associated with a product, as compared to its competitors, that makes it very attractive to its target markets or turns them off. The level of service, or the quality of the materials and workmanship in the product, must warrant the price being asked. Historically, dietitians have charged very little for their services and products, that is slowly changing. We still tend to underestimate the size of the market willing to buy a "Cadillac" option. Perhaps we have worked with limited budgets too long.

The six common pricing strategies are (1):

1. **Skimming**: you charge a very high price to reach a small, elite and profitable market.
2. **Trading down**: you add a lower priced, less prestigious service to your existing elite service; this is used to expand to a less elite or affluent market segment.
3. **Trading up**: you introduce an elite expensive service to increase the status of other generally lower priced services and to attract new buyers.
4. **Cost plus**: you start with what it costs you to have the service or product and then add mark up according to institution policy (commonly used on books, clothing, etc.).
5. **Demand oriented**: you set the price according to what you think the market is willing to pay, all the strategies use a little of this method.
6. **Under bidding**: you set the price with a low profit to be more attractive than competitors; this is a very common method used by dietitians,

but it often makes you work very hard with nothing to show for your efforts.

COMMON QUESTION

There seems to be great variation in the cost of nutrition services. As a new consulting nutritionist, I am struggling to create an image and become known. How do I charge?

In any transaction, each party gives up something to obtain something else. The value of whatever is exchanged may be referred to as price. Price must reflect the perception of a fair exchange by both parties, or win/win.

Even when no money is exchanged such as with free public health services, donation of time to dietetic or trade organizations, giving free speeches, and the like. There is still an exchange of something valued, and if you don't feel the exchange is fair, you usually won't continue doing it.

In addition to monetary value, price may reflect the value of your time, effort, personal services, caring, loyalty, power or prestige, goodwill, and many other nonmonetary components. And, since quality is not free, a higher price generally connotes more value placed on the product or service a client receives. Unless there is some advantage to your service as compared to the competition, you will only be able to compete on price.

Traditionally, dietitians have not been very good at playing the pricing game. Their fee- for-service is often based only on monetary value as speculated by the dietitian, rather than on what the market would bear. It appears that the nonmonetary variables such as the uniqueness of the knowledge we share, the highly individualized care, and the initial program development time often has not been considered. Also, many dietitians jeopardize their ability to give time-consuming higher quality services because they sell their services so inexpensively that they must instruct many more people to make a living or make the clinic profitable. There is a current trend toward change.

All professionals face added pressure to set their fees correctly because fees are not frequently changed, as compared to retail pricing. You do not see professionals offering two- for-one sales or fifteen percent off coupons to be more competitive in the marketplace.

No matter the price you charge, the "perceived value" felt by the buyer must be equal to or higher than the fee to continue to attract customers. The best way to justify your worth is through measuring the outcome you produce through your consultation.

(Answered by Marianne Franz, MBA, R.D., Louisiana Tech)

Establishing Fees

It is illegal (price-fixing) for us to discuss what charges you could ask for your services. It is also illegal for you to call around your area to ask the going rates of other health professionals. You decide for yourself what you need to charge. We can, however, discuss the factors to evaluate when you establish fees for your work:

- How much expertise and experience does the work require?

- How difficult or demanding is the job?

- How much total time will the job, paperwork and follow-up take?

- How much direct overhead cost (handouts, teaching materials, travel expense, hiring another consultant to help, secretarial time, computer use, etc.) and indirect overhead (to maintain office, telephone, insurance, etc.) will be expensed to this job?

- What will the market bear, so that you don't price yourself out of it?

After you have considered all of the variables in establishing fees, charge whatever you want since it's your business and your decision.

Fees are a curious item. If you charge a small fee, sometimes, not always, patients, physicians, and clients think that you are not as good as the competition. If you charge a fee that your reputation, years of experience, or expertise can't support, no one will pay it. Arriving at "correct" fees for different types of jobs is more a process of negotiation and learning from experience. As a practitioner becomes known for quality work and a good reputation, new business will come his or her way. The fee will become less important because people are willing to pay for what they feel is the best.

FEE STRUCTURES (2)

Flat Rates The same fee is charged for the same service to any client. Used when selling the same service again and again because you have a good idea of the time and expense involved. Easy to use for speaking engagements, routine clinical consults and group classes.

Per Hour Rates The hours of work are variable or may be unknown in advance so a fee is charged only for the hours worked. Used for subcontracting, long therapy sessions and consulting projects. Clients are most comfortable with an approximate time frame or maximum number of hours.

Per Head Rate This rate charges according to the number of individuals who participate. This rate is often used for workshops, teaching or speaking to groups who "pay at the door." It does involve some risk, but if attendance is good you can do very well. You can couple this rate with a flat rate to charge for a minimum number with each extra person at an added fee.

Project Rate This rate covers the development of a project like writing a series of educational booklets or comparing bids from contract food service companies for client accounts. Clients like project rates because they are easy to compare and unless you have an agreement otherwise, you usually cover cost overruns. This rate includes your expenses, overhead, profit and some room for miscalculations or unexpected delays. If the client is at fault for the delays, your agreement could make him responsible for any added costs. If the project is cancelled through no fault of your's after the agreement is made, you should have agreed upon in writing some compensation for your lost income. To protect yourself from nonpayment, consider asking for your fee in thirds (1/3 upon signing an agreement, 1/3 midway and 1/3 at the end upon completion and approval) or half the amount up front.

Retainer Fee You can ask for a retainer fee when you are asked to be "available" by a consultant account or physician's office or for a Board of Directors of some organization. The amount you charge may be based on your normal hourly rate or whatever you feel your availability is worth. A retainer should be tied to a limit (such as one eight-hour day per week or forty hours per month or whatever) and anything over that amount should be charged extra.

If you presently work at a site on commission where you take all the risk and the client-load is inconsistent, and you feel the clinic people want a nutritionist's services, you might negotiate to have the job changed to a retainer so you could depend on a more stable income.

Contingency Fee or Commission Payment is made to you only if the project is successful or you work somewhere like a clinic and you take the full risk on whether patients pay. Writers are sometimes asked to work on speculation, and employment recruiters or many salespersons work on commission. The risk is high because a lot of time and overhead may be invested without any promise of income, but the income is usually hefty when it does come. If someone asks that you work on commission, make sure the reward is worth it either financially or professionally.

FEES IN DIFFERENT SETTINGS

Diet instruction fees should be consistent so that patients feel that they are charged fairly. There is no standardized way of charging for nutrition consultations. Some practitioners charge by the hour, but charge a minimum fee for very short appointments. They give their patients an estimate when asked how much the fees are. Other practitioners charge by the visit and then try to keep the appointment within a certain time range.

Several practitioners have programs where the diet consultation "package" takes three to eight or more visits. Printed diets are given out only after much education and assessment has taken place. The program commitment is made clear in the beginning. The fees are either paid in cash or credit card up front, or paid as they go, or payments are heavily weighed up front.

Following this same way of thinking, many practitioners automatically include several follow-up visits in the fees charged to clients. It is commonly agreed that a one-visit instruction *rarely* changes behavior. Patients aren't always aware of that and will not always attend follow-up visits unless their

118

importance is stressed. By paying in advance, patients make more effort to attend appointments.

Practitioners do not agree on whether offering flexible fees to certain clients produces the desired results, but it is an option. It is not uncommon for patients to remain uncommitted to making the desired changes in counseling when they have very little financially invested. For example, you give a "special" rate to a your friend or a physician's relative or a chronic dieter who has "tried everything." Of course there are exceptions and each counselor can decide what works best.

Group classes for weight loss, gourmet, "natural, " or heart healthy cooking are very popular with the public. For the private practitioner or employee group classes represent challenge, a creative outlet, and the possibility of making more income per hour because of reaching more people at a time. Here are two hints that may be helpful to a practitioner thinking about doing group classes: First, preregister attendees instead of letting them show up at the door, so that you can cancel if attendance will be poor or adjust your room and handouts if a large number plan to come.   Second, collect the fee for ongoing classes at the first session, or when preregistering so that attendance will be better and your budget more stable.

Public   speaking or speaking to professional groups can be very satisfying and fun. It should be financially rewarding. Organizers often work harder to have a better audience turnout when they are excited about the speaker and there is a fee to cover. Occasionally, there will be times when you choose to give a free talk, but at that time let the organizers know that you are waiving the normal fee, so they don't tell everyone you work for free. If the organization is nonprofit, either ask for a receipt showing that you donated your fee, or ask that they write you a check, which you will deposit, and write one back to them. Check with your accountant, they don't always agree on what is necessary for tax purposes.

When you first begin public speaking, you may not be familiar with what organizations are willing to pay. The best way to find out is to ask the person who calls to set up an engagement.   They know what their fee boundaries are, and most local people are very willing to share and negotiate with you. If the fee is low, try asking for more; also ask that your travel and handout costs be covered, or include an extra amount in your fee to cover local travel expenses. Always take your business cards and brochures to pass out and let everyone know where to find you. An easy alternative is printing the information on the handouts for your presentation.

As you become an established and sought-after speaker or an author of some note, your fees can reflect this. Travel and accommodations will be included for out-of-town travel. However, although the fees will be much higher, when you consider the travel time to distant speeches and any lost income while away from the business, the actual net income may be modest. Speakers often look on the opportunity as one to grow professionally, to travel and meet new people, and to sell books, products, consultative services, or whatever. With the cost of air travel today, many program planners schedule their meetings so that speakers and attendees can stay over a Saturday night. This can save 1/2 to 3/4 the cost of the airline ticket. If you are asked to stay over a day or two, negotiate for all your expenses if you want the job.

Consulting to business, media, or sports teams usually comes after years of specialized training or experience in the field. However, young practitioners with expertise in nutrition assessment, wellness, and other new emerging areas are also being asked to consult at this time.

If you are stumped on how much to ask for a consultant job, ask the client to make an offer, like a daily rate to make a media tour. At least then you would know the ballpark they are in, and you can then negotiate if it is too low. Don't answer too quickly and agree to a figure without doing your own calculations first. Clients are often hesitant about mentioning a fee first, in case you would have been willing to work for much less.

If you set the fee yourself, use your best calculations on what it will cost you to do the job, estimate your hours, supplies, computer usage, secretarial time, telephone, FAX, mail, travel and needed profit, and then estimate more hours to do the job by approximately one-fourth to one-third. Most often the problem is not that we set our fee too low, but that we underestimate how long a job will take and we barely break even. Coming in under budget is always acceptable, if it happens. More negotiating suggestions are found in Chapter 21.

Charging commercial clients is different than charging a patient in a private consultation because what you produce, like a menu, video script, article for publication or whatever will potentially bring in revenue to the client. You can always negotiate to arrive at the final agreement. What you want to avoid is coming in too low so you don't make money or coming in so high that you sour the client on using your services. You are looking for a well-thought-out beginning asking price with room to negotiate.

The factors to consider in pricing your services are:

- The popularity and recognition factor of your name and reputation.

- How the product will be used and the profit potential for the client.

- Your best estimate plus a cushion on the number of hours and other resources this project will cost you.

- Consider asking for a royalty for as long as the item is in use. Ask for editorial or revision rights to up date the product as needed or yearly. And finally, if the client wants to state that you are a staff member or consultant, ask for a retainer fee and have a letter of agreement on your rights and liability limitations. Talk to your professional advisors concerning your protection, proposal, fees, and before signing anything.

- Have your agreement on fees, expected outcomes, review process, project aborting, etc. down in writing and signed before you start work.

120

- Ask for a nonrefundable portion of your fee up front to cover some expenses in case the project plans change.

COMMON QUESTION

What can I use for arguments to substantiate why as a consultant , I should be paid $50 per hour? I am competing with dietitians who are willing to work as an employee for $12 per hour.

First, realize a few things about our profession and our marketplaces. Professionally, we are in a state of transition from being somewhat passive home economics majors to more assertive nutrition experts who initiate programs and ask a competitive fee for service or as a wage. Each of us is making the transition according to our own timetables and by what our lifestyles dictate. If someone loses a job to a more flamboyant peer or suddenly becomes the family's sole support, awareness and attitude changes evolve more quickly.

Next, not every client or consultant position is willing to pay the higher fee, no matter how good you are. In other words, you won't get every job, nor will you want every job you go after. Some jobs aren't worth more than $12 per hour.

In some instances if you really want the position, your only other option is to negotiate to do all of the required work in fewer hours for the same total income. For example, if there is $1050 budgeted for nutrition consultation each month, sell the client on the idea that that money is a flat fee paid to have the job completed and not tied to being on the job physically for eighty-seven hours per month or whatever. You will complete all the group classes, counseling, assessments, documentation, menu review, or whatever is required, and be at the job twenty to twenty-five hours per month or more often if needed. You will have to use your time well and produce for the client, but the pay is better ($42-$52 / hour), and you didn't lose the job. The client will have her or his nutrition needs met and still be within budget.

If a prospective client is comparing your consultant fee against that of a $12 per hour employee, there are some good points that may help your case, but first and foremost you must realize that *the client must believe and be convinced that you are worth that fee* or no amount of logic will sway him otherwise! **Possible selling points are:**

- As a consultant, you are bringing your own teaching materials, films, weight loss program, and previously successful seminars. The client does not have to pay for development time and hit or miss programming.

- When the cost of fringe benefits and Social Security, etc., are added to the hourly wage, the amount increases by one-third to one-half.

- As a consultant, you are not paid for meal times and breaks. And you come prepared for the job and can produce better work in a shorter period of time. You will even agree to fewer hours (at the higher fee).

121

- If you have been marketing well and using the media or other types of exposure to build recognition of your name, this is a selling point that may help attract more business to the client.

- If you have expertise in computers, culinary skills, kitchen layout, marketing, eating disorder programs, or you know people who could be beneficial to the client's programs or staff, try sharing enough to interest the client in the additional benefits you could bring to the job.

Once a "sell" is made to the client, realize that your arguments cannot be just campaign promises if you want to keep the position. You promised short-term excellence and the client will expect you to deliver.

SELLING AN INVENTION

When you want to sell an invention there are several things you must know. First, manufacturers are contacted by thousands of people each year who have "good" ideas for new products. So don't be discouraged if you have to sign a form stating that the manufacturer does not owe you anything unless they use your idea and had not thought of it themselves first. Also, most large manufacturers have their own Research and Development (R&D) departments that come up with new ideas, and they often discourage their bosses from buying an idea that could be developed in-house.

If you cannot patent your product (in other words it does not contain any new ingredients or process or outcome), then often its value is not as great because other companies can copy it legally and exactly, if it becomes popular. Also, if you have an unrefined product that still needs work or one that is only for a small select population, such as for patients with high uric acid levels, or one that has never proven itself on the market, it is usually not worth as much to the manufacturer. Today, because of the cost of introducing a new product on the market, many companies would rather buy out a small profitable company with products that are selling than try an unknown product on their own. Today, according to *Advertising Age* it costs $10-20 million to test market, advertise and then introduce a new cereal product nationwide into grocery stores.

Charlie McCann, a former new products manager for Coca-Cola of New York, once told me that the only way a small, underfinanced company can make a lot of money on a new idea is as the granola inventors did it. Come out with a product that sells like wildfire and then sell out to General Mills or Kellogg before everyone else jumps on the bandwagon and puts you out of business. There are thousands of exceptions to that rule, most notably, Ben and Jerry's Ice Cream, Stephen Job's Apple Computers, and American Beverage Company's SoHo.

Along with product samples, a "package" to interest a manufacturer could include a proposal with a market analysis and the product positioning. It could have a label sample, package design, and trademarked name, slogan and logo. The positioning entails determining who this product is designed to sell to, and why they would but it.

122

When you have developed a product you are proud of, it is time to contact a patent and contract lawyer to get feedback on how to protect your specific product. You must determine what you want from an agreement with a manufacturer. A business person with experience in this area is also very valuable, especially in determining whom to contact and how.

If you have any contacts with someone who could open doors for you or introduce you to the right people, use them. In some instances you may choose to use someone as an agent who knows the industry and offer him a finder's fee if he brings a buyer to you. From my own experience, do not expect someone else to come in and do all the work unless you can pay them well or they get part ownership in the product.

Several Options For Selling A Product

A manufacturer may show more than a casual interest in your product and want to offer a **90-day contract to look it over.** You will have to decide if you want to take it off the market for that period and allow a company to get to know the product inside out. It may be your best chance to make a sale (and to make some money because you will charge for the contract), or it could be a mistake. If several companies want it, others might not be interested if the first one rejects it.

An outright sale of your product to the company that will manufacture it and take it to market. Some companies have a policy of always owning everything they manufacture---it's cleaner that way---no inventors get in the way. You could sell outright for one lump sum or sell for an up front sum and a percentage of future sales. Or, to make the agreement work, you may accept only a percentage of sales, but that is risky unless you really trust that the company will produce as promised. The more risk you take, the more assurances you must have that the manufacturer will not sit on the product, reduce the quality of the product below the expectations of the target market, price it above what the market will pay, package it poorly, or not promote it.

Another option is a license-use agreement where you retain ownership of the product but sell the manufacturer the exclusive or nonexclusive right to produce the product for a specific period of time and/or location. This offers the advantage that you still ultimately own the product, but if you chose the wrong partner again, the product may not be worth much when it's returned. When you still own the product and a customer is hurt by it, whether from the original formulation or how it was manufactured, you could still have some liability risk.

Dietitians have become partners with programmers, venture capitalists, small manufacturers, marketing specialists, and others in order to get their products to market. Call your advisors and lawyer, and involve them in securing a contract that will protect you and your product.

There are no guidelines on how much you can sell a product for or how much percentage to negotiate for. It all depends on how much a buyer is willing to pay and how bad you want to work with that buyer. The value is influenced by the uniqueness of the product, the size of the potential market, the markup and profit potential, the strength of the competition, and whether the product is already a proven success with packaging, tradename, patents, and copyrights established. The more you have done on the product, the greater the value.

REFERENCES

1. *Competitive Edge* marketing seminar notebook: The American Dietetic Association, 1987.
2. Kelly, K.: *How To Set Your Fees and Get Them,* Visibility Enterprises, New York, 1984.

Chapter 17

Third Party Reimbursement

When someone other than the patient pays your fee for nutrition counseling, that is called third party payment. That "other" party is usually an insurance company or government program. At this time independent private practitioners report only inconsistent and sporadic coverage of their fees by third party payers, but it is improving.

As insurance coverage for nutrition services becomes a reality, it is hoped that more people in need of nutrition counseling will seek it out. We know that good nutritional care can make a big difference in the maintenance of good health. Unfortunately, third party programs, both public and private, have been slow to recognize the contributions registered dietitian can offer their beneficiaries. They have been particularly hesitant to cover nutrition services offered by an independent practitioner outside the standard institutional setting or physician's office. As the cost of health care continues to rise, perhaps the public will demand that nutrition services be covered to prevent and treat disease.

In California nutrition consultations by naturopaths and chiropractors are routinely covered but not nutrition consultations by registered dietitians, except under the auspices of an outpatient clinic or physician's office (1). The explanation for this from the insurance companies is not due to perceived poor care, but instead one of lack of legal recognition of dietitians by states.

The American Dietetic Association's Nutrition Services Payment Systems committee's publication *Reimbursement and Insurance Coverage for Nutrition Services* published in the fall of 1991 explains to members the payment options available in today's health care financing system. It guides members through the intricacies of billing third party payers to maximize reimbursement in many different practice settings (2). This publication, along with the cost benefit literature review, published as an April 1989 Journal supplement and the November 1991 JADA supplement which reviews four areas of critical care, should provide self-employed and employed dietitians with valuable information on how to improve their patients' chances for reimbursement.

COVERAGE CRITERIA

The major criteria that insurers use in deciding whether to offer coverage of a new service is whether the public is already willing to pay for it and whether there are requests for coverage for it. In other words there must be public demand and willingness to pay for the services, not just professional pressure. As new insurance policies are negotiated, nutrition counseling could be an added "perk" offered by employers or a new coverage item used by insurance companies to attract new business. However, if there are no private practitioners or hospital outpatient clinics in the area to make the public or the companies aware of the valued services, no changes are likely to be made. Most insurance policies are written for specific businesses or regions; very few are national. Therefore, changes will have to be initiated on a local or statewide basis. It should not be assumed that because a company offers coverage in one state or region, it will automatically offer it somewhere else.

Patients usually have the best chance of being reimbursed for nutrition consultation charges when the dietitian works out of a hospital-based clinic. There is a very good chance charges will be covered when the dietitian works as a consultant in a physician's office, but coverage is improved if the dietitian is an employee. Medicare can only be charged if the dietitian is an employee. Independent practitioners can improve their patients' chances of reimbursement by using a professional appearing billing form and having the patient attach the physician's request for nutrition consultation.

A major criteria insurance companies use in deciding what services to cover is whether the service provides cost/benefits. Will it save health care costs in the future for the patient to see a dietitian? Are the services vital and effective? Studies are available that help prove the cost/benefits of nutrition counseling, but each of us can develop statistics in our own setting.

To date twenty-six states offer some sort of legal recognition of dietitians in the form of a license or similar certification. In the other states presumably anyone calling themselves a nutritionist or dietitian can do so legally. This also keeps many providers from offering coverage on nutrition counseling by a registered dietitian.

BILLING SUGGESTIONS

Consultants suggest that, for purposes of cash flow and effective fee collection, nutrition consultants ask for payment of their fees at the time of the visit. It is then the responsibility of the patient to make sure the forms are filled out correctly and sent into the insurance company. If less than the entire fee is reimbursed, the patient, not the consultant, absorbs the difference. If patients delay payments and expect you to fill out their insurance forms, it could mean added problems and financial burdens for the practitioner.

Claims should be sent to insurers even when a patient is told over the phone that funding is probably not available. This may help create an increased awareness of the nutrition services and would check whether different people interpret their company policies differently.

126

GROUNDWORK FOR PAYMENT

The seven major steps to implementation of a Nutrition Services Payment System in any dietetic setting are (2):

1. Establish a rationale and plan for implementation.
2. Identify, define, and describe the services provided in the practice setting.
3. Establish fees.
4. Process charges and bill appropriate parties.
5. Monitor payment and reimbursement.
6. Document services rendered.
7. Educate users---market nutrition services.

Reimbursement

To help improve the patients' chances of obtaining reimbursement, the following suggestions are given:

1. **Have the referring physician write the request** for a diet instruction down on a prescription pad or a pad provided specifically for nutrition referrals. Include this order along with the paid bill when the patient sends in her or his insurance claim. The chances are poor if a client is self-referred for nutrition consultation. Practitioners can telephone the patient's physician to ask for a referral.

2. **On the nutritionist's bill, state the medical reason(s) for the nutrition consultation,** being careful not to list obesity as the primary diagnosis, unless there are complications. The bill should also show the referring physician, date, the services offered, the amount of time spent and the dietitian's registration and license numbers. Do not use the words "nutrition education" since it does not sound medically based.

3. **Consultants should make a special effort to document improvement in patient's health** not only in subjective terms, but also in lab values, skinfolds, and other anthropometric, physiologic, or cardiac values. Documentation of results may prove very beneficial in future negotiations on the need for third party coverage and the contribution of nutrition consultation.

MARKETING TO INSURERS

You are encouraged to contact your local insurance headquarters offices to see what steps they would suggest to have nutrition consultation become a covered service. You may also contact state agencies that govern Workers' Compensation and Medicaid programs. Some private practitioners have offered academic credentials, resumes, nutrition services definitions, plus their approximate cost and time allotments and patients' outcomes as supporting evidence of the quality and validity of their care. Letters may be written to third party payers to introduce your service or to defend patients' requests for coverage.

CONCLUSION

On the negative side, there is the potential that has already happened in other medical professions when third party coverage arrived---that it did not guarantee better patient care. And, it supported a few incompetent professionals who took advantage of the program.

A positive result of third party payment, is that more patients will seek help for their nutritional problems and may come for help sooner. Some financial relief through third party coverage, would mean follow up could last longer. This should result in better and more comprehensive nutritional care and more success in changing clients' behavior. An increase in third party coverage probably will not produce a dramatic increase in client referrals or a long line of patients waiting to get in the door. Counselors must still build a reputation for being successful and effective so that patients and other health professionals have a high "perceived value" for nutrition services.

REFERENCES

1. Williams, William, insurance consultant to The American Dietetic Association, Chicago, 1983.
2. *Reimbursement and Insurance Coverage for Nutrition Services,* The American Dietetic Association, Chicago, 1991.

Chapter 18

Start-up Decisions and Costs

The cost of starting a business venture can vary greatly depending on the region of the country and the tastes of the practitioner. Some feel that if they are going to start a business, they are going to do it right. Others try to see how little they can spend to make the venture fly. Both can be successful, but both have also failed.

Investing a large sum each month in overhead to cover prime office space, extensive advertising, a secretary's salary, and new furnishings can create a successful stable image right from the start. This should logically attract more business---eventually. Eventually is the important word. There is a point where adding more money to create a good business will not necessarily bring in more clientele faster. However, an equally bad error can be made by not investing enough to give clients the feeling that you will be there next week.

Before trying to guess how much you are willing to spend on this venture, first decide what kind of office, furnishings, services, staffing, and marketing you would ideally like to have. Then estimate the cost to see if you can afford it. Compromises may have to be made. It may be that the office must be shared with another professional to cut the rental fee, the computer diet analyses and photocopying sent out, or a typing service called in as needed.

As mentioned earlier, most business consultants encourage new business owners to buy only the essentials, look for affordable quality, and keep the overhead low, especially the first year. The second year, increase the profit and savings, and ordinarily, wait until the third year to expand and invest in more expensive ventures. The years involved are not as important as the business and financial growth that should logically take place first.

It is a well-known fact in business that the more metropolitan the area and the more ideal the rental space, the higher the cost, unless the area is overbuilt. This is especially true on the East and West coasts as compared to rural America. Competition for office space and higher service fees drive up costs that you must pay to run your business. Fees that a consultant charges can reflect these higher costs. The figures that follow are just rough estimates of the costs involved. Call around in your local area to get more accurate figures (see Figure 18.1).

IMPORTANCE OF WORKING CAPITAL

Up-front money will be invested to buy or rent the essentials to start your business, for example, office space, printed materials, calling cards, scale, calipers, insurance, telephone, answering service, furniture, and so on. The money that maintains these essentials and your salary is the working capital. Therefore, when estimating your expenses, recognize that there are two categories: up-front money to open the doors and maintenance money (working capital) to sustain the business. When planning a business, these two categories do not include the money being generated by clients.

The working capital should be readily available, but it does not have to be in your checking account. It could be a prearranged line of credit from your bank that isn't used unless it is needed---or any one of a number of other choices mentioned in Chapter 15. As a reminder, for your peace of mind, arrange to have six months' working capital available.

OFFICE SPACE

Choosing the correct office location, along with good marketing, may decide your ultimate success in business more than your nutritional expertise. Your office space can be instrumental in conveying stability, credibility, and success to patients and clients---or just the opposite.

Novices to business often do not know what kind of office space to look for. Some choose office space that costs very little, but unfortunately, they often get the quality they paid for. Others sign leases for beautiful space that destines them to work just to pay the rent. Some practitioners have found that sharing office space with a physician or even renting space in the same building as an influential or controversial physician may keep other physicians from referring patients.

Knowing that some practitioners work successfully out of their homes, others try it, but have dismal luck. You can avoid most of these problems with a little research and objective evaluation.

Rental Office Space

The ideal office location is convenient, accessible, and presents a good image. Clients will become more tolerant of inconveniences such as limited or paid parking, no elevator service, and little or no waiting room space as your reputation grows. However, these problems possibly could be avoided by anticipating them and seeking a better location.

It may take several years before your business will attract clients from very far away. Practitioners suggest that offices be located near prospective clientele. Market research should help identify that area of town.

If you choose office space in a medical complex instead of an office building, you may find that you will attract more business, if the physicians in the building are good referral agents. Fewer patients may get "lost" between being referred and actually scheduling a nutrition consultation.

Although "store-front" businesses in shopping malls or corner retail centers can do very well, private practitioners are not known for choosing these locations---yet. As emergency medical centers and daytime outpatient services become more prevalent in retail areas, maybe dietitians will opt to be there too.

There is one final point on a rental location: before signing a lease closely evaluate your neighbors, surrounding businesses, and the landlord. If you are signing a long-term lease, it is important to know if the area is going downhill, if neighboring renters are disruptive, or if the landlord maintains the property well.

Figure 18.1 Sample Start-up Cost Estimates

Working Capital
Have six months' capital available before starting.

Lease
Deposit: Damage and last month's rent?
Monthly rent: $6 to $30+/square foot/year.
Nameplates: $5 to $150 (be sure to check).
Parking: Is staff parking included in rent? Is cost high for clients?

Utilities
Deposit: Amount varies.

Telephone
Deposit: Amount varies, but may run from $100 to over $400.
Installation: $60 to $800; you may have to buy a phone system.
Monthly rate: $15 to $65+ per line.
Yellow Pages listing: One line is free; everything else is extra.
White Pages listing: Listing is free, but boldface is extra.
Long-distance service: $5 to $20/ month, plus phone bill.

Services
Answering service: $40 to $100 month.
Answering machine: $150 to $300, depending on features.
Call Forwarding: $2+/ month.
Call Waiting: $5 or less/ month.
Accountant fees: $60 to $175.0+/ hour.
Attorney fees: $65 to $150 + / hour.
Temporary secretarial service: $8 to $24.00/ hour.
Typing service: $7 to $24/ hour.
Receptionist-secretary: Salary varies, but the best are expensive.
Cleaning service: cost varies.

Insurance
Office liability and fire: $50 to $125.00+/ year.
Malpractice: About $83/year when working part-time for $200,000 coverage;
        $186 on up/ year for $200,000 coverage when working full-time.
Disability: $20 to $40.00/ month.
Health: Amount varies.
Life: Amount varies.

131

Office Supplies
Announcements: $25 to $65 per 100.
Business cards: $25 to $65 per 1000.
Letterheads: $10 to $30 per 100 (next 100s are less).
Envelopes: $18 to $30 per 100 (next 100s are less).
Brochure: Varies greatly; get several quotes. Ranges from 15 to 35 cents per
       brochure plus typesetting.
Logo: Artist fees vary greatly; an art student or teacher costs less than a
       commercial artist.
Bookkeeping system: $40 to $650 to establish.
Copying and printing: Price around; prices vary greatly.
Postage and miscellaneous: Keep supplies in modest amounts.
Handouts and teaching materials: Keep in modest supply.

Equipment and Furniture
Medical scale: $200+.
Typewriter/ Word Processor: $250+.
Copier: $50+/month to rent or $1500+ to buy.
Calipers: $175 to $450.
Computer and software: $1500 to $6000 to buy; may be leased, or send food
       lists out for analysis.
Fax machine: $500 on up, can be a combination answer machine and fax.
Furnishings and carpet: Amount varies greatly.

Advertising
Experts suggest 15% of the budget for advertising first year.

Incorporation
$800 to $3500.

Seeing Patients at Your Home
Before starting a private practice out of your own home, realize that the home environment can be a blessing or a big mistake. The home setting should be as professional as any private office. That means no family interruptions or phone calls during patient interviews and a comfortable yet clean and uncluttered setting. If the home does not have an appropriate waiting area, it may be necessary to allow more time between patient appointments.

A positive benefit of working out of one's home is that patients and clients seem to relax more quickly. This eases sessions or interviews. Also, it is convenient, requires no travel, and overhead is reduced; therefore profit per hour can be higher.

On the negative side of using the home: it may be an intrusion into the family's privacy, patients or physicians may be hesitant to use your services, and the dietitian may feel tied to the work setting. Some dietitians report they do not work out of their homes because they are concerned that their business images would not appear as established and successful. It is inconvenient and a very poor business decision to use your home to see patients when it is in a large apartment or condominium complex, and difficult to find.

If a den or other room is used exclusively for seeing patients or as your office, a percentage of the square footage and a portion of the related expenses or a rental fee may be a business tax deduction. A multipurpose room such as a living room or den with the family TV cannot be used as a deduction. Consult with your financial advisor on your specific situation.

Zoning laws for your neighborhood should be checked before starting to see patients at your home. The laws were written to protect the neighborhood quality of life from any undue disruption, excessive traffic, or commercialism. Practitioners who already work quietly out of their homes and have only one or two patients per hour have not found that zoning was a problem. If it becomes one, it may be possible to obtain a zoning variance for your business. Unless the zoning is correct for a business at home, an outside sign is usually not permitted.

Home Visits

Private practitioners in both rural and affluent areas have had success seeing patients in their own homes. Patients enjoy the convenience and are willing to pay extra, if they can afford it.

For the practitioner home visits are not an efficient use of time, if they pull him away from the office where other patients could be seen. If, however, the practitioner works at home and does home visits instead of renting an office, the savings could make it a good option.

Travel time, gas, and other related costs must be figured to help decide home visit fees. Some practitioners charge their patients a flat rate, while others charge according to the total time involved.

As home visits become more commonplace, or when insurance coverage more readily applies to home rehabilitation, this option may be very viable and popular.

Office Layout

If you can afford it, it is always a nice touch to have a receptionist or secretary--even one shared in common with other offices--to greet patients as they arrive. Patients expect to have a place to sit and wait and a more private place for the diet consultation. Except for group meetings and large families, there will seldom be times when the waiting room will need more than four chairs and your office more than two for patients.

Most practitioners decorate their offices to fit their own tastes, not as a medical clinic. Patients seem more at ease with warmer surroundings and the break from what is traditional.

To establish credibility immediately, practitioners' certificates, diplomas, and awards should be framed and displayed in their offices. Patients do notice and read these items.

Office Safety

For the sake of safety, it is advisable to have an office fire extinguisher, flashlight, and smoke alarm. A diagram of the exits should be attached to

133

the back of the main door. The furniture and decorations in the waiting room and your office should not be obviously dangerous or fragile. Any steps should be well marked and lighted.

When clients are being seen in the evenings it is best to ask group members to leave together or to call the building security person to make sure the client, or you, get into your cars without problems. When you are working before or after normal business hours (when few people are around), care should be taken to keep the office door locked. This precaution also applies whenever working out of your home---do not just let people walk into an unlocked house. With a little care, potentially negative situations may be avoided.

OFFICE AGREEMENTS

Rental or Lease
The following guidelines may be helpful to you when renting space:

- Do not accept the stated rental fee at face value. Virtually all rents are negotiable.

- Be on the lookout for especially attractive bargains caused by the economy or overbuilding. Many property owners are strapped for cash and are willing to make attractive offers.

- Look for ways to operate with a minimum amount of space. Should the firm be successful, chances are good you will be able to find additional space when it is needed.

- Practitioners seeking to serve a large market area should consider renting two smaller offices at different locations (one close to downtown and one in the suburbs) rather than one large one. This can double the firm's exposure and convenience to clients without doubling the cost of doing business, if it is planned well.

- Be aware that many leases have additions that boost the space costs well above the base price per square foot. Maintenance or management fees may not have limitations on escalation. Compute these costs into the amount of the lease.

- In negotiating for consulting space, be sure to mention that your business will not need special plumbing, extra electrical outlets or lavatory facilities--this will mean less expense and fewer problems for the building owner and rental could begin sooner.

- Be sure to ask what the rental fee includes, such as, shared waiting room, receptionist, utilities, insurance, carpeting, and so on. Discuss who will own any shelving, carpeting, or other additions you may pay for in your office--usually the landlord takes ownership unless another arrangement was agreed upon. If you want to cover the floor but not leave the carpet, use an Oriental or Southwestern-style rug.

- Will any months of free rent be offered to you as an enticement to rent?

134

- Check to see that the lease allows you to sublease your space in case the need arises.

- Most leases run a minimum of one to three years, but occasionally special concessions can be made for new or small businesses. Realize that the shorter the term of the lease, probably the sooner the rent will go up.

- Have a lawyer review the terms of the lease.

The major advantages of having a rental space of your own are that you can control its use, you can decorate it to your tastes, materials and records are readily available, and a business phone can be permanently installed. All of these elements help contribute to a more smoothly run operation and the appearance of order and prosperity. In a food management or similar practice, the office locale can be more flexible, especially when clients seldom come to the office.

Before moving into rented space it may be necessary to pay not only the first month's rent, but also the last month's rent and a sizable damage deposit. In all it may amount to three or more times the monthly rent! Ask your financial advisor about local state laws governing the money held by the landlord and your rights to interest, early payback, and so on.

Rental fees are quoted in two basic ways: a monthly rate, such as $350 per month, or as cost per square foot. The cost per square foot is usually for one year unless indicated otherwise. It may range from $6 per square foot in some locales to $30 or more in others. To figure your rent first determine the total numher of square feet to be rented then multiply that figure times the cost per square foot to arrive at the total cost per year; divide by 12 months to arrive at your monthly rent.

Coleasing

Coleasing takes place when two partners or other people agree to rent an office jointly. This is often an advantage when the square footage is too large for one and it is useful to share the cost. If the office space is only large enough for one person at a time, the days are alternated.

It is not advisable to colease with another nutritionist, unless you are partners and working for the same goals. Otherwise, trying to advertise two businesses selling the same or similar service under the same telephone number and handling "walk-in" patients without intruding on each other's territory could prove too troublesome.

It is again extremely important that you choose a coleasee well, and that a lawyer review the lease agreement. The agreement may hold you both responsible for damage or theft that your coleasee or his clients inflict. It may leave you with the full responsibility if the other person moves or leaves and does not fulfill the entire lease agreement. No doubt if you and the other coleasee present yourselves as "one" to the landlord, he or she will expect you both to be responsible for the property and the terms of the lease. You could therefore have an agreement with the other leasee that each of you is responsible for any damage and for the rent for the term of the agreement. Again, make sure you can sublease the space if necessary. Read the agreement carefully, change terms as necessary, have your lawyer review and make additions, and then submit it back to the landlord.

Sharing Office Space or Subleasing

Sharing office space is an alternative for those who want all of the amenities of a nice office and locale, but at less expense. In addition to the office, the telephone and answering service, copy machine and receptionist/secretary may be shared. Again, all agreements should be in writing and reviewed by a lawyer.

An office may be subleased from another professional such as a speech therapist or psychologist who only needs the office several days per week or who has too much space for his or her business. The office rent and expenses can be split according to the percentage of the week each uses the office or for whatever amount you agree upon. Be sure to negotiate and get the best deal for yourself as you would with a landlord.

Office space can be shared with a physician or clinic. Several different options are possible in this instance (see Chapter 24). The private practitioner could remain independent and do his own billing, marketing, printing of materials, and scheduling of own appointments while subleasing or renting space. Another option would be to give a percentage of the consultant fee in return for the use of the office and its amenities. A third option is to negotiate a retainer fee where you would always be available to see patients for the physician or clinic during a designated time in return for your receiving a specified fee--this is a good option when your services are sought after but the patient load is variable. A final option that some practitioners are still able to find is office space offered for free so that nutrition services are more accessible to the patient.

As you negotiate rent with a physician or clinic, consultants warn that doctors sometimes tend to overestimate the number of persons you will see. Agree on a fee that you can afford, not one that is based on ultimate expectations.

Close association with other professionals can provide numerous benefits. Several very successful practitioners report that much of their success when they first started in business came from having one or more "mentor" physicians who promoted them. Some of the physicians sublet space to the dietitians, but others just did it out of friendship and respect for the practitioner and aid to the patients.

Depending upon your individual situation, some important questions need to be discussed with the physician: Will you be able to see other doctors' patients at the office? Who will schedule patient appointments, pull and file charts, and bill patients? Can you use the copy machine? Who will market you and how? Remember the more services you request the more you may have to spend. Write down all agreements and have a signed copy for each party. A simple letter of agreement will work. A termination clause is advisable. When a contract is coming up for renewal, you should start negotiating at least a month in advance to allow both parties a chance to work out differences.

Parking

In some locations parking space is at a premium, especially in downtown or medical center areas. If a parking lot is owned by your building, are spaces included for the leasee? Can they be added when negotiating the lease?

Name Plates and Floor Directories
Most office buildings have some kind of directory outside the building, in the main lobby, or on each floor, in addition to door name plates. Seldom will a landlord of a medical building allow you to print your own--they like them standardized. This again could be a lease option to negotiate. Don't assume anything; one practitioner had to pay up to $26 per line for four partners on six floors.

Utilities
When utilities are not included in the lease, the utility companies can give you an estimate of your monthly bill. For electricity they will need to know the number of watts of each light and how many hours per week it will be used, in addition to the estimated usage of other equipment such as air conditioning, a typewriter, or computer. For gas heating, the square footage of your office can be used in determining an estimate. A money deposit or a letter of credit may be necessary to obtain new service, if you live in the area, try to negotiate using your established good credit.

Telephone
The ongoing changes after the break up of AT&T will necessitate that each practitioner check on the best telephone coverage available locally. To survive a business must have good telephone service and coverage.

A new business phone system costs approximately $800 to install. Converting an existing private line in an office or at home is usually only a fraction of that cost. If you have never had a business line, the telephone company may ask for a deposit--call for an estimate. The monthly fee for the telephone line will range from approximately $10-$85 per line.

Other services that you may consider for your phone are call waiting, call forwarding, conference lines, and a limited service line. Call waiting will allow you to accept a second incoming call while keeping the first call on the line. Call forwarding allows you to transfer your incoming phone calls to another phone number where you or your answering service can answer it. Limited service lines are not available everywhere, but the line allows a limited number of outgoing calls to be made each month for a reduced rate. Calls above the limit are charged extra; in-coming calls are not counted. The rates and availability of these services vary--call your local company for more information.

Whenever you pay for a telephone line, business or personal, you will be given a listing in the white pages for free; bold print is extra. To have a Yellow Pages listing, you must have a business line. One listing under the most appropriate heading (probably "Dietitian" or "Nutritionist") will be given to you. Additional listings, bold print, extra lines, logo, a large ad, and so on will cost extra and will be billed monthly or however you arrange. If you share office space with someone who already has a business phone, for an added fee you can have your name added to that line. It will then be in directory information and in the Yellow Pages.

Answering Service
When you begin your business the phone should be answered during normal business hours, Monday through Friday. An answering service or recording machine can give you coverage when you are away from the phone. An answering service that receives your call through call forwarding and does not answer with your company name is the most inexpensive while giving a personal touch.

A telephone answering machine with a remote call device can give you coverage. The public is becoming more familiar with talking to a machine. If the message is clear, creative, and of good quality, callers will use it.

SERVICES

Secretary/Receptionist
There is little doubt that a small business owner would enjoy using the services of a secretary/receptionist, however, there are ways to have the duties covered without having the full cost of an employee. According to surveys conducted by popular women's magazines, a good, experienced secretary is usually paid as much as a good dietitian with years of experience. Some alternatives are to hire someone part-time for several mornings per week, send out your typing, set up your office so that you can handle it yourself, use a temporary secretarial service at peak times, or find office space where a secretary's services are included.

INSURANCE

Malpractice
Call The American Dietetic Association to find out the most current malpractice carrier and policy information. Prices vary according to the number of hours worked and the desired limits on coverage.

Office Liability and Furnishings
When a practitioner opens an office people will visit, there is always the risk that someone will get hurt on the premises. In rental space the landlord usually carries liability coverage, but often on a limited basis. When sharing space at a physician's office or clinic, good liability coverage may already be available to you under their policy--check. When working out of your home, home insurance companies ask that they be notified so that coverage can be increased. Insurance for office contents in case of fire, theft, or other loss is easily acquired along with the liability coverage.

Disability
Disability insurance will provide a certain level of limited income while you are ill. The most expensive coverage begins after only 15 days of illness and

138

lasts for up to life. To reduce the cost disability payments could begin after 60 or 90 days of illness and last for only one year.

The premium and disability coverage are dependent upon your age, health, and present income. Unfortunately self-employed individuals have a more difficult time qualifying for this type of insurance according to several companies. Check with several insurance companies, including ADA to see what they have to offer and compare costs and coverage.

Health

Health insurance is a necessity with today's health care costs. One hospital stay for one week or more could wipe out an uninsured person's savings. To help reduce the cost of a policy, try to join under a spouse's policy, contact local HMOs or PPOs, or join a group policy (through The American Dietetic Association, executive clubs, rural cooperatives, small business owners, local chambers of commerce, or those offered by local insurance brokers). In some cases if you have two or more employees in your business, you can qualify as a group. Another way to keep premium payments lower, is to choose major medical coverage instead of a comprehensive top-of-the-line policy. You would have to pay the first $500 or $1000 of a bill but then coverage may be 80 to 100 percent after that. Prices and coverage vary so greatly that you will need to take the time to get several quotes.

Life

Life insurance to pay off your loans and debts, as well as to help support your family in case of your death, is an important consideration. Term life insurance is usually the least expensive for the amount of coverage if you are younger and in good health. However, as the person grows older, the yearly premiums may increase quickly. Variations of whole life policies are readily available today. This type of policy is more expensive from the beginning, but eventually can act as a savings account to be borrowed against. This type of policy has a definite total price; therefore, premiums do not continue indefinitely as with term insurance.

OFFICE SUPPLIES

Business Cards

Before ordering cards make sure that your address and phone number will be more than temporary. Several practitioners have had cards printed with either the phone or address missing and had the information calligraphied in later. Allow two weeks to have cards printed. Because of the cost savings, most businesses order 500 or 1000 cards at a time. Cost for printing depends upon the layout, paper, ink, embossing, and number of different colors of ink. For the first run there usually are typesetting and layout fees.

Letterheads

Paper that is standard stock can be printed easily when more is needed. When the letterhead is on special paper, it can be more economical and time efficient to order the paper by the ream and keep it on hand yourself. Take it to be printed as you need it. If the letterhead printing or ink is special, it is more economical to print a larger amount because of the one-time fees to change ink colors, emboss, imprint, and so on.

An economical way to send out a large mailing or form letter is to type the letter on one of your letterheads and have it reproduced on good paper (logo, your name and address, letter, and all). The date, heading, and your signature can be added whenever you use the letter.

To have a professional looking letter it is important that the color of paper you choose has correction tape or liquid to match. Plain paper should be purchased to match the letterhead for additional pages of a letter. Business letters are usually sent on 81/2" x 11" paper, but notes can be any size with the appropriate size envelopes.

Brochures
Good quality brochures are an asset to a business; typesetting or desktop publishing is highly recommended. To save money the brochure could be a self-mailer, but for times when the best image is required, use an envelope. Before printing your brochure have several people read it and offer suggestions. Some pharmaceutical companies have offered to print brochures for private practitioners as a professional service. If you are interested in this service check with your local representatives.

Bookkeeping System
A beginning bookkeeping system with an appointment book, cash ledger, receipts, file folders, and yearly ledger can be purchased for under $40. Your accountant or CPA may request that you purchase a definite kind of system, but most are reasonable.

Diets and Handouts
The most important aspect about printed materials given to a client is to keep them simple, clear, and impressive. Also, don't load the patient down with every free booklet available on a subject--pick the best ones, free or not.

EQUIPMENT AND FURNISHINGS

Medical Scale
If a scale is used, a good balance beam medical scale is suggested. A waist-high balance beam is not suggested because it is awkward for very heavy patients to stand on the scale without touching the beam. Spring scales are not always accurate.

Skinfold Calipers
For consultants who work with weight loss, sports nutrition, or nutrition assessment, calipers are a must. They range in price from approximately $.50 for the plastic ones to $175-$250 for the metal ones to $450 for the computerized ones.

Typewriter
If you decide to buy a typewriter, look for one that is a word processor so that the manuscripts can be easily edited and printed. It is suggested that it

be pica-size type so that elderly patients can easily read it, not script style that is not appropriate for business writing.

Computer

A computer, its components, printer and software can be a tax deduction if they are used for business; if used for both business and home, only a percentage is deductible. Businesses are springing up that rent computer or word processor time--you just supply the software. Systems may be leased monthly for a minimum number of months. For businesses where you will write, search databases and communicate often with big businesses, a computer, modem and FAX are becoming standard office equipment.

Copier

When the volume warrants it, consider buying a photocopier. Many practitioners state that having a plain paper copier that can reproduce office forms, bills, bulk mailings, instruction materials, and so on is a necessity. At the start of a business it may be more economical to share a copier or find a convenient quick copy store. Used copiers may be available for reasonable prices.

Office Furniture

Prices will vary with personal taste. Make the setting comfortable for yourself and the client. For dietitians who will be seeing very large patients, buy sturdy chairs without armrests or with a wide area between armrests, and not so soft so that standing up becomes embarrassing.

MARKETING

Advertising

Business consultants suggest that at least fifteen percent of your budget be allocated to cover the cost of the first year's kick-off campaign in marketing, such as newspaper ads, business lunches, brochures, direct mail letters, and so on. Also allow five to ten percent or more of each additional year's budget for on-going marketing.

MISCELLANEOUS

Although we like to feel that we have anticipated all of the applicable expenses, we of course haven't. Memberships and subscriptions will need to be budgeted. A dependable car may have to be purchased. A "cushion" needs to be planned to cover petty cash expenses and unexpected larger expenses.

Good preplanning makes the evolution of a business an anticipated pleasure instead of a crisis management seminar.

section 5

Managing Your Business

Words of Wisdom:

"Unless you try to do something beyond what you have already mastered, you will never grow."

Ronald E. Osborn

"To dream anything that you want to dream. That is the beauty of the human mind. To do anything that you want to do. That is the strength of the human will. To trust yourself to test your limits. That is the courage to succeed."

Bernard Edmonds

Chapter 19

Creating a Good Business Image

Every new business and its owner will eventually develop an image in the mind of the public. The important thing is that the image be a good one. Having a positive, successful image is what many large corporations, politicians, and movie stars spend untold amounts of money to achieve. They know that their image will usually decide success--whether their products sell, they get a vote, or remain a star (1).

Consultant nutritionists report that as their professional images grow to look successful, their businesses attract new clientele with a minimum of effort. Good images make patients, physicians, and business people want to use their services. Everyone likes to feel that their nutritionist (also physician and dentist) is the best, the most sought after, the most qualified and successful.

YOUR OWN STYLE

When creating an image the first thing that comes to mind is physical appearance. Also, it is important who we are, what we stand for, our "message," tactfulness, stability, credibility, and appearance of success.

Successful entrepreneurs have a variety of professional approaches. There are those that are very conservative in dress and manner and traditional in instructing patients. Others have flashy appearances and seek out unconventional nutrition information. As long as the person's practice is ethical and meets the clients' needs, it is not necessary for everyone's approach to be the same.

Creativity and uniqueness in the development of a business will help create an image that is distinctive from its competition. One image is only better than another if the practitioner feels more comfortable with it, or if it is more successful in reaching more people and producing more income.

WHO WE ARE AND WHAT WE STAND FOR

Choose battles carefully. Others' opinions of us are greatly influenced by what we choose to defend, our honesty and how we fight our battles. It is important that we have opinions, and that they are well thought out and researched. Do not appear to be a person who lacks loyalty and changes

143

opinions to please whoever is ahead. Defend your arguments with facts and fairly listen to other points of view. Also, be willing to accept a majority vote or new evidence that substantiates another point of view. Become known for your honesty, integrity and fairness.

APPEARANCE AND FIRST IMPRESSIONS

Because of stiff competition and the fast-paced nature of this society a person seldom has the opportunity to make up for a poor first impression. A well-qualified dietitian may never get the chance to show what he knows because he did not "first get his foot in the door."

Having a good appearance increases the chances that a consultant's creative ideas will be heard. A counselor's effectiveness on the job is also influenced by appearance. Part of whether a patient or his family respond to counseling is dependent upon their first impression of the counselor, and whether credibility has been established.

Although it may seem vain and foolish to put too much emphasis on outward appearance, it is equally fool hardy to put too little value on it. A story about an East Coast student illustrates the importance the public places on overall appearance and clothing. A student was dressed in two different ways on two different days and then went to ask people for money in a New York City subway. He used the same words both days, "I've lost my wallet; can I borrow 30¢ to get home?" The first day the student had a day's growth of beard and was dressed slovenly in old clothes. The second day he was clean shaven and dressed in a three-piece suit. The difference in the amount of money he collected was astounding--about $19 the first day and over $300 the second day! The public responded to how he took care of himself, dressed, and the status or power it implied.

To show examples of how dress and appearance influence feelings about someone, think how you would feel when:

1. A very close relative of yours is in the hospital and while you are visiting, a young medical person comes into the room. The fellow is wearing a white jacket with a stethoscope around his neck. He is also wearing a loud-colored paisley tie. Do you wonder whether he is really the physician in charge or just a student? Do you question his seriousness?

2. You are down to the two final candidates to be the dietitian to head a corporate wellness marketing campaign. You must hire the best one for the job. Both women speak equally well and have similar grooming. One candidate has worn floral shirtwaist dresses to both interviews and the other wore a linen suit the first interview and a black, feminine suit at the second interview. Do you feel a tendency to hire the candidate who dresses more like a corporate executive?

A dietitian should strive to be a good example of the nutrition and health professions and "practice what he preaches." That means he or she should have near normal weight, eat well, and have a healthy appearance. Carolyn Worthington, a registered dietitian who specializes in recruiting

144

dietitians, states that, "Nothing diminishes a candidate's job prospects more than being very overweight. The overweight dietitian destroys her or his credibility with clients and medical staffs." Just as a cardiologist who smokes or a preacher who swears loses credibility in the eyes of some of his or her clients, extreme obesity and poor health habits can create a credibility problem for a dietitian.

Other aspects of a good physical image and appearance are posture, direct eye contact while speaking, a firm handshake, and body language that is confident and positive, not filled with nervous movement. Speaking in a clear, bold manner and making sure that the statements are well thought out also contribute to good image.

HERMAN

"Are you eating properly and getting plenty of exercise?"

TACTFULNESS AND MANNER

Along with physical appearance, people notice and respond to a professional's tactfulness and manner. The old adage holds true, "He was right, but he lost the argument because of the way he handled it." People in business find that they are not only selling a commodity or service, but also themselves to the client, their families, and professional peers.

Business people have the task of finding the happy medium between being aggressive and knowing when to be passive and pull back. They must learn when to make a point and when to let another person's point of view dominate. Novices tend to experience greater swings and react in one extreme manner or the other. Experience and self-confidence help develop a more self-assured, moderate attitude and approach. This transition is difficult for most. Until recently women have never been encouraged to be assertive. Consultant nutritionists have definitely experienced this confusion coming from meeker hospital roles into trying to distinguish themselves as businesspersons. Time and experience in the field prove to be the best teachers.

The "Rule of 250," developed by a sales trainer, briefly states that every person we meet has a sphere of influence with other people, such as employer, family, neighbors, and so on, that may affect as many as 250 other people. That means that a tactless comment or a bad encounter or a very positive experience can have influence on a potentially large number of people. A businessperson's image in the eyes of the public is greatly affected by the small day-to-day dealings and the manner in which they are handled.

Some suggestions that could improve tactfulness with your patients, clients, referring physicians, leasing agents, professional counselors, etc., include:

1. Be very cautious about what is said when you feel that you have been attacked. Becoming defensive and "striking back" is *not* the best response. Instead try to relax and state something like, "I am sorry you feel that way" or "I don't feel that was necessary to say."

2. Be brief and direct in your word choices and speak in a slow, nonemotional tone. Conduct your business directly with the individuals involved and do not leave long messages with spouses or secretaries. Secondhand messages have a way of being misinterpreted.

3. When people ask, "Are you worth that much money?" consultants can answer by saying, "I certainly am; let me explain what I can do for you."

4. If a physician states that he or she only charges $45 for a visit, why do you charge $65, a good answer is, "that is true, but the difference may be in how long we spend with the patient. I spend 45 minutes to one hour with a patient for that fee."

146

5. If a patient is not responding to the counseling and probably has no intention of doing so, it is not out of line to suggest that, "We evidently do not respond well to each other, and I feel that perhaps another counselor could help you more. Would you like for me to refer you to someone else?"

6. If a professional advisor (lawyer, accountant, etc.) has not performed your work well, talk directly with the individual and state, "I am not happy with what I see of your work. Are you interested in my business, and if so, what can you do to take care of this situation?" or "Your work is not the quality that I expected and I am disappointed. Some of it is not what we discussed. I would like you to reevaluate the charges on the bill you sent me."

STABILITY AND CREDIBILITY

In his book *Winning Images*, Robert Shook states, "People need to know that their relationships with you are durable. Everyone realizes that flash-in-the-pan types cannot be counted on, and such an image scares people away" (1).

A service type of business such as nutrition counseling is, by its nature, intangible, therefore, its need to look stable and credible, is even greater. Most beginning practitioners will not be in a financial position to afford an expensive office in the best location, so other means to look stable and prosperous must be found.

Using high-quality business cards and brochures, as well as handout materials, gives the appearance of professionalism and can engender a sense of trust in others. Offering personalized instruction and development of high-quality programs gives a business and its owners credibility. Completing projects by the deadline and within the projected budget builds a good reputation. Doing something when you say you are going to do it sounds simple, but it is a rare individual or company that actually follows this principle.

Keeping appointments and arriving on time is important and is appreciated. Clients and patients also expect to come and meet with a consultant nutritionist at or near the appointment time. Physicians who are notoriously late in seeing their patients are finding that patients will not accept this discourtesy as they used to.

Second chances are seldom given today to professionals who do not perform as promised. Many people whose talents border on genius achieve only mediocre results in their careers because they lack the necessary follow-through and persistence to perform well. In business less-gifted people continually outperform highly educated and gifted persons because they provide consistently good service (1).

To enjoy a long and rewarding career, an entrepreneur should provide outstanding work and good, timely information. The clients should feel that they receive full value of the services rendered.

SUCCESS BREEDS SUCCESS

People like to deal with successful people because being successful must mean they are good at what they do. When given a choice, people want to deal with the best. To create an image of success do outstanding work and become successful. The performance and reputation of a professional will attract the public and bring in business referrals as time passes.

When starting a new business there are some lessons that can be incorporated to reduce the amount of time needed to appear as a winner. First appear busy to the clients. Patients question how good a professional is if they can make an appointment at any time on any day they call. It is not misrepresentation to state several available appointment times during the week instead of saying, "Any time you want Tuesday or Wednesday--I'm open." Honesty may be interpreted to represent poor business and poor service for the money(1). One practitioner found that as she traveled on business and became less available in the office, demand for her services increased because her professional image was becoming more successful.

One practitioner in California, after being in business for three years, had an actual eight-month waiting period for nonemergency patients to get an appointment. Patients must have felt privileged to see such a successful nutritionist. Why else would they have agreed to wait so long? The practitioner now has two associates and the three of them see several hundred patients per week.

When working in a medical complex or clinic area, it is not suggested that a professional regularly take extended breaks in the public areas. Prospective clients and referring physicians take notice of others who appear not to be busy.

Framed diplomas, degrees, or awards displayed on office walls are also a graphic way to show success and accomplishment. Desk sets and trophies have adorned businessmen's offices for years, so there is no reason for plastic food models and free calorie charts to be the only highlights of a nutritionist's office!

The image of success is undoubtedly the most significant reason many people are able to demand such high prices for their work. The artist, for example, who establishes the reputation of being distinctive and expensive soon gets more for his work than many unknown artists who have as much or more talent. The secret is in his ability to build a winning image, not in his talent to paint on canvas (1).

CONCLUSION

When entrepreneurs become successful in business, they usually find that other people who could not be bothered before now seek advice and agree with them on the issues, just like in the musical *Fiddler on the Roof* during the song "If I Were A Rich Man." Referrals of new clients and jobs are received with minimum effort as compared to that needed to start the business. Fees go up to improve the profit margin. More importantly, job satisfaction increases because more options open in the nutritionists' lives.

REFERENCES

1. Shook, Robert: *Winning Images*, Macmillan Publishers, New York, 1977.

148

Chapter 20

Promoting Your Venture

A commitment to marketing is essential in any business small or large. Lack of sufficient marketing and promotion is one reason so many businesses stagnate or fail to attract customers.

All too often, an entrepreneur assumes marketing falls under the heading of selling and promotion or advertising. In fact, it is the other way around. Selling and promotion are key elements in a marketing plan, but on their own they are only short-term tactics (1). Tactics alone may boost you in your chosen market today, but market assessment and long-range planning prepare you for the new markets.

MARKETING AN INTANGIBLE--- COUNSELING, MANAGEMENT

Marketing is concerned with getting and keeping customers. Product intangibility has its greatest effect on the process of trying to get customers. How do you propose to sell something like nutrition counseling or consulting that a customer can't hold in his hand, feel, or see?

Intangible products can seldom be tried out in advance. Prospective buyers are generally forced to depend on surrogates to assess what they probably will get. They can look at before and after pictures of weight loss patients. They can talk to current users of your services. They can see and hold your elegant calling card, brochure, or business proposal in its attractive binder.

Similarly, companies develop elaborate packaging to best show off their products and not only entice the buyer but also reassure him. Theodore Levitt relates in his article "Marketing Intangible Products and Product Intangibles" that, "The product will be judged in part by who offers it---not just who the vendor corporation is but who is the corporation's representative. The vendor and the vendor's representative are both inextricably and inevitably part of the 'product' that prospects must judge before they buy. The less tangible the generic product, the more powerfully and persistently the judgment about it gets shaped by the packaging, how it is presented, who presents it, and what's implied by metaphor, simile, symbol, and other surrogates for reality "(2).

It is easy to understand why banks build large, sturdy buildings and hire articulate consultants in business suits. Also, why proposals are in "executive" typeset and leather bindings, and why architects laboriously draw renderings of buildings. It explains why insurance companies offer "a piece of the rock," put you under a "blanket of protection," or in "good hands."

PUBLIC RELATION'S ROLE IN MARKETING

Public relations programs are designed to create a positive climate in which a company or group can do business, earn recognition and gain acceptance. Marketing programs set forth strategies for selling or promoting products and services for which funding is sought or consideration is to be gained. Such strategies define an organization's competitive edge and its position within the marketplace (3).

Public relations (PR) is primarily a communications tool, whereas marketing also includes needs assessment, product development, pricing and distribution. PR seeks to influence attitudes, whereas marketing tries to elicit specific behaviors such as buying, joining, etc. PR defines the image of an organization, whereas marketing defines the organization's goals, business mission, customers, services, and so on (3).

Selling products or services, or soliciting funds should take place after public relations and marketing campaigns have opened the doors, creating a favorable climate for success (3). Effective public relations does not necessarily require costly expenditures. It does require a clear under-standing of an organization's image, products and marketplace.

Elements of successful PR and marketing campaigns (3):

- Planned, not left to chance

- Continuous, not single shot

- Pro-active, not just reactive to events and problems

- Clearly focused with well-defined goals, timetables and specific assignments

- Well-managed, evaluated, and revised regularly

PROMOTION

Promotion is the communication you use to help others become familiar with you, your services or product. Promotion is becoming more important to dietitians than ever before because of the changes in the marketplace.

First, consumers are now shopping around to find the best nutrition services and products for their money. Second, there is confusion today in the public's mind about who to believe in the nutrition field. Finally, dietitians aren't the only legitimate players in the nutrition arena. Where we may have had ownership in the past in some market areas through default, today that is no longer the case. Nutrition is in demand by the consumer; it is therefore a competitive area of business (4).

Dietitians often neglect to plan and oversee adequate promotion for programs, not realizing that poor attendance or lackluster promotion reflects back on the program. Actually, it shows lack of foresight and follow-through if a practitioner devotes total attention to the development of an excellent program that could produce client satisfaction and yet fails to insure the program success through adequate promotion (5).

Promotion will attract far more clients to our doors than any form of legislation. Because the health-care focus is evolving to more health promotion and to attracting the "well" individual, we must accept that our services are among the many nutrition options available to each consumer. Therefore, dietitians must learn how to promote themselves and their products.

PROMOTION TOOLS

There are many tools that can be used in promotion. Which techniques you select are usually determined by the target market, your budget, and the degree of competition. Some promotional tools are far more effective in reaching the target market but may (like television or color ads in magazines) also be very expensive. Other techniques may better meet the expectations of the target markets, for example, tasteful brochures mailed to clients' and physicians' offices. Medical professionals have been slow in using less traditional promotion tools such as billboards and neon signs because of their own value judgments and what they perceive would be their potential clients' reactions.

Some forms of promotion may make your peers uncomfortable because they are new. If your peers are not your buying market, then you must keep their disapproval in perspective. To play a viable role in the marketplace, dietitians must continually innovate or they will be left behind. Innovation, quality service, and promotion are the lifeblood of success in business (5).

When trying to evaluate which forms of promotion to use, public relations experts suggest that you go down a list of the promotion options and hypothetically try to fit the service or product to it. Look for ideas that are creative, unique, and in good taste.

Promotion is most successful when a plan is designed for multiple exposure of the name or message to the target market over an extended period. For a weight-loss program at a fitness center, promotion could include newspaper and radio ads, free media publicity, direct mail promotion and in-house newsletter promotion to members. You could give gym bags printed with the program name and logo at registration, and program T-shirts when fitness goals are met. These are just a few promotion ideas; there are dozens more.

There are advertising and public relations firms and individual consultants that can create promotional campaigns for a fee. For most dietitians with many projects, that is not always an affordable option, but it may be a wise investment for selected projects. Promotion costs should be seen as part of the necessary expense and investment made to create demand for nutrition services. The challenge is to choose wisely and be cost effective when investing in promotional programs The question could be asked, "Can you afford not to promote?"

Following is a listing and brief overview of promotional tools that are commonly used to market dietitians services and products:

One-on-One Communication

One-on-one communication can be your most effective form of promotion. It affords the opportunity to speak, hear, see, and exchange viewpoints face to face. As the promoter, you have the opportunity to read the body language and expressions of your listener and then adjust your presentation for best impact.

Satisfied customers are walking promoters of inestimable value. Through word-of-mouth advertising, listeners may be more influenced to try a dietitian's service because the promoter lends credibility as a satisfied customer.

Public Speaking

As discussed earlier, speaking to individuals and groups is considered the most efficient way to market, according to surveys of small business owners. It lets you get your messages across and establish your credibility at the same time to large numbers of people.

Business Name

A good business name can be a marketing asset to a practitioner. Business consultants suggest that the name be distinctive or descriptive. Many practitioners use their own names for their business name. They find that as they become better known, people remember both them and their company since they have the same name.

Other consultants choose descriptive easy-to-remember business names such as Nutrition Consultants, The Nutrition Group, or Gourmet Services. Less common are names that do not give a clue to the type of business such as Creative Concepts, Hinton Associates, or Lifeline, Inc. Potentially, names could also indicate the area of specialty: Sports Cuisine, Nutrition Communicators, or Kitchen Designs.

In time all practitioners become identified with their business names---if the name is used regularly. Don't waste your time on trying to come up with a creative name, if you end up using only your personal name on promotional materials and when conducting business. Also, it is costly to change your business name, so be sure to research it well before advertising under it.

Logo

A logo is a symbol. If it is used to identify a product, it is called a trademark. If it is used for a service, it is called servicemark. Logos can be fun and very comical or highbrow and sophisticated, or somewhere in between. Logos are used to draw attention to whatever they are used on, such as stationery, posters, business cards, brochures, or billboards (see Figure 20.1).

Business Owner

Private practitioners are potentially their own best marketing asset. Your personality, image, communication and business skills, and expertise in nutrition will be ultimately responsible for attracting and keeping clients.

Business advisors suggest that business people use at least the following four practices to help promote their business. First, use the phone

152

Figure 20.1

A Selection of Logos

(*Source:* Reprinted by permission of the business owners.)

and all of its marketing potential, in other words, talk to clients regularly, confirm appointments, respond to referring physicians, and call for more interviews to let people know about your business. Use the phone to interest new prospective patients into coming for an appointment. Take the time to show an interest in their needs, to tell them briefly what you have to offer, to

153

let them know what you will expect from them, and to discuss an appointment time and your fees. By taking time to market your services instead of just to schedule an appointment, the client will become excited about the expected personalized care.

Second, use your writing skills to correspond with people on a timely basis and to publish. For those who feel weak in this area there are adult education classes, books, and editors or writers for hire to help you.

Third, use public speaking to make yourself more visible in your community and to interest people in nutrition. Speaking to clubs, community groups, PTAs, and at conferences will make people recognize you as a nutrition specialist.

Fourth, become involved in several local or national organizations that could benefit you personally or professionally. Attend meetings, support activities, and run for offices. Dietetic organizations, including Dietetic Practice Groups need input from active, assertive dietitians on their way up. Small business owners' groups, executive clubs, Toastmasters, and local political groups offer opportunities to become involved.

Writing for Publication
Writing is an ideal medium for practitioners to distinguish and promote themselves by communicating with the public or their peers. Writing for lay periodicals or books provides the opportunity to reach a potentially large audience, to share your views, to be paid for your work with more frequency, and to become known.

Writing for publication in professional journals does not pay directly, but it helps establish you as a knowledgeable, qualified professional and excellent resource. Articles may also lend credibility to your programs and services. This type of promotion also may attract more business in the form of referrals or consultation opportunities.

Business Cards
Business cards should always be carried and handed out. They can be powerful marketing tools and one of the least expensive. Other peoples' cards should be saved and used the next time you want to network or you need some information or service. Business cards should list your name, credentials, business name, phone number with area code, and full address.

Some considerations to think about: Do you want to print appointment information on the back of the card? Does the card look too cluttered as it is laid out? Can everyone read the typeface (script and Old English are difficult to read)? Since card sizes are fairly standard, will choosing another size card make your card stand out or be thrown away? How can you best use color, style, paper and design to attract attention to your card?" (See Figure 20.2.)

Letters
Letters that are well written and to the point have boosted the careers of many business persons. All too often we overlook the contribution that impressive correspondence can provide. As important as the content of a letter is, its neatness and grammatical correctness can influence a reader

Figure 20.2

Sample Business Cards
(*Source:* Reprinted by permission of the business owners.)

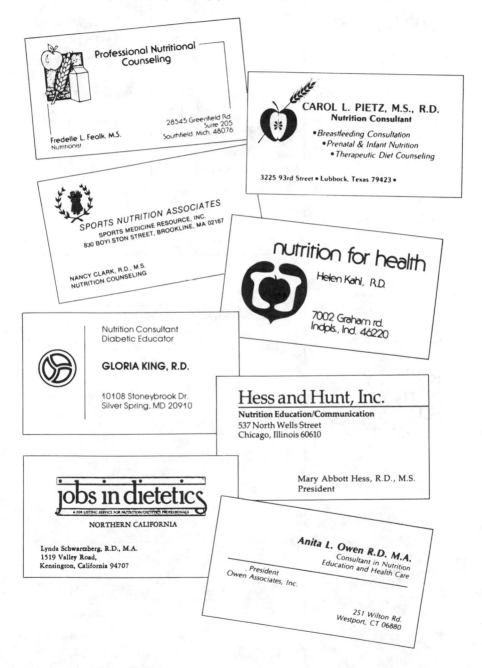

Figure 20.3

Sample Envelope Layouts
(*Source:* Reprinted by permission of the business owners.)

Soft Bite

NUTRITION
SOFTWARE

P.O. Box 1484
East Lansing, Michigan 48823

Nutrition Consultants Inc.

677 N. New Ballas Road
St. Louis, Missouri 63141
Suite 218

111 S. Tremont Street
Kewanee, Illinois 61443

SMITH AND MANTERNACH
NUTRITION ASSOCIATES

One Dubuque Plaza • Dubuque, Iowa 52001

**KATHY
SCHWAB
R.D.**

NUTRITION
CONSULTANT

1 0 1 1
S. W. Curry - 4
Portland
Oregon
9 7 2 0 1
503/295-1119
503/233-4567
EXTENSION 194

Nutrition & Diet Counseling of Rockland

24 South Main Street, New City, N.Y. 10956

NUTRITION SPECIALTIES,™
INC.

The Nutrition Experts™

St. Paul Business & Technology Center
245 East Sixth Street
P.O. Box 905
St. Paul, Minnesota 55101

just as much. Letters with numerous corrections or misspelled words are poorly received (see envelope address layouts in Figure 20.3).

Busy people will often refuse to read obvious mass mailings, such as those addressed to "Dear Sirs" or "Dear Philadelphia Physicians" or those that are poorly photocopied. Creativity, time, effort, and money must be invested to ensure that your letters are read. Business consultants suggest that even on mass mailings, the signature and heading should be individualized whenever possible.

Direct Mail

Direct mail is used when you know specifically whom you want to contact (usually either potential clients or referral agents) and when you want to increase your chances of attracting a higher-percentage response.

Direct mail should be personally addressed instead of "To whom it may concern." Personalize mail as much as possible to increase the readership. Direct mail is used for marketing surveys, announcements of a new office location or new services, and to acquaint potential clients or referral agents to your services. Membership lists of your local medical society or national dietetic practice groups, the Yellow Pages, and shared business cards are good sources of names and addresses. Many organizations ask for a fee and an explanation of how the membership lists will be used before use is granted.

Resume

A resume can be a very effective marketing tool. It should highlight the aspects about you and your experience that best qualify you for a position you are seeking. In other words, you may need several different resumes. It can either be a chronological (listing your experience in reverse chronological order) or functional (highlighting your skills and responsibilities). Resumes also can be used along with letters of introduction in business to open doors for you, or to establish credibility in a proposal, or to help introduce you at a speaking engagement.

A variation of the resume would be a curriculum vitae or vita (an expanded version that includes published books and papers) and the biographical sketch (in paragraph form) often used for introduction purposes at speeches.

Typeset or laser printed resumes look impressive. Word processing can make updating a resume very easy. However, the most important qualities are that it not have any typographical errors and that it is interesting and accurate. There is hope that content may actually count.

Letters of Reference

Letters of reference or introduction written by prominent, objective people who know you and your work personally or professionally are impressive. They help establish credibility and may help open doors for you. Keep the original on file and use good prints or photocopies.

Brochures

157

Brochures are used to introduce and promote. It is not imperative that a private practitioner have a brochure, but many have found that attractive, clever ones attract business and easily pay for themselves.

The four most important things to remember about a brochure are to write the information with the customers' needs utmost in mind; talk about "benefits"---in other words how will your product or services make the customer happier, healthier, more fulfilled and so on---*Don't just list what you have to offer!* Also, make the brochure attractive, simple to read, and interesting. Leave open space and use bullets to make scanning easier. Your readers may be interested in seeing a good picture of yourself and hearing statements from satisfied customers. You may need several brochures to hit several different target markets.

Brochures seldom list fees because it dates them and sometimes makes them poorly received. If insurance sometimes covers your services or there is an employer co-pay program, it could be mentioned in the brochure. Your name, business name, address, and phone number should be highlighted. It is highly suggested that brochures be typeset and printed on good quality paper. (See brochures in Figures 20.4 and 20.5.)

Portfolio

There are times when dietitians want to show the scope of their creativity and samples of their work such as creative menus, educational materials, media work, or catering ideas. When a business is new and its reputation and yours are unknown a portfolio may be the marketing tool you need.

A portfolio is similar to a scrapbook or a slide show designed to show graphically what you have to sell. The portfolio may be in a commercially available portfolio folder, on a tripod display with charts, on slides or on audio or video tapes for dietitians who do media work. Presenting a portfolio to the client helps make the intangible promise tangible, enticing, and clearly defined.

The cost of a portfolio can vary greatly, depending upon what is included. Items may range from professionally produced food photos or renderings to just copies or samples of educational materials, authored articles, menus, snapshots, letters of reference, and newspaper coverage. Occasionally it is worth paying a professional artist or calligrapher to add a special touch. Unfortunately, many of us never use samples of our past creativity to help us win the next contract.

Posters

Using posters to promote seminars and classes has proven to be successful for some practitioners. To save money on printing costs, a large number of poster shells (ones with only partial information) can be printed at one time with the logo, business name, and phone number. The date, place, time, and event can be added as the posters are used. Sometimes a pad is attached with tear-off cards to send in for more information.

If the posters are not too large, most stores, health clubs, beauty shops, and so on that allow posters are willing to let you have display space to solicit their customers. When you use this type of marketing and you want

158

Figure 20.4

Sample Brochure Cover

Figure 20.5 Sample Brochure Cover

Sample Personal Promotion Brochure

Hess and Hunt helps the foodservice and health care industry and its agencies. . . .

- Meet the needs of consumers who have health concerns.
- Promote nutritious products by providing responsible spokespersons and developing publicity materials.
- Educate the public and health professionals by making presentations and teaching courses.

Hess and Hunt helps foodservice organizations. . . .

- Write menus and expand current offerings of light, healthful items.
- Create effective nutrition promotions.
- Sell products to markets with specific health needs.

Hess and Hunt helps social service and government agencies. . .

- Develop innovative nutrition education materials.
- Improve services to the community by teaching staff and client groups.
- Formulate food specifications, menus and evaluation tools to improve program quality and meet federal requirements.

Hess and Hunt helps print and electronic media . . . .

- Obtain responsible nutrition information.
- Inform the public about popular nutrition topics by writing articles and appearing on radio and television programs.
- Translate scientific jargon into language that ordinary mortals can understand.

Mary Abbott Hess   Anne Hunt

Since 1979, **Hess and Hunt, Inc.** has provided insightful professional nutrition expertise for business, industry and government. The firm brings together the broad knowledge of Mary Abbott Hess, a registered dietitian and associate professor of nutrition, and the communication background of Anne Hunt, a food public relations specialist formerly food editor of *Sphere* (now *Cuisine*) magazine. Hess and Hunt with a support staff of experts in nutrition education, foodservice, marketing and graphic design offers nutrition communications that are both creative and dependable.

Hess and Hunt can translate the science of nutrition into language consumers understand. The firm is experienced in all print and electronic media, as well as in the preparation of booklets, educational programs, brochures, radio scripts, posters, displays, slide presentations, menus and recipes. Hundreds of speeches have been made to professional and general audiences.

Mary Abbott Hess and Anne Hunt were recently honored with the Morris Fishbein Award for excellence in medical writing for their book, *Pickles & Ice Cream: The Complete Guide To Nutrition During Pregnancy* (McGraw-Hill, 1982; Dell Paperback, 1984). Hess is the coauthor of *The Art Of Cooking For The Diabetic* (Contemporary Books, 1978) which has sold over 200,000 copies.

Both Hess and Hunt are active in professional organizations, including the American Medical Writers Association and Society for Nutrition Education. Mary Abbott Hess, R.D., M.S., has been elected to leadership positions in the American Dietetic Association and the Chicago Nutrition Association. She is a member of the Institute of Food Technologists and the Roundtable for Women in Foodservice. Anne Hunt is a member of the American Home Economics Association and has served on the Board of Directors of Chicago Home Economists in Business. She is editor of the Nutrition Educators With Industry newsletter.

Mary Abbott Hess has a B.S. from Simmons College in Boston and an M.S. from Northern Illinois University. Anne Hunt is a graduate of Wooster College, Wooster, Ohio, and completed a post graduate course of study in food and nutrition at Mundelein College in Chicago.

Figure 20.6   Sample Media Bio

KATHY HELM

Nothing dominates the nation's consciousness and (pocketbook) like nutrition and fitness. Your listeners can now have a nationally renowned expert to answer their questions about this vital aspect of their lives. She is Registered Dietitian, Kathy Helm.

Kathy has 16 years of media experience. In 1989, she hosted her own nationally syndicated radio talk show on "American Know How." She has guested on ABC-TV's "Nightline", NBC's magazine show "1986" and conducted over 600 interviews. Kathy Helm also hosted a nutritional television segment four years on the NBC affiliate in Denver.

In her private practice she has counseled over 6,000 persons . . . she won't be thrown by questions from your audience. Her specific areas of expertise include weight loss, consumer & environmental issues, as well as sports nutrition. As a part of her private practice, Kathy was a nutritionist with the Denver Bronco Football Team, and the spa associated with Neiman Marcus, The Greenhouse. She offers your audience advice that some of America's most important and famous people pay thousands of dollars to receive.

Your listeners want to know about wellness, new foods, organic gardening, food controversies, vitamin supplements, weight loss and disease prevention. No one is better equipped to give them the answers than Kathy Helm.

KATHRYN HELM PRODUCTIONS, INC.
P. O. Box 1295 • #5 Hickory Hills • Lake Dallas, TX 75065 • (817) 497-3558

to use the locations more than once, call or stop by when the event is over to take the posters down and check in with the owner.

Press Kits

Press kits are commonly used to interest the media in writing or broadcasting a story to help you promote your services, product, book, or speaking engagement. The kit may include a variety of items:

- A cover letter addressed to the person

- A press release on the service, product, or book you wish to publicize

- A sample of the product or book, or a copy of newspaper articles, or critical reviews

- A resume and short biographical sketch, or media bio (see Figure 20.6)

- 5" x 7" black and white glossy photo of you or the product

Press kits should be descriptive, attractive, and to the point. They should explain why the public would be interested in the topic. Although press kits can be very elaborate with printed covers and numerous photos, they can also be as simple as several of the above items placed in a large folder with pockets.

Banners

Banners draw attention and create name recognition. They can be used at a "fun run" finish line, in a lobby during a Wellness Festival, or over the cafeteria door to promote the new line of "Light and Natural" foods. Banners can be made with paper and paint; however, they can be reused many times if they are made from cloth or heavy plastic. They are a great promotional tool for a large area where crowds are gathered and also create a festive mood (5).

Give-Aways

Give-aways (T-shirts, notebooks, mugs, gym bags, etc.) with the program name or logo are popular promotion items. The more useful and practical the item, the more it will be used and the name or logo displayed. (These items are sometimes sold as fund raisers rather than given away.)

FREE PROMOTION

Media

Working with the media---radio, television, and newspapers---gives free marketing exposure to practitioners. One can do years of public speaking and not reach a fraction of the number of people who watch one television program or read a newspaper.

Nutrition, fitness, and health are "hot" topics right now and probably will be for several years to come. Experts in these fields who have a flair for this type of work and have something unique to say are sought after.

162

Media people are looking for stories and information that will interest their public. It can be classified as controversial, human interest, new research, exposes, practical, or a scoop story, but it has to have a "hook" or a "handle"---some unique element to attract the audience. Working with the media is discussed in Chapter 30.

Many practitioners got their first start with the media during National Nutrition Month. We sometimes forget that there are eleven other months to work with also. We do not have to wait until we are invited to contribute. If you plan to have a successful business, it is imperative that people know about you. Through a phone call, introductory letter, over lunch or at an office interview, however possible, try to talk to the local media program directors and newspaper writers. A private practitioner in Chicago reports that she has been quoted or consulted on articles over fifty times in the last year in local newspapers. She sent her card, introduced herself, and offered to act as a resource person. Eventually, she was credited with a by-line or in the article for what she contributed.

Public Service Announcements PSAs are welcomed by the media. The PSA can announce a new series of classes, a seminar, or a new associate's arrival. The announcement must be short, concise, and cover a subject or event that is in the public interest. It can be printed in a newspaper or read on the air. Obvious commercial promotions for your business or to sell something are not permitted unless you pay for commercial time or space. The lead time for PSAs ranges from three to eight weeks, so call ahead and plan accordingly.

Radio and television stations support PSAs because of the service they provide to the community and because it looks good on their record when they reapply for their broadcast licenses. Newspapers usually feel that PSAs increase readership.

It is becoming more common for commercial food and beverage companies to hire dietitians as media spokespeople to offer PSAs. The dietitians are trained to provide interviews on an educational topic relating to food or nutrition and to interject the information about the company's product.

Publicity

Publicity is free media coverage of some newsworthy story, program, or event. It is easily recognized as the media coverage of a local Health Fair or of the local school children during National Nutrition Month. In a recent newspaper article, it mentioned that a man named Lawrence "Herkie" Herkimer was going to be in the *Sports Illustrated* magazine for the second time in forty years talking about cheerleading and cheerleading camps. "I've got a soft spot in my heart for *SI*," says Herkie. "Back in the mid-'50s, they did a story on me and it really helped establish my company." That is what good publicity can do for you.

Practitioners can call or write the media with their requests for publicity. For planned events such as the beginning of weight loss classes for teenagers, or a sports nutrition conference, the media should be contacted several weeks in advance. When planning a special event consider including a local celebrity or co-sponsorship with a philanthropic organization to improve the possibility of media coverage and to attract a larger attendance.

Publicity comes for no cost, but it may be sporadic or completely upstaged if a bigger news item breaks the same day as your story.

In an article by Peter Miller, "Be Your Own Publicist," he suggests the following references if you want to reach the media yourself, many libraries will have them (6):

- Bacon's *Publicity Checker* ($195). Lists more than 18,000 newspapers and magazines as well as 100,000 media contacts. (800) 621-0561.

- *Broadcasting Yearbook* ($95 prepaid, $115 if billed). Covers radio, TV, and cable and their staffs. (800) 638-7827.

- *Gale Directory of Publications* ($265). Information on 25,000 newspapers, magazines, journals and newsletters. (313) 961-2242.

- *Hudson's Newsletter Directory* ($99). A listing of 4,000 newsletters by subject. (914) 876-2081.

Small companies can compete with large corporations with megabucks for media coverage, if you follow some very basic premises tested and proven by publicist Peter Miller (6):

- Write about a topic, not about yourself

- Be factual

- Include your name, address, and phone number at the top of the page

- Be brief: Limit the news release to one page, but also include a cover page addressed to the individual reporter or editor, there may be a brief biography of yourself, and a short history of the business or product

- State on the news release "For Immediate Release," that means use it anytime

- Describe your material as a "news release"

Using this approach, Miller helped a small contact lens company in Washington, D.C., go from five employees working in an apartment to a forty percent increase in sales and offers from all over the world to buy the firm. The publicity program cost approximately $200 over a period of seven months (6). The money paid for printing, postage, and photocopying. His time was donated because he was using them in his master's thesis. They were able to generate exposure in *Newsweek,* the *Washington Post,* and in the UPI (United Press International).

PAID ADVERTISING

It is ethical, professional, and highly recommended that you consider using advertising. The U.S. government encourages professionals to advertise in hopes of producing more competitive services and better values for the

164

public. Professional organizations are recognizing that it is becoming a fact of life for their members and stress that it be done tastefully.

Advertising is used by some practitioners as an ongoing budget item used to attract clients. Others use it only at times for special events, new program announcements, and at the beginning of seasonal peak periods (September and February-March). Whenever it is used there are two guidelines that should always be followed:

- First, make it clever and distinctive.

- Second, plan to have a campaign, not just a single ad. Estimates vary that the average person must see or hear an ad between five and eleven times before he or she remembers it, so repetition is necessary.

A good rule of thumb to determine how much to spend on advertising is five to ten percent of the gross annual budget. This is after the initial expense of fifteen percent for the first year. Another way would be to divide the cost of the advertising by the cost of the product you are selling or initial consultation fee. Evaluate if the number of new clients needed to break even on the advertising is reasonable (if it's too expensive, you may have to see twenty-five new patients/ clients per week just to pay for advertising). There is a point where putting more money into ads will not bring more clients or profit to your office. When you first begin a business, budget an amount that you can afford to spend and look for other previously mentioned ways to market yourself for less cost.

Most dietitians cannot afford to compete with the amount of advertising purchased by commercial weight loss and other nutrition programs. For that reason where we spend our advertising money and the distinctiveness of our advertising are all the more important. To help determine what works for you, *ask clients and patients how they heard about your business.*

The Yellow Pages and the media all have free sales personnel that can assist clients in determining the best way to use their advertising dollar and help with ad ideas on a limited basis.

If a practitioner wants help on an overall advertising strategy, plus artwork and a slogan an advertising agency or public relations firm can do it, as well as students and professors at your local colleges and universities. Obtain estimates before you agree to have work done because good firms are usually expensive.

Fees often range from $1,500 to $15,000 on up (advertising not included) to set up an advertising campaign with a logo and slogan for a small business. Fees are less if you come up with the ideas and do some of the leg work for yourself or limit the items they contribute.

Yellow Pages

The Yellow Pages offer a business the opportunity to advertise to everyone who owns a telephone for a year. Most businesses find this type of advertising very productive.

Patients and clients know to look under "Dietitians" or "Nutritionists" to find a consulting nutritionist listing. Occasionally, practitioners also list under such titles as "Reducing and Weight Loss," "Physical Fitness," "Catering," or along with a contract clinic or spa. One listing in the Yellow Pages and white pages is offered when you have a business phone. All other listings, display ads, extra lines, or bold print are an extra charge.

It is highly recommended that a Yellow Pages listing include the words "Registered Dietitian." The telephone company does not police their listings so anyone can list themselves under a title we and the public assume to be ours alone. When a private practitioner chooses a business name that does not indicate that the business is run by a trained professional and there are no credentials listed, there is a good chance that business is lost. Examples would be "Big Pines Consultant Services" or "Moore & Associates, Inc."

To help save money but still have a good size ad and several listings, buy only one larger ad and refer the other listings to it, such as " See ad under 'Nutritionists'. " Put the ad under the listing where you think it will be seen best and where clients would look for your name first (see Figure 20.7).

The Yellow Pages closing date for having your ad ordered is usually three to five months before the books are available. Plan ahead and call and ask for assistance. Evaluate your listings and ad each year and try new ideas that might work better. By asking new clients how they heard about you, you will know if your ad works.

Figure 20.7

Sample Yellow Pages Advertisements

Dietitians- Cont.

MCCULLY REBECCA L MSRD
CONSULTING DIETITIAN
MEMBER AMERICAN DIETETIC ASSN
HOURS: BY APPOINTMENT
5300 N Meridian

Nutrition Counseling Service
106 Preston Forest Village
Therapeutic Nutrition
308 E Main St

WEIGHT PLACE THE
NUTRITION CONSULTANTS
● REGISTERED DIETICIANS
BY APPOINTMENT ONLY
3400 NW Expwy

ALICE ZIMMERMAN NUTRITION LIFELINE

REGISTERED DIETITIAN
CONSULTATION FOR
● WEIGHT REDUCTION
● DIABETES
● HIGHBLOOD PRESSURE
● HEART DISEASE
● PREGNANT WOMEN
PUBLIC SPEAKING

Zimmerman Alice
8140 Walnut Hill Ln

Nutritionists

Banister Carol A RD MS
4200 W Memorial Rd

CHEHAK ANASTASIA MARIE RD
Consulting practice in nutritional
science related to health,
medical disorders and prevention
2912 Persimmon Creek Dr Edm

Nutrionics Health Systems
510 24 Avenue SW Nrm
Nutrition Consultants
1621 Oakwood Dr Nrm

NUTRITION CONSULTANTS OF TULSA

WEIGHT CONTROL - DIABETES EDUCATION
THERAPEUTIC DIETS - PRENATAL COUNSELING
INFANT NUTRITION - NUTRITION SPEAKERS
CLASSES
JUDY M. CORRELL, R.D.
CECILIA L. DAVIS, R.D.
GEORGIA W. KIMMEL, R.D.

3010 S Harvard

NUTRITIONAL COUNSELING CLINIC
2140-A S Memorial Dr

Newspapers

Newspaper ads are commonly used by dietitians with varying degrees of success. The wording and placement of the ad are critical. It must be distinctive enough to catch the reader's eye. The competition to attract attention is very stiff in a newspaper, especially a large daily one. Ads should run on a regular basis in order to be remembered. Scheduling ads regularly also makes the cost of each individual ad more reasonable.

Large daily newspapers have good exposure but are only partly read by most people. Readers go to the sections that interest them most and skim the rest. Fortunately, newspapers know what sections are read most and by whom. Advice columns, horoscopes, cartoons, letters to the editors, sports' scores pages, and, in small towns, the obituaries are usually read closely. Although women's sections are read well, on coupon day that is often not the case, according to a practitioner from Rhode Island who advertised regularly. Request that the ad be placed on a page that is mostly writing so that your ad will stand out and not be lost between the huge furniture display ads.

Small newspapers and weekly papers are usually read more closely and have a loyal but smaller readership. The cost of advertising is more reasonable. The placement guidelines for an ad are the same as mentioned for large newspapers. Also, smaller papers are usually more open to the idea of a nutrition column written by a local person or articles that are contributed locally.

An ad should catch your attention with either a catchy word, phrase, graphic design, photo, or something. It should be easy to read and understand, plus be clever. The phone number should stand out. It is not necessary to condense your brochure or calling card into an ad. In fact, you will attract more attention with the headline "Ready for Bikini Season?" than with "Nutritional Consultation by Professional." If you cannot think of an idea you like, check the ads that other businesses are using and see what you like and dislike about them. If you have an idea but need artwork, go to a graphic artist. If you cannot think of a good idea, budget in an advertising firm or advertising student for the creation of the ad.

Radio

Radio advertising can be geared to a very specific group of the population. Depending upon the type of music played and the time of day, radio stations know from national surveys their listeners' average ages, the percentages of men and women, their approximate income, and educational levels.

Radio ads must be repeated to be remembered. Sales people from stations will offer several "packages" of ad lengths and airing times to make the campaign more reasonable. They often will help with writing the ad and having a station person record it or read it live. Smaller stations have lower advertising fees because fewer people listen to them. In fact, it's the listenership that determines how much a station charges in a given market, but all fees are negotiable. The longer you decide to commit to their station, the lower the rate that you will be charged. Don't accept the first figures that you are quoted. Take your time and check for the best air times and prices for the target market you want. Classical stations are sometimes a very good choice for private consults and "easy listening" for the over 40 years old group, and so on.

Businesses that can afford regular radio advertising report that it is very successful. Smaller businesses with lower budgets and irregular use of radio advertising report hit or miss success. According to business consultants if you plan to use advertising, you need to commit enough financial support to produce results or you should not do it at all.

Television
A television ad is extremely expensive to produce and to show on the air. Again, it must be repeated to be effective, and target audiences can be determined by the type of programs being shown. Television advertising reaches a large number of viewers, but is so expensive it would be very difficult for a consultant working alone to break even on the number of added customers it would attract. Not enough income is usually generated by one person in one hour to support this expenditure and other overhead too. It may be possible that several consultants working together or working for one person could generate enough added income to warrant television advertising, but exhaust all avenues for getting free television exposure first.

A reasonable TV ad can be produced for $2,000 to $15,000 depending upon whether you hire someone to act or speak or you do it yourself.   The air time varies greatly depending upon whether it is a small local cable station or prime time on a major network. As you would expect, the better the viewership and time slot, the higher the cost from $1,500 to $50,000 or more per week for a daily ad.

One private practitioner did invest with a partner in TV advertising to promote their quick weight loss program in the fall during the popular afternoon talk shows.   The ads cost $30,000 per week for several weeks and they did fill 50 weight loss classes with 12 people each at about $400 per person up front (plus a weekly fee for meal-replacement beverages) or over $1/4 million in gross income in 30 days. Figuring the cost of the ad, the air time, the meeting rooms, the secretarial time, the educational materials and the instructors to handle all those people, there was still a good profit. But very high risk if it had not worked.

KEEPING CUSTOMERS

After you have marketed successfully enough to attract customers, it is important to keep them. Experts suggest that businesses spend six times more trying to attract new clients than trying to market to former ones.

Customers are assets for more than just a source of revenue. They are "walking promotion" of your services and an advertising medium of great value. Each person has a sphere of influence that reaches far beyond his immediate family and business peers to a potential of several hundred people.

There are numerous ways to strengthen relationships with clients or referral agents that can be carried out with a minimum amount of effort on your part once the system is established.

Some examples of how private practitioners as well as other professionals have strengthened their relationships with customers include:

For patients Begin having a strong relationship with your patients when the appointment is scheduled and again at the first visit by providing personalized care. Continue with the same quality of care on the follow-up

168

visits so that patients feel your initial concern was genuine. Use phone calls or mail notes to reconfirm appointments. Periodically call patients in between visits to see how they are progressing or when the call would be significant to the patient. Send out announcements when new group classes are forming or to let athletic patients know that you can now do computer analysis of their food intakes. When a new diet program is particularly dangerous and you send a letter to discuss the pros and cons, patients appreciate the communication.

For physicians Follow-up after patient visits can include not only written notes or referral acknowledgment, but also a phone call. Periodic letters or phone calls can be used to discuss ongoing patient progress. Newsletters, regular office visits, or luncheon appointments to discuss new services and nutritional information or research are appreciated. Offering to conduct noon in-service seminars for the office staff has worked well. A thank you card or Holiday card is always welcomed. For special accounts, try delivering gourmet fruit or other food baskets or food samples for special low salt or low fat diets.

For consultant accounts Depending upon the situation, check in monthly with the people higher up and send copies of your reports to them. If appropriate, offer to do in-services, weight loss, or wellness talks to employees outside your regular contract agreement. Use many of the above suggestions for physicians and for consultant accounts too.

CONCLUSION

Attracting and keeping clients is necessary to survive in business. Selling and promotion should always be major priorities of any business whether new or established. Private practitioners soon learn to carry a supply of calling cards wherever they go. Stepping forward to shake hands and introduce themselves becomes second nature. Although many things seem awkward at first, after so many hours and days are invested in a project we love, it becomes very easy to talk about it and encourage others to use it.

REFERENCES

1. Mancuso, Joseph: "What Business Are You Really In?," *Success*, September 1985.
2. Levitt, Theodore: Marketing Intangible Products and Product Intangibles, *Harvard Business Review*, May-June 1981.
3. Joan-Patricia O'Connor, O'Connor PR & Marketing, 1523 31st St, NW, Washington, DC.
4. Rose, James: *The Competitive Edge*, The American Dietetic Association, 1987.
5. Helm, Kathy King: "Promotion Strategies" in *The Competitive Edge*, The American Dietetic Association, 1987.
6. Miller, P.: How To Be Your Own Publicist, *Home-Office Computing,* December 1990.

Chapter 21

Negotiating and Selling

Historically, negotiating was an arena where one person was the victor and the other was the victim. Stronger individuals used negotiations to control the opposition. As a result, the final agreement usually heavily favored the victor. The victim accepted the agreement, but later often either did not produce in good faith or learned to manipulate or sabotage to gain back lost ground.

WIN-WIN NEGOTIATING

In the last ten years or so a new era of negotiation strategy has evolved in business called win-win negotiation (1). With this strategy both parties feel they benefit from the agreement. Now with the win-win philosophy everyone can become quite adept at representing themselves and their ideas and expecting the other party to negotiate in good faith. Some compromise may be necessary by both parties.

When negotiations stall on an unbalanced or unfairly weighted agreement, it is not uncommon today to hear the "victim" try to bring the other party into a win-win agreement. This can sometimes be done by stating, "I can't see how I will benefit from this agreement as it stands. Would you be willing to compromise on . . . ?" Or, "We have tried to be very fair and negotiate in good faith. You haven't offered any inducements or compromises that show that you feel the same."

Successful Negotiations

There are many good books published on the art of negotiation. In reality, though, the only way to gain expertise is through experience. One session of negotiation prepares you for the next one. One often learns as much by a session that went poorly as by one easily won that lacked challenge.

Negotiation should be seen as a game of minds each vying for its needs to be met without having to give up too much in return. When taken in this light negotiation can be fun and challenging, worthy of thorough research and time to develop the strategy.

When negotiating, don't share all of your information up front. Clarify each point during your discussions. Document each concession as each party makes it so opponents can't renege later. Determine who the other party's leader is as soon as possible; it may not be the person speaking. **Consider the following points to avoid (2).**

- Don't be overwhelmed by the successful position or status of the other party.

- Don't worry about the results.

- Don't negotiate over the phone.

- Don't oversell and push too far.

- Don't appear too up tight, but don't relax!

- Don't "lose your cool" and get angry unless it's needed for dramatic effect.

Advantage Points to Remember (3)

- Try to set up the negotiations on your own ground or somewhere neutral where you feel comfortable. The other party's home ground or office may be intimidating.

- Wear your " power" outfit so that you feel comfortable and in control. Overdressing in business attire may prove to be successful in some instances.

- Don't say something you are later sorry about. Don't quote figures and offer services until you have a chance to think about them because once spoken they may be difficult to change. If you don't know what to say, try, "I am very interested in what you're suggesting. Let me research it and get back to you tomorrow."

- Be aware of your body language. Sometimes it gives information that may be to the other party's advantage. Nervous movements may sabotage an otherwise strong presentation.

- If you are not comfortable with negotiating for yourself hire a qualified lawyer or other business advisor to go with you to help carry the session. Or, have them coach you before you go into the negotiation session.

STEPS IN NEGOTIATING

Step 1 Qualify the other party. Is the other party a "middle man" who can only pass on information or the one in charge? Are the businesspersons who want you to write restaurant menus truly solid and well financed? Does the fitness center have any intention of contracting with you after you share your nutrition proposal with them? How do you know that the other party is worth your investment of time, effort, and money?

      The best answer to all of the above questions is to ask tactful, straightforward questions of the other party. Don't be so caught up in trying to impress them, that you fail to evaluate them! Another method of qualifying someone is to ask for references or a financial statement (when appropriate).

The reputation of a business or its owner can give a clue whether they are credible and honest.

Step 2 What are the other party's "needs " and are they "over a barrel " for some reason? By knowing as much as you can about what the other party "needs" from the negotiation, and any reasons why they are motivated, you have a better negotiating position.   Examples could be that the Health Department has given them a 30-day ultimatum to clean up the food service, or that business is poor and your name and reputation will draw more clients.

Use this information to your advantage, but don't always share the fact that you know their problems. One of the greatest challenges in negotiating is to evaluate the other party and decide how open you should be and how much not to share.

Step 3   Are there any "desires" that are strong? In some instances people or businesses may be motivated more by what they would like than what they need. They may want to be the first hospital to offer corporate wellness in the city and may disproportionately allocate funds to it. Or, the team coach may want a nutritionist to work with the players. Or, a restauranteur may want his menu to appeal to more clientele by offering nutritious menu items.

Step 4 Determine how low you can go. What do you need and want from the negotiations? Determine your financial breakeven point and the amount of profit you will need to make the project worth your time. Develop statistics, illustrations and logical arguments to support and defend your views. What can you ask for, but be willing to give up as a concession? Never ask for the least you will accept up front. Ask for more and then expect that the final agreement will probably be a compromise.

Step 5   Do you have a "Sears Plan " ready?   Jean Yancey, a small business advisor in Denver, Colorado, counsels people to offer the "Sears Plan:" good, better, and best alternatives. If the other party doesn't like one alternative you offer, have another ready to go. The *best* offer would be the most comprehensive and costly. The *better* offer is a good compromise. The *good* offer will at least get your foot in the door or provide an option in case negotiations stall.

Step 6 Determine what other items besides money you will ask for in the agreement. What interim payments and reports will you want? Ask for regular monthly payments, or for some projects, perhaps one-third up front, a third at midpoint, and the final payment on completion. What about royalties for as long as your materials are used? What about editorial or revision rights when programs become dated? Travel, office, mail and phone expenses--- are they included? What staffing or support services will you expect?   What marketing support will you request?

SELLING

172

A sale takes place when a client or patient agrees to pay for a service or product, or more globally, when someone agrees to do what you want done. To survive in business, sales must happen. Of course, everyone wants to offer products that are in such demand that they "sell themselves," but that is a rarity.

Dietitians can increase their sales by improving their sales presentation skills and by better taking advantage of sales opportunities. Constantly be aware of instances where your nutrition services can be appropriately sold.

Getting Your Foot In The Door

Often before you can sell a physician or corporate leader on your services, you must first get passed their secretaries. In a corporation go as high as you can to give your sales presentation. You want the decision-maker(s), but you may have to start several levels below.

Some tricks of the trade shared by Barry Wishner, R.D., are to make the client feel like he or she is special, part of an exclusive club. Say, "I have heard that your OB practice is one of the most progressive, patient education-oriented practices in the area. I have a nutrition service that OB patients love that also will generate increased revenue for your practice. Can I have five minutes of Dr. Johnson's time to explain it to her?" It also works to appeal to their human nature by saying something like, "I had a baby five years ago. I am a dietitian, but I know how difficult it is keep your weight gain under control. Do you offer a nutrition seminar to your new OB patients? I have my brochure and sample patient booklet, could I have five minutes of Dr. Jones' time to explain my program?"

Sometimes it works to stop by a physician's office, and ask to schedule an appointment to talk to the physician. If he or she is unavailable, then ask to talk with the head nurse. If the nurse will talk to you, and your message sounds interesting, you may be scooted into the physician's office inbetween the next two patients.

Try using someone as a referral to get to see the top person. Once you have established good rapport with a businessperson or physician, it is not out of place to ask if he or she knows of other CEOs, wellness directors, or physicians who might be interested in your program. Ask if you could use their name as a referral.

A-B-C Accounts

In any business, no matter what you are selling there will be some people who use your services or buy your products more than others. Sales experts suggest many different numbers, but everyone agrees that the majority of your time and resources should be spent maintaining and keeping your "A" accounts happy. "B" accounts use your services on an irregular basis, but given good service, or added attention some might become "A" accounts. "C" accounts refer you patients or buy your product only when the moon turns blue. They might be contacted yearly in a mass mailing.

All three accounts could be in the same medical practice or may be very cordial to you at local Chamber of Commerce meetings. Some will be major clients and some won't. The important lesson to learn is that you spend your time and resources where they are most effective. **Take the time to identify who supports you. Keep your "A" accounts happy!**

The Sales Presentation

The sales presentation includes four major components, each with a specific purpose (3):

1. Introduction. The purpose of the introduction is to establish with the prospective client how you are different from all the others waiting to sell the same product. You do this by making statements that either focus attention, specify direct benefits, or warn of danger. For example "From your year end report I saw that your company spends more than $2,500 per employee on health insurance. We have a wellness program that reduced medical expenses at the Reed Company by twenty percent last year."

2. Investigative Phase. This phase is one of the most important in the modern-day sales process. Get the buyer to define his or her other needs, wants, and expectations. Do this by asking open-ended questions and by listening to the answers. The information obtained in this exchange will help you personalize your presentation and perhaps think of new products to sell. For example, "Have you ever tried any employee education seminars and did they work?" or "What are your three worst employee health problems in your opinion?"

3. Presentation Phase. During this phase present facts carefully chosen for their effect on your client. Show how his or her needs will be met by what you have to offer. Buyers base their decisions on fact and emotion. Garner emotional support for you and your services. If you see that the buyer is drifting or does not appear to understand, go back to the investigative phase and refocus attention by asking more questions. You need to be flexible. The outcome of this phase should be a natural progression to the close.

4. Closing. This is the time to bring the presentation to closure, either by asking for a sale's or other commitment. This can best be accomplished by summarizing the client's needs and identifying solutions that you have to offer. Ask when you can begin or how you can provide more assistance or when you can provide more information. Your purpose may have been to introduce yourself and explain your services. Several ideas for closings might be: "If we have an agreement next week, how soon can I get started?"or "What more can I give you to help you make your decision?" or "Is there any reason why you wouldn't want to offer a weight loss program to your employees given all the possible benefits?"or "Can I count on your commitment to this program for the coming year?"

Even if the client is not interested in your services at this time, leave the session as friends and on a positive note. If the client isn't ready to give an answer, ask when you can call for his answer. Don't give up. After the sales call, drop a note into the mail thanking the prospect for his or her time.

PROPOSALS

A proposal is a comprehensive marketing tool used to present the selling points of an idea. One could be used to interest a corporation in using you in their wellness program. Or, sell an obesity seminar to a clinic director, or to interest a financial backer in a new product or business venture.

Proposals can range from a simple one-page typewritten information sheet to a typeset, bound presentation containing a volume of pages, along with a slide show and taste session. The scope of the proposal is determined in a large part by what is expected, what is used by the competition, and what will be impressive enough to make the sell. The experienced practitioner is not the only one to use a proposal. The novice may find it to be the very marketing boost to build her or his business more quickly.

Proposals should only be long enough to interest the client and make the sell. Care should be exercised so that explanations are not so detailed that clients can carry them out themselves without you.

Proposals usually represent many hours or days of research of the market and the client so that the proposed item is "positioned" correctly. It will fit the client's needs. One may include:

· An introduction or explanation of the scope of the proposal

· An overview of the market and its potential

· A short analysis of the competition

· Background information about the client and his needs

· Your answer to fulfilling the client's needs

· Why you are best for the job (include resume and references)

· Estimates of costs and potential income

· Any final selling points

A proposal should build in excitement and interest as it leads to the answers you have to offer. Determination of which points to use and their order are at your discretion. You want the client to feel that they can't live without you and what you have to offer.

Whenever possible, the proposal should be made in person to the entire staff of decision makers. Questions and any confusion can be handled immediately. An experienced negotiator may choose to paraphrase the proposal and offer a shorter written copy.

However, instances may arise when a proposal must be mailed or left at an office. When you are not there to give the introduction and to promote the concept with tact and enthusiasm, a letter of introduction and the written document must do it for you. A phone call should be timed to coincide with the day the person receives the document. If the contact person must sell the concept to others, when preparing the proposal enlist his or her help. Ask what selling points, statistics, or other information she or he feels will be needed to impress the others? Ordinarily, the answers you receive will give you great insight into the client company and their real interests.

There is always some fear about the risk in giving a potential client the opportunity to see a truly unique, clever idea such as an invention or new business concept. A proposal should never be detailed on how you will do your job, in most proposals you are selling the client on using you, your creativity and expertise. It is fairly standard to ask before the proposal is offered that the ideas be considered privy information or to have "Confidential" stamped on the proposal. As an added safeguard, if you are very worried about controlling the concept, it is acceptable to bring another person with you as an associate (and witness). Finally, you can ask that the client sign a Non-Disclosure Agreement (see Chapter 22). However, some people will take offense to being asked, or will refuse to do so on legal grounds (they may have already had plans to pursue the idea). For example, you may be one of several people presenting proposals on starting a wellness program.

If an agreement is never reached, and yet your unique idea is used by the client, you could sue if your case is strong enough (a witness or written agreement may be necessary to do so). You will have to be able to prove that the unique idea was owned by you through copyrights, trademarks, or patents.

A proposal provides a perfect opportunity again to offer the "Sears Plan" to a client: the good, better, and best approach. Anticipate that the client may be hesitant to buy the most comprehensive plan you have to offer. Be ready to promote the contingency plan of lesser cost and involvement in case the first one doesn't sell. A third "at least you got your foot in the door" plan could be either offered initially, or you could wait and use it if all else fails.

Making a proposal may set the beginning groundwork that will lead to other new ideas or ventures between you and the client. Or it may only help your client decide what he doesn't want to do. Whatever the extent of the agreement to work together, it should be outlined, and all parties should have a copy.

Assertiveness in Business Grows in Time

As Herb Cohen states in his book, *You Can Negotiate Anything, we* actually negotiate several times per day every day of our lives. Whether we need a refund on poor service, a package delivered on time, or the secretary to answer the phone more pleasantly, we are trying to have our wishes met. We sometimes have to become more assertive to do it.

To be more effective in your work and to negotiate better contracts and consultant fees, it helps to know when and how to stand your ground. For persons who are not used to being assertive, finding a happy medium between being passive and being overbearing or stubborn, is a necessity. Finesse will develop in time. Consider how you would have handled the following situation:

Situation A

Two businessmen called the nutritionist to ask if she felt she had expertise in menu development for their proposed natural food restaurant. They told her they had heard good things about her professionally and wanted her services. They also mentioned that they were well financed and planned to start a concept that could be franchised nationwide. A meeting was scheduled for the three on the coming Thursday.

The nutritionist was very excited about the concept. At the meeting the two men asked verbally for her confidentiality, and she agreed. They then explained in general terms what they planned to do, where, when, and how successful it would be. The two men were dressed in business suits and were apparently successful and trustworthy if appearances meant anything.

The two men asked to see some of the nutritionist's work in menu and recipe development and she agreed (she had brought her restaurant portfolio on her past client accounts). The businessmen were impressed. They told the nutritionist that they might even have a staff or consultant position for her at a very good salary, if she would consider taking a chance with them by working in return for a "piece of the action."

The nutritionist was always willing to pursue new, exciting concepts, but she had heard too many similar proposals before to go blindly into another one. She knew it was her turn to start asking some questions: Who was backing the venture? What experience did the two have in the restaurant business; if it was very little, who was going to be hired to develop and manage the concept? What did they want her to do besides menu and recipe development, some marketing, personnel training, ongoing updating and testing of food items, or whatever? For what amount of time? Also, what did they propose would be her fair share of "piece of the action?" Would it mean she would be a partner or shareholder? Legally, how would it be set up?

The reason for this battery of questions was the fact that they had first said they were well financed, and then asked her to work without pay, at least initially. The questions were probing, but the businessmen were asking her to participate in their business venture in return for nonpayment of her services. She had every right to find out as much as she could before calling her own lawyer and other business consultants to discuss the offer.

Too often less assertive or business-wise nutritionists accept appearances as the truth and unwisely believe that other people always have their best interests at heart. The businessmen were there because they wanted something that they thought the dietitian could supply (good recipes, expertise, credibility, or whatever). It is always better to try to find out up front if a business relationship is honest and open, than to assume everything is okay. You risk not being paid, or being professionally burned by people who misrepresent themselves and their capabilities.

AGREEMENTS

Agreements or exchanges of promises between two parties can take several forms. The more common are a verbal agreement, a bid, letter of agreement, or contract. Some forms do not offer the business novice much protection in case the other party does not perform as expected. Contracts are more detailed, but are sometimes too complex and expensive to be useful. The best agreements are between two reputable people who have adequately discussed their expectations of the other person.

Verbal or Gentleman's Agreements

Verbal or gentleman's agreements for fees and services are usually considered legally binding in most states and are very common. Professional consultants and advisors often quote their fees for certain services and we agree to them verbally. We may agree to consult at a physician's office or a health club on a handshake. Verbal agreements are fine when you know the other party, and both of you know what is expected and perform accordingly. In cases where there are misunderstandings or one person does not produce as expected, a verbal agreement can prove to be inadequate protection.

COMMON QUESTION: **Keeping a Successful Account**

I am negotiating with a physician to offer nutrition consultation in his office. I am willing to work hard, take a financial risk, and build the program. But what guarantees do I have that as soon as I have become successful financially, I won't be replaced? How can I protect myself before I make the investment?

If the physician is a fair and honest person there are ways to avoid problems. If she or he is not, the situation probably will be out of your control. First, realize that it is only a good deal if you both feel you have been fairly compensated for what you have each contributed. So get out in the open what you each are offering the other. You may be offering time, effort, and some money, and the physician is offering client referrals, facilities, and some money. Later on as you succeed the possibility of being replaced is reduced if the following have taken place:

- You have a working relationship with the physician and the staff and you are considered an asset.

- You are closely identified with the nutrition program, and if you go, so will the program and client load.

178

- Each of you feels fairly compensated. Also, incentives should be built in so that extra work or effort on your part is rewarded.

- You developed the teaching materials on your own time and copyrighted them. The programs can only be used as long as you are a consultant there.

- Finally, before beginning, you and the physician should put your agreement in writing. At this time try to add a simple partnership buy-out agreement in case the physician wants the program, but wants to replace you.

You may be surprised, it may be the physician who fears you leaving more than the other way around.

Bids

A bid or cost estimate for a job is legal. It can be a good agreement if it is specific as to quality and date of completion, and both parties agree to any changes in writing. The most common shortcomings of bids are too little shared information. To help remedy this, bids may be accompanied by an explanation or sample of a similar finished product or a proposal (see Figure 21.1).

Figure 21.1

Sample Bid

SMITH & JONES NUTRITION SERVICES, INC.
2530 Ridgeway
Tucson, AZ 85728
BID

Development of a diet manual for EARTH GROWN FOODS on lacto-ovo vegetarian diets for the following limitations:

Low Calorie
Low Cholesterol
Diabetic
Low Salt

The manual will include sample menus, nutrient charts, references for recipes, and a brand-name food guide. The finished manual will contain approximately 100 pages.

Completion date: One (1) month from the acceptance of this bid.

Project cost: $10,000

EARTH GROWN FOODS   DATE

Letter of Agreement

A letter of agreement is also legally binding, but less formal or complicated than a contract. For many people a letter is also less intimidating. To be good this form of agreement must be comprehensive and may include the following information:

- What the agreement is for, i.e., services, product, etc.

- Who is providing it

- When

- Where

- For how much

- How often

- Who is paying for it on what schedule or by what process, i.e., billing, monthly fee, etc.

- Any additional provisions

- Term of the agreement

- Termination clause by either party

A letter of agreement may be written in the form of a short exchange of promises (see Figure 21.2). It may be in the form of a business or personal letter that outlines what the agreement is as the writer understands it .

It is suggested that both parties sign the agreement. However, courts of law will often stand behind a letter that was sent by certified mail (return receipt requested) when no rebuttal was made, and the work was allowed to progress as if the agreement were accepted.

It is highly suggested that you consult with your lawyer concerning the provisions you should include in your letters of agreement to cover your particular business. After you are more familiar with this type of agreement, you will seldom need legal input except in cases of higher risk.

Contracts

Contracts are usually used when the risk is greater, the money is higher, and/or when more control is needed. Legal input is highly suggested for the development or review of all contracts before one is signed.

A contract may have any number of provisions and limitations and the contract is usually biased to the advantage of the side that writes the contract. Included provisions may or may not be reasonable, so read them carefully. Most items of a contract are negotiable, especially if the other party is highly motivated to get a signed contract.

One item of great concern to consultants, employees, and subcontractors is the noncompete clause in a contract. If one is used, it must

180

be reasonable. Most noncompete clauses state that clients provided by the contractor or employer are not to be taken or approached for a period of time after the consultant or employee leaves. No directly competing business can be started by the consultant within a certain radius of the business for a period of time. Recently courts of law have said that special training or proprietary information must be taught to the employee or consultant by an employer in order for a noncompete clause to be used. Check with a lawyer in your state before signing an agreement with a noncompete clause.

Figure 21.2 Sample Personal Letter of Agreement

THE WOMAN'S HOSPITAL
7600 Jones Street
Atlanta, GA 30303

January 19, 1993

Ms. Stephany White, R.D.
Nutrition Consultant Services of Atlanta, Inc.
7800 Fannin, Suite 203
Atlanta, GA 30310

Dear Stephany:

This letter is to confirm our telephone conversation of January 18, 1993.

As agreed in our conversation, your firm will provide its services to this hospital according to the following provisions:

1. The hospital agrees to pay $45 per outpatient consultation to Nutrition Consultant Services of Atlanta, Inc.
2. This agreement shall be for six months (6) months and automatically renewable at the end of each six month period.
3. Requests for services shall be coordinated by the Food Service Department and Nursing Service.
4. Statements remitted by Nutrition Consultant Services of Atlanta, Inc., shall detail each consultation.
5. This agreement can be terminated by either party with 30 days written notice.

Thanks for your assistance. If you have any questions concerning the agreement, please do not hesitate to contact my office.

Sincerely,

Cary D. Henry
Administrator

Figure 21.3 Sample Contract

AGREEMENT

AGREEMENT dated the 20th day of October, 1988, between DIET SERVICES IN FOOD AND NUTRITION, INC. (hereinafter called the "Corporation"), and JAMES GORE.

WHEREAS the Corporation is in the business of providing consulting services and assistance normally associated with clients and

WHEREAS from time to time the Corporation may require outside assistance in rendering said services; and

WHEREAS JAMES GORE wishes to provide said services from time to time when required by the Corporation; and

WHEREAS the Corporation and JAMES GORE desire to set forth herein their understandings and agreement:

NOW, THEREFORE, in consideration of the foregoing, the mutual promises herein set forth, and other good and valuable consideration, the receipt and sufficiency of which are hereby acknowledged, the parties hereto, intending to be legally bound, hereby agree as follows:

1. PREVIOUS AGREEMENTS CANCELLED

All prior agreements, whether written or oral, between the parties hereto are hereby cancelled and of no further force and effect.

2. ACTIVITIES OF JAMES GORE

During the term of this agreement, specified in Section 4 hereof, JAMES GORE shall undertake for and on behalf of, and to the extent specifically requested in writing by, the Corporation, subject to his availability and the other limitations set forth herein, to provide the Corporation with systems and other services normally associated with projects for clients of the Corporation.

3. COMPENSATION OF JAMES GORE

The Corporation hereby covenants and agrees to pay JAMES GORE at the rate of $300 per day and to reimburse him promptly for all travel, telephone, and other expenses paid or incurred by him in connection with the performance of his activities, responsibilities, and services under this agreement, upon presentation of expense statements, vouchers, or other evidence of expense and receipt of payment from the client by the Corporation for such out-of-pocket expenses. Payment for services will not include travel time to a client's location unless client has agreed to pay the Corporation for such travel time. JAMES GORE will submit invoices and time sheets to the Corporation on a monthly basis.

4. TERM

The term of this agreement shall commence as of the date hereof and shall continue until terminated by either party at any time upon thirty (30) days' written notice to the other. Notwithstanding the foregoing, JAMES GORE agrees that he will complete in a timely manner any project in progress at the time of said notice of termination.

5. INDEPENDENT CONTRACTOR

JAMES GORE shall at all times be an independent contractor, rather than a co-venturer, agent, employee, or representative of the Corporation.

6. DISCLOSURE OF INFORMATION

JAMES GORE recognizes and acknowledges that the list of the Corporation's customers, programs, designs, or products, as they may exist from

Figure 21.3 (Continued)

time to time, are valuable, special, and unique assets of the Corporation's business. JAMES GORE shall not, during or after the term of this agreement for a period of three (3) years, solicit the Corporation's customers or disclose the list of the Corporation's customers or any part thereof to any person, firm, corporation, association, or other entity for any reason or purpose whatsoever, without the written consent of the Corporation. In addition, at and after any termination, JAMES GORE shall not utilize the Corporation's programs, designs, or products for any purpose without the express written consent of the Corporation. In the event of a breach or a threatened breach by JAMES GORE of the provisions of this paragraph, the Corporation shall be entitled to an injunction restraining disclosing, in whole or in part, the list of the Corporation's customers, or from rendering any services to any person, firm, corporation, association, or other entity to whom such list, in whole or in part, has been disclosed or is threatened to be disclosed. Nothing herein shall be construed as prohibiting the Corporation from pursuing any other remedies available to the Corporation for such breach or threatened breach, including the recovery of damages.

7. BINDING EFFECTS; ASSIGNMENT

This agreement shall be binding upon and shall inure to the benefit of JAMES GORE and the Corporation and their respective heirs, executors, or administrators, personal and legal representatives, estate, legatees, and successors. The obligations under this agreement may not be assigned by JAMES GORE without the prior written consent of the Corporation.

8. NOTICES

All notices and other communications hereunder or in connection herewith shall be deemed to have been duly given if they are in writing and delivered personally or sent by registered or certified mail, return receipt requested and first-class postage prepaid. Unless notice of change of address is given to either party by the other pursuant to the provisions of this section, all communications shall be addressed:

(a) If to the Corporation:
   DIET SERVICES IN FOOD AND NUTRITION, INC.
   1967 Sage Circle
   Golden, CO 80401

(b) If to the consultant:
   Mr. James Gore, R.D.
   JAMES GORE ASSOCIATES
   1414 Clarkson
   Denver, CO 80218

9. GOVERNING LAW

This agreement shall be governed by and construed under the laws of the State of Colorado.

10. MISCELLANEOUS

No modification or waiver of any provision of this agreement shall be valid unless it is in writing and signed by the party against whom it is sought to be enforced. No waiver at any time of any provision of this agreement shall be deemed a waiver of any other provision of this agreement at that time or a waiver of that or any other provision at any other time.

The captions and headings contained herein are solely for convenience and reference and do not constitute a part of this agreement.

Figure 21.3 (Continued)

JAMES GORE agrees to provide his own insurance coverages and to indemnify and hold harmless the Corporation from any injury or liability arising out of the negligence, misfeasance, malfeasance, or omission in the performance of services to or on behalf of the Corporation.

JAMES GORE agrees to execute any agreement required by a client of the Corporation in order to protect the secrecy and confidentiality of past, present, and future plans, provisions, designs, forms, formats, procedures, methods, customer data, employee data, technical data, know-how, research and development data and programs, financial data, legal data, marketing data, and other technical and business data belonging to said client of the Corporation.

IN WITNESS WHEREOF, the parties hereto have set their hands and seals this 20th day of October, 1988.

DIET SERVICES IN FOOD AND NUTRITION, INC.

_____   _____
Signature   Date

JAMES GORE

_____   _____
Signature   Date

Generating a contract can be expensive and time consuming. Your legal bill will be less if you know what you want. Tell your lawyer to make the contract practical, easy to understand, and complete enough to protect your reasonable interests (see Figure 21.3). Unless cautioned otherwise, some lawyers produce documents that are so detailed and intimidating that no one will sign them.

CONCLUSION

Underlying this discussion on negotiating and agreements should be the awareness that usually the best outcomes evolve when both parties feel they benefit from the agreement--also, when both parties are honest and produce work in good faith. Learning how to "read" the other party and keep control of your advantage points becomes easier with experience and trial and error.

REFERENCES

1. Warschaw, T. A.: *Winning By Negotiation,* McGraw-Hill, New York, 1980.
2. *Negotiating Tricks,* Report No. 200, 1978 by Chase Revel, Inc.
3. Cohen, Herb: *You Can Negotiate Anything,* Bantam Books, New York, 1980.

Chapter 22

Protecting Your Ideas and Interests

Business owners want to know how to keep others from taking their ideas and how to protect their property from lawsuits. The better known means of protection are copyrights, patents, and insurance, but there are many other options, including written agreements, personal discretion, and incorporation.

With time and experience the ability to "read" an individual or situation and evaluate the risk involved will come easily. Through contacts and networking over the years, and your own savvy, the development of ideas will become relatively non-fearful.

PUBLIC DOMAIN

A distinction needs to be made about what kinds of ideas can be protected legally or claimed for ownership. Any new and original literary, graphic, audio, mechanical, video, process series, or ingredient may be protected as belonging to an individual or company. All items, names, and so on, that are considered common knowledge and nonunique are in the "public domain." They cannot be the sole property of any one person or business. Examples of common items are the words "food," "juice," and "nutritionist," the Basic Four Food Group listings, and the common medical diets (although unique diet manuals can be copyrighted that use that information). Everyone can use all items in the "public domain."

HAVE IT IN WRITING

To avoid confusion and lawsuits the best advice is not to assume anything about even a simple agreement; discuss it thoroughly and have it in writing. Initially, use lawyers to look over all agreements and later use their services especially on all risky, important, and costly agreements. No one should start a job "on good faith" unless he is willing *not* to collect for the services.

PERSONAL DISCRETION

Many good creative ideas become public property because the originator of the thought talked about it indiscreetly. Exceptionally different and quality ideas are of great value personally also financially, and should be treated as such. Obviously, in the development of your ideas consultants or professional advisors may need to be involved, but there is better legal recourse if any of these individuals take an idea. Business people will tell you that the best way to avoid being fearful in business is to work only with very ethical, honest people who come highly recommended or whom you have checked out through references.

If an original idea must be discussed with a company or individual you do not know, have a trusted acquaintance present who could witness the conversation, or ask to tape record the session, or ask that a simple Nondisclosure Agreement be signed (see Figure 22.1). If handled tactfully, no one will be embarrassed or threatened by the precautions.

TRADE SECRETS AND INTELLECTUAL PROPERTY

Trade secrets and intellectual property are ideas and materials that make the business unique. A trade secret may be protected by not telling anyone about it, which may hinder its usefulness, or by having nondisclosure agreements. Intellectual property may be protected by copyrighting, trademarking, or patenting.

Copyrights

Copyrights are issued by the U.S. Copyright Office for books and pamphlets, for new diet programs with original elements that have not been used before, and for other artistic, musical, dramatic, audiovisual, choreographic, or literary creations. The copyright notice should appear on all published works that are distributed to the public. The use of the copyright notice is the responsibility of the copyright owner and does not require advance permission from the Copyright Office.

Figure 22.1

Sample Nondisclosure Agreement

NONDISCLOSURE AGREEMENT

_____ agrees to maintain the confidentiality of all proprietary information and trade secrets concerning Diet Control, Inc., or Diet Control, Inc.'s products, and printed information of which he or she becomes aware. This obligation of confidentiality shall survive the termination of this Agreement.

Agreed and Accepted:

Diet Control, Inc.

_____   _____

Date: _____

186

The copyright law grants copyright owners certain exclusive rights to their works, including the rights of reproduction and of public performance. Only copyright owners have the right to make or authorize copies of their educational materials, slides, articles, or videotapes and to show their videos publicly (1). An owner may grant permission to others for limited use of one or more of these exclusive rights. Some owners will charge a fee, while others will allow free use.

The notice should be on the copies "in such manner and location as to give reasonable notice of the claim of copyright." The required copyright generally consists of three elements. The first is the " " symbol, the word "Copyright," or the abbreviation "Copr." The second is the year of first publication, and the third is the name of the copyright owner. An example of a typical copyright is " Copyright 1992 Nutrition Daily" (1).

In books, pamphlets, and other publications a printed reminder is usually added that states, "This material may not be copied or reproduced in any manner without the written permission of the author." Lawyers who specialize in copyright law suggest that newly published material with the copyright notice be sent to someone out of state by certified mail. The postage receipt will show when the copyright was first used. In case of a copyright dispute the documented date may prove to be significant.

Copyright forms and information may be obtained by calling or writing: Register of Copyrights, Library of Congress, Washington, D.C. 20559 or a local federally authorized library, or call (202) 707-9100. It is usually advisable to initially contact a qualified lawyer who can answer questions on the subject. The copyright application filing fee is $20 plus several copies of the completed work (1). The form is simple enough for most persons to fill out. It is highly recommended that you register your copyright within three months of going public with the copyrighted material because you may be awarded statutory damages and attorney's fees in infringement litigation (or an additional $50,000 over actual damages and profit) (2).

The copyright term is effective for the life of the author and fifty years after the author's death. Works created for hire, and certain anonymous and pseudonymous works, can be copyrighted for seventy-five years from publication or 100 years from creation whichever is shorter.

As the copyright owner, you, not the government, are responsible for protecting the use of the copyrighted material. If the copyright is abused, you or your lawyer can send a "cease and desist" order to the infringing person or organization to ask that use be stopped. Going to court is costly, but it can be used as a last resort.

As an example of how a copyright infringement can be handled, one consulting nutritionist found out that one of her contract OB-GYN clinics where she worked as a consultant was photocopying her copyrighted prenatal brochure and handing it out to all new patients. She made an appointment to discuss the situation with the clinic director. She stated that her contract agreement did not allow uncontrolled use of her copyrighted materials. The clinic agreed to purchase the brochures at a bulk rate of $1 each with 500 brochures being the minimum order.

Figure 22.2

Application for Registration of a Copyright

(*Source:* U.S. Copyright Office.)

FORM TX

UNITED STATES COPYRIGHT OFFICE

REGISTRATION NUMBER

TX TXU

EFFECTIVE DATE OF REGISTRATION

(Month) (Day) (Year)

DO NOT WRITE ABOVE THIS LINE. IF YOU NEED MORE SPACE, USE CONTINUATION SHEET (FORM TX/CON)

1 Title

TITLE OF THIS WORK:

If a periodical or serial give: Vol. ...... No. ...... Issue Date ......

PREVIOUS OR ALTERNATIVE TITLES:

PUBLICATION AS A CONTRIBUTION: (If this work was published as a contribution to a periodical, serial, or collection, give information about the collective work in which the contribution appeared.)

Title of Collective Work ...... Vol. ...... No. ...... Date ...... Pages ......

2 Author(s)

IMPORTANT: Under the law, the "author" of a "work made for hire" is generally the employer, not the employee (see instructions). If any part of this work was "made for hire" check "Yes" in the space provided, give the employer (or other person for whom the work was prepared) as "Author" of that part, and leave the space for dates blank.

1

NAME OF AUTHOR:

Was this author's contribution to the work a "work made for hire"? Yes ...... No ......

DATES OF BIRTH AND DEATH: Born ...... (Year) Died ...... (Year)

AUTHOR'S NATIONALITY OR DOMICILE:

Citizen of ...... (Name of Country) } or { Domiciled in ...... (Name of Country)

WAS THIS AUTHOR'S CONTRIBUTION TO THE WORK: Anonymous? Yes No; Pseudonymous? Yes No

If the answer to either of these questions is "Yes," see detailed instructions attached.

AUTHOR OF: (Briefly describe nature of this author's contribution)

2

NAME OF AUTHOR:

Was this author's contribution to the work a "work made for hire"? Yes ...... No ......

DATES OF BIRTH AND DEATH: Born ...... (Year) Died ...... (Year)

AUTHOR'S NATIONALITY OR DOMICILE:

Citizen of ...... (Name of Country) } or { Domiciled in ...... (Name of Country)

WAS THIS AUTHOR'S CONTRIBUTION TO THE WORK: Anonymous? Yes No; Pseudonymous? Yes No

If the answer to either of these questions is "Yes," see detailed instructions attached.

AUTHOR OF (Briefly describe nature of this author's contribution)

3

NAME OF AUTHOR:

Was this author's contribution to the work a "work made for hire"? Yes ...... No ......

DATES OF BIRTH AND DEATH: Born ...... (Year) Died ...... (Year)

AUTHOR'S NATIONALITY OR DOMICILE:

Citizen of ...... (Name of Country) } or { Domiciled in ...... (Name of Country)

WAS THIS AUTHOR'S CONTRIBUTION TO THE WORK: Anonymous? Yes No; Pseudonymous? Yes No

If the answer to either of these questions is "Yes," see detailed instructions attached.

AUTHOR OF: (Briefly describe nature of this author's contribution)

3 Creation and Publication

YEAR IN WHICH CREATION OF THIS WORK WAS COMPLETED:

Year ......

(This information must be given in all cases.)

DATE AND NATION OF FIRST PUBLICATION:

Date ...... (Month) (Day) (Year)

Nation ...... (Name of Country)

(Complete this block ONLY if this work has been published.)

4 Claimant(s)

NAME(S) AND ADDRESS(ES) OF COPYRIGHT CLAIMANT(S):

TRANSFER: (If the copyright claimant(s) named here in space 4 are different from the author(s) named in space 2, give a brief statement of how the claimant(s) obtained ownership of the copyright.)

- *Complete all applicable spaces (numbers 5-11) on the reverse side of this page*
- *Follow detailed instructions attached*
- *Sign the form at line 10*

DO NOT WRITE HERE

Page 1 of .... pages

Other ways to discourage misuse of your copyrighted material include the use of odd size paper that does not easily fit on a photocopier, use of blue or brown ink that does not photocopy well, and use of the new paper and inks that do not reproduce at all on a photocopier.

Formerly employed dietitians are usually in a quandary about ownership of materials and programs they develop while employed.

Figure 22.3

Sample Request to Reprint Copyrighted Material

Dear _____ :

I am preparing an educational exercise and nutrition booklet for the patients at the Medical Treatment Center, Garland, Texas. May I please have your permission to include the following:

Unless you indicate otherwise, I will use the following credit line:

I would greatly appreciate your consent to this request. For your convenience a release statement is found below. Please sign and return this letter to me. A copy has been included for your files.

Permission is hereby granted for the use requested above.

Sincerely,

_____
Signature

_____
Date

Jan Jones, R.D.
1010 Harland
Garland, TX 75075

Lawyers agree that if you were paid as an employee when you developed the copyrighted materials for your employer, and if you do not have another prearranged agreement, the employer owns them. A former employer however, can not keep you from practicing your profession or using your expertise, so you can create different materials on the same subject. If you want to develop unique materials to use at work, and you want to own the copyright, do the work on your own time and at your own expense. This is assumes you have not signed an agreement giving your employer rights to all your ideas while employed (common in Research & Development).

If you want to use reprints or copies of other persons' copyrighted material, articles, newspaper stories and so on, you should request permission first. See Copyright Release Form in Figure 22.3.

COMMON QUESTIONS: USING COPYRIGHTED MATERIAL

I recently purchased several videotapes on exercise at the store, can I show them during my group weight loss class at the hospital?
No. The exemption allowing teachers to show videotapes in the classroom applies only to nonprofit educational institutions, such as K-12, colleges, and universities (*section 110*) (1).

When I give lectures, I show slides of charts and cartoons from books and the newspaper. Is this legal?

189

No, not without permission of the copyright owner. Photographs in books and magazines are protected by copyright, just like the written material (*section 102*) (1).

My public library has books on nutrition. May I photocopy from them?
Yes, but only small portions may be copied. The library photocopying exception to the copyright law allows an individual to make a single copy of one article from a magazine or one chapter from a book owned by a public library, provided the copy is made only for the personal use of the individual (*section 108*) (1).

I live in a small town and I am sure no one will know whether I have the permission of the copyright owner to photocopy her educational materials in a book from Aspen Publishers. Aspen can't give me permission---I've already called. Why should I write for permission?
By using the material without permission, you are stealing or trespassing on the owner's rights. Infringement of copyright can result either in a civil lawsuit brought by the copyright owner and/or criminal lawsuit brought by the U.S. government, which carries heavy fines and possible prison sentence (1). Do you really want to risk getting caught when it's so easy to write? You can find publishers' addresses at the library and The American Dietetic Association will help you contact any dietitian.

What if I write and I never hear back, or the owner wants me to pay $100 for the rights?
Do not use the copyrighted work unless you have written permission (keep the letters on file), and you pay whatever fee is charged. There may also be other restrictions like the number of copies or size of the group or whatever.

Trademarks

Trademarks are issued by the U.S. Patent and Trademark Office to provide national recognition of a name, logo, or phrase that denote certain products or services. Examples of common product trademarks include: Coca Cola, Vivonex, Kleenex, and Crayola. When a trademark stands for a service offered by a business instead of a product it is referred to as a "service mark." Examples of common service marks include: the logo of The American Dietetic Association, McDonald's name, and Prudential's rock.

A trade or commercial name is a business name used to identify a partnership, company, or other organization. Incorporation of the business will protect the company name from use by others in the original state and where the business legally expands its markets. There is no provision in the trademark law for the registration of trade names used merely to identify a business. However, you can control your name if it is written or spelled in an unusual manner or it's in artwork created to stand for your company (3).

Before filing an application, a search of trademarks should be made in the Search Room of the Trademark Examining Operation located in the Crystal Plaza Building No. 2, 2011 Jefferson Davis Highway, Arlington,

Virginia. Any trademark that is too similar to one already filed will not be accepted for registration. The search can be done by any individual. Trademark lawyers have contacts with persons who can do the research for a fee. You can also call the Chamber of Commerce in Arlington, Virginia, and get the names of several trademark search companies that will research a trademark for around $40-50. Applications and more information can be obtained from the Patent and Trademark Office, Washington, D.C. 20231 or call (703) 557-INFO.

To establish rights to a trademark, you can either file an "intent-to-use" form with a drawing and pay a $100 fee or file a trademark application with three copies of the mark as it is actually used in commerce along with $175 fee for each class of goods. The term of the trademark registration is twenty years from the date of issue, and it may be renewed at the end of each twenty-year term as long as the mark is still used in commerce (2).

Trademark rights are protected under common law; in other words, the mark belongs to the first user as soon as it is used, whether or not it is ever registered. However, registering a trademark does have its advantages: it shows official claim of ownership and exclusive right to use the mark on the goods mentioned in the registration. There is no time limitation on when an application for registering a trademark can be filed.

Once a registration is issued, you may give notice of registration by using the "R" in a circle symbol, or the phrase "Registered in U.S. Patent and Trademark Office." Although registration symbols may not be used prior to registration, many trademark owners use a "TM" or "SM" (for service mark) to indicate claim of ownership.

The owner of the trademark, not the government, is responsible for protecting the mark from being used by others. In hopes of fooling the public, some companies create products with trademarks that are very similar to older, well-known trademarks. In these cases, the established company hires lawyers to start legal proceedings to stop the infringement.

If you are going to go to the trouble and expense of trademarking a name, make it distinctive as well as meaningful.

Patents

Patents are issued to inventors to help protect inventions from being used without the inventor's permission. To be patented, an invention must have a useful purpose for existing and it must have some new, never before patented element that makes it unique. A new patent can be issued on a new process, machine, composition of matter, or any new and useful improvements on an old patent.

A patent is effective for seventeen years. Thereafter the invention is considered to be in the "public domain" and anyone can use it. Because of this fact some inventors decide not to patent a product that cannot be duplicated so that they own it exclusively. The owners of Coca Cola chose not to patent their product many years ago so that the formula (which was only recently disclosed) would remain a company trade secret.

191

Patent claims and/or designs must be researched either at the Patent Office or at one of the federally designated libraries across the United States. The search will tell you what claims have already been issued patents. You may have to alter your product's claims after you conduct a search. A search by a lawyer will range from $500-$1500 or more depending upon the complexity of the item researched. There are firms in your Yellow Pages and others like: Affiliated Inventors Foundation, Inc., 2132 E. Bijou Street, Colorado Springs, CO 80909 that will do searches for you for about $300-450, but you should check out any firm first before using it.

What does it take to patent the new product you've dreamed up? "Persistence and perseverance," says patent attorney Ken Schaefer (4). The patenting process can be costly and lengthy, too. Filing cost ranges from $315 to $630, and the lawyer's time may add another $1500 to $3000 or more. If there are designs and intricate circuitry, you may need an engineer for the drawings. Once you get a "notice of allowance"---which means your patent has been approved--- you have to pay an "issue fee" of up to $620. The entire process takes about twenty months. Even with all that time and money involved, the Patent and Trademark Office issues about 1,400 patents every week. More information and an application can be obtained from the Patent and Trademark Office, Washington, D.C. 20231.

INSURANCE

Insurance was originally devised as a means of spreading the risk of having bad luck through a group instead of being shouldered by one individual. It has always been common to insure material possessions, but when starting a private practice, insurance to pay salary in case of disability and malpractice insurance are recommended. The cost of business insurance premiums is deductible as a business expense.

Malpractice insurance is available to cover the high cost of legal representation and the high incidence of threatened and actual lawsuits against not only physicians, but all persons who come in contact with the patient. Malpractice is discussed in detail in Chapter 18.

Disability insurance pays income when the insured person becomes ill or disabled, and is not able to work up to capacity. It is encouraged for sole supported, self-employed people because they are not eligible for worker's compensation, unemployment benefits, or sick time except through programs set up by their own company. Social Security disability insurance requires six months of no income before payments can begin. No income for an extended period could mean loss of the business as well as personal property. It is sometimes difficult to qualify for this type of insurance if you have a business based out of your home, so if you work or consult somewhere else, highlight that location for disability insurance purposes.

Office insurance would include fire, theft, and liability coverage. This coverage is common and can usually be obtained from a practitioner's existing home insurance company. Office coverage is necessary because many medical buildings' insurance policies do not cover tenants' furnishings, possessions, loss of business, or visitors' accidents. When working out of your home, it is still necessary to carry extra insurance for times when clients visit and to cover your computer and other office equipment.

Auto insurance on business-owned vehicles is common and necessary. In case of an accident involving the business car, the liability coverage should be especially good because the public believes that a business has more assets, and the possibility of a lawsuit after an accident may be greater. The cost of the coverage is comparable to personal auto insurance unless younger members of the family or persons with poor driving records are allowed to drive the car.

INCORPORATION

Many persons choose to incorporate their businesses to reduce the risk of losing their personal property for business dealings. A corporation is a complete, legal entity separate from its shareholders with its own assets. If all business is conducted in the corporate name and under its umbrella, the corporation's assets alone are at jeopardy for the business' failures, and lawsuits (see Chapter 13 for more information).

HOW MUCH RISK IS THERE?

Starting a business venture is not a risk free endeavor. In fact, it requires an individual to constantly be confronted with numerous important decisions, to initiate new untried ideas, to counsel patients on medical-associated nutrition programs, and risk financial loss.

The best ways to protect oneself are to be ethical, to ask advice of people who are successful in business, to make well-thought-out decisions, to document all important agreements and client visits in writing, and to learn from experience. Most people who have been in business for some time suggest that a person "take reasonable precautionary measures and then go on with business and living."

REFERENCES

1. Dukelow, Ruth H: *The Library Copyright Guide,* excerpt in *Quilting,* August 1991.
2. Sitarz, D.: *The Desktop Publisher's Legal Handbook,* NOVA Publishing, IL, 1990.
3. Helm, Kathy King: *Becoming An Entrepreneur In Your Own Setting,* Study Kit #3, The American Dietetic Association, 1991.
4. "Have you built a better mousetrap?," *Family Circle,* August 15, 1989.

Chapter 23

Ethics, Malpractice, and Libel

The ethical manner in which people conduct their businesses determines to a large extent the loyalty of clients and the support of peers. Clients want to feel that they are being honestly served for a fair price. Our peers expect us to conduct ourselves professionally, honestly, and within the law. Others expect us to give accurate information and not engage in questionable dealings that will reflect poorly upon ourselves and, possibly, the dietetic profession.

Unfortunately, historically, professionals too often were ridiculed and ousted from their professional groups because they tried or believed something that was new and different but perfectly ethical. For a profession and its members to lead in their area of expertise, exploration of new ideas is mandatory. Some tolerance must be exercised by peers and organizations in judging the merit or ethical nature of a new idea.

Commonly, business people who get into trouble ethically or from malpractice close shop because business becomes so poor. Occasionally, there is that rare instance where the person benefits from all of the publicity and ends up with a booming business. If the breach is bad enough, a lawsuit, loss of license or professional membership may occur.

WHO JUDGES ETHICS?

Ethics in private practice may be "judged" by our professional and business peers, by government agencies such as the judicial system, the Internal Revenue Service, or the Public Health Department, and by business organizations such as the Better Business Bureau and the local Chamber of Commerce. As long as no one complains, no one probably will ever be concerned about you or your business. That is one good reason to take complaints seriously and follow them to resolution. However, fear of ethical breaches should not paralyze you or make you compromise on all matters that you feel very strongly are right.

Professional Process

If the person is an employee or contractual consultant, an ethical matter could be simply addressed in-house. If the person is in private practice, more

194

than likely it will be the local or state dietetic organization or state licensing board that first questions a professional ethics problem. If the matter is serious enough, the House of Delegates Ethics Committee of The American Dietetic Association will review the case in terms of considering censoring or revocation of membership.

Peers have the obligation to handle an ethical review in a professional manner and not commit slander, libel, and character assassination. The accused individual has the basic right to be considered in the right until proven otherwise.

The Individual

Ultimately, of course, it is individual practitioners who must live with their own decisions. We all have varying degrees of restrictions that we place on our actions according to our value systems. We tempt our ethical boundaries every time we don't simply refuse a physician who wants a kickback, or when we give less than our best care because we run short of time, or when we discuss our fees at the local dietetic meeting (could be interpreted as price-fixing).

Honesty In Business

In an article, "Why be honest if honesty doesn't pay?," authors Bhide and Stevenson found in extensive interviews that treachery can pay. There is no compelling economic reason to tell the truth or to keep one's word. In the real world punishment for the treacherous is neither swift nor sure, even when wrongdoing has been clearly shown. Conscience rather than calculation explains why most businesspeople keep their word and deal fairly with one another. It is the absence of predictable financial rewards that makes honesty a moral quality to be cherished (1).

WHAT THEN IS ETHICAL?

The American Dietetic Association and its credentialing agency, the Commission on Dietetic Registration have written a Code of Ethics for the Profession of Dietetics. A copy can be obtained from the ADA. The main components of the standards include the following (2):

- That a member provide professional services with objectivity and with respect for the unique needs and values of individuals

- That professional qualifications are presented accurately

- That conflicts of interest are avoided

- That competency of practice is maintained

- That confidentiality of information is respected

- That controversial material is substantiated and given an unbiased interpretation
- That a member practices honesty, integrity, and fairness

Up to-Date Knowledge
As professional dietitians, we are expected to give the best quality of work we are capable of doing. To do that, we have an obligation to remain current and up to date in our field of knowledge. Our knowledge is what we have to market. Therefore, every effort should be made to have our knowledge timely, unbiased, well thought out, and of such quality that the competition cannot compete.

Self-referrals
Established private practitioners normally consider it ethical to accept new patients who refer themselves. The professional relationship is between the patient and the practitioner, similar to when a patient goes to see a family guidance or stop smoking counselor--no referral is needed. Why should eating food be controlled by a medical referral? The dietitian is the trained expert in the nutrition field, and nutrition is the area of service. The practitioners do not make medical diagnoses. They make nutrition assessments and provide nutritional care plans. Patients who need medical care are given the names of competent medical professionals or are referred to the local medical society.

Computing Diets
Computing diet limits for all patients is becoming commonplace in private practice. Most private practitioners find that as referring physicians gain more confidence in them, diet orders change from specific limits to only diagnoses or chemical scores. It seems we have all come to realize it is premature to guess a calorie level before a diet history and assessment are made.

Patient Records
Your patients' records need to be kept confidential. A patient has the right to see his own chart; therefore, care should be taken when comments not related to the patient's nutritional care are made or even repeated by you. If a patient requests that his records be sent to his physician, clinic, or another dietitian, photocopy the materials--keep one copy and send the other. It is recommended that you keep the old patient charts for as long as you are in business. If office storage space becomes a problem, box the charts that have not been used for many years, label the box, and store it at home.

Referrals to Other Professionals
It is considered good patient care to refer patients to other professionals that you feel could help the patients with their problems. This is often done in the cases of anorexia nervosa, when suicidal statements are made, when the patient needs medical care, or when more testing is needed. If the patient has a referring physician, you should try to work through him or her to help the patient.

Referring patients to other professionals does carry some risk with it for you, especially if you only give one or two names. You may be held responsible if the patient is very unhappy with the care they receive from the other professional--both of you may be sued. Therefore, if you give several names of specialists you highly respect, also suggest the patient seek help from the local medical society, the county health department, or look in the Yellow Pages.

It is ethical to suggest to patients to seek a second opinion in matters of health. Care should be taken not to alarm the patient unnecessarily or to condemn their medical care. Consulting nutritionists state that seeing questionable medical care is not an uncommon occurrence. The hope is that it will not be compounded with questionable nutritional care!

Questioning Diet Orders

It is ethical, if not mandatory, for a nutritionist to question a diet order that is not clear, reasonable, or correct. Part of what the patient and the public expects from a professionally trained nutritionist is that decisions are made in the best interest of the patient.

"Ordering" Laboratory Tests

According to Sue Rodwell Williams, Ph.D., R.D., from California, some private practitioners "order" appropriate laboratory tests for their patients through arrangements made with a local physician. To do this at least two major criteria must be met: first, the dietitian must be a clinical nutrition specialist and be recognized by the medical community as such; and second, sound protocols must be written jointly by the practitioner and a physician and filed with a nearby reputable clinical laboratory. Periodically the protocols should be reviewed and updated by the dietitian and physician. Additionally, there should not be hesitancy by a practitioner to recommend to a physician that certain tests would be appropriate for nutrition assessment. Mutual respect and good working relationships are prerequisites for this kind of trust to take place. (See "Finger-Stick Blood Screening" under the "Malpractice" heading.)

WHAT IS UNETHICAL?

Other than failing to follow the previously mentioned ethical practices, it is also unethical to commit theft, fraud, and other illegal acts. Many unethical acts are open to interpretation, while others are very clearly defined by the local and federal governments.

Price and Territory Fixing

Price fixing is said to exist when professionals discuss in writing or verbally what to charge for services. This includes when current fees are published as examples. Encouraging someone to set their fees by calling around and checking the "going prices" of any allied health professionals is considered price fixing. The concern is that the buying public is not getting the best deal because everyone who provides a certain service is influenced to charge a certain fee--instead of allowing competition to prevail.

197

When professionals agree to territorial boundaries, where patients can only see the dietitian in a certain area, it is considered territory fixing. This also is illegal. By the way, it is also illegal for someone to try to keep you from practicing in "their territory."

Restraint of Trade

When you are asked to suggest referral names of professionals, there are several guidelines to help avoid restraint of trade:

1. Give more than one name and only suggest people you highly respect.
2. Suggest that the individual check for other names at the local dietetic organization, medical society, public health department, or Yellow Pages.

Practicing Medicine

Local medical licensing boards and medical societies are very concerned when they feel people are overstepping their professional scopes of practice into practicing medicine. The line is not always clearly defined, but it usually involves *making diagnoses* from the patient's symptoms and tests (X-rays, CAT scans, blood tests, etc.), and representing oneself as "curing" a patient. *Screening* for glucose or cholesterol problems is now so common in grocery stores and malls that by itself, *without diagnosing it* is not considered practicing medicine.

Several private practitioners have been accused by local physicians for what the physicians perceived to be practicing medicine. The known instances revolved around allergy testing, passing out a medical diet based upon symptoms, and miswording an advertisement. The problems were resolved, but only after much trouble and embarrassment. Care must be taken not to insinuate that diagnoses are being made.

Misrepresentation of Ownership of Ideas

Ideas have value. That is why the processes of copyrighting, patenting, and trademarking were started by the government--to protect the ownership of new ideas. Most ideas are evolutions or conglomerations of thoughts from many sources. "New" ideas are often better ways of stating or doing an old concept.

As we progress in business, we evaluate our ideas and keep the ones that work and discard the rest. We also evaluate ideas, programs, materials, speeches, and business techniques that we see and adopt what we think will work for us.

Ethically, the important point to remember is that we should respect the protection offered by the copyright, patent, or trademark. There are also many unique business ideas or concepts that are the pride and joy of another person. If that person feels that by adopting his or her idea, you have "stolen" or infringed upon her or his business, you may be heading for a legal confrontation.

Given the opportunity many people are happy to give a copyright release or negotiate some equitable agreement. All too often it seems the very people who become upset when their own work is taken by another, don't give a second thought about photocopying someone else's brochure, teaching materials, or book chapter.

What is a "kickback" and is it ethical?

As it relates to our profession, a "kickback" is a payment resulting from noncontractual favoritism, usually involving restraint of trade. For example, a referring physician or clinic wants to charge you a fee merely for the referral of a patient, and if you refuse, the referral would be made instead to a competitor. It also can occur when a consultant dietitian awards a contract for food or services for a client account to a company in return for receiving remuneration "under the table." Kickbacks are illegal.

The government feels that patients should not have to pay to be referred for proper care (fees would no doubt be raised to cover the cost of kickbacks). Client accounts should be able to have fair, honest contracts without the negotiator making a profit, unless that was part of the agreement.

A point of clarification should be made here concerning office sharing and paying percentage of your income for it. If office space or services are being exchanged in return for you seeing patients, it is not considered a kickback to pay for the space.

Certainly, not all ethical issues have been discussed, just some of the major reason of concern for private practitioners. For answers to other questions, call the appropriate legal or business advisor or the American Dietetic Association.

MALPRACTICE

Nutritional malpractice occurs when a dietitian fails to meet the accepted standard of care, and the action results in harm to the patient. Although there have been only a few cases where dietitians have been sued for malpractice (all known cases have either been dropped or settled out of court, except for one), the possibility of more cases in the future is very real. As dietitians become more visible professionally, as they take the initiative to prescribe diets, and as more attorneys use "blind pleading" in suits for their clients where more professionals other than just physicians are implicated, the risk of a suit is more likely (3).

Life and business are not risk free. However, having a basic understanding of the legal system as it applies to malpractice may help to minimize the risk, and its accompanying expense and embarrassment.

Legal Principles

In their article "Malpractice Law and the Dietitian," *JADA*, October, 1975, Elizabeth and Daniel Reidy state, "Each person is required by law to exercise a certain standard of care in order to avoid causing injury to the person or property of others. If a person fails to meet that standard and that failure causes harm to another's person or property, then the person is liable for the damage. This is the basic law of negligence. Dietitians-- like physicians, lawyers, accountants, and other professionals--must exercise the skill and knowledge normally possessed by members in good standing of their profession" (4).

There is no theoretical minimum harm that a patient has to prove. Simply demonstrating that negligence of proper care on the part of the dietitian caused discomfort or delayed the recovery process constitutes the basis for a lawsuit. However, if the patient does not prove that the dietitian's care caused some injury to him, there can't be a finding of liability against the dietitian (2).

Possible Liability Situations
Whenever dietitians practice their profession, whether or not they are paid for it, they are potentially risking liability and must meet the professional standards of practice. Other instances where liability may be tested are in situations where food from a kitchen gives food poisoning, where a nursing home patient dies and/or is diagnosed with malnutrition and where there are miscalculations on diet instructions, such as protein or potassium on a renal diet (2). Dietitians violating accepted management principles run the risk of being charged with administrative malpractice.

Protecting Yourself Against Malpractice
Along with giving good care, a dietitian should stay current with new advances or practices in the field of nutrition. In a court of law documentation of proper care and communication about the patient's poor eating habits to the proper channels is extremely important. Records should show that the proper information was given to the patient, that his progress was adequately followed, or if he did not return or follow it, it should be so stated, and that the referring physician was advised of the patient's progress in writing.

Finger-Stick Bloodscreening
According to an announcement in the May 1990 ADA Courier, "Members covered by ADA-sponsored liability insurance are protected against malpractice suits when performing finger-stick bloodscreening, a procedure many dietetic professionals include in their practice as a client service. This simple screening technique can identify possible health problems related to blood sugar and cholesterol. When questionable results are obtained, the client is referred to his or her physician for further laboratory analysis. Diet modifications are made only after the client's condition has been assessed. Malpractice insurance coverage for eligible members is effective, provided the RD practitioner has received training on the finger-stick blood screening techniques" (5).

WHAT IS LIBEL AND HOW IS IT DIFFERENT?

Legally, libel is any statement or representation published without just cause or excuse, or by pictures, effigies, or other signs tending to expose another person, corporation, or product to public hatred, contempt or ridicule. Calling someone a "quack," or "incompetent" could cause defamation. However, you should not be discouraged from stating the facts as you know them, backed up with scientific evidence. Such subjects as the danger of a severe low calorie diet regime and the nutritional inadequacy of some foods are

200

important to the public, and it is the responsibility of our profession to warn the public.

Don Reuben, an attorney for Reuben and Proctor in Chicago, Illinois, has stated, that in cases where a dietitian makes a public statement about an issue, "A dietitian's key defense against a public person (corporation) or government official who sues for libel is that the suing party must prove the dietitian knew it was libelous at the time of the statement. A dietitian is an expert and professionally trained authority who has the right to express nutrition facts as she sees them under fair comment protection" (6).

Victor Herbert, who is both a physician and a lawyer, has stated, "If a private individual or company sues you for speaking the truth as you see it, without malice, countersue on the grounds of malicious harassment and abuse of process. Ask the court to order the plaintiff to pay your legal fees, as suggested by Federal Judge A. Sofaer in NNFA (National Nutritional Foods Association) vs. *Whelan and Stare* (78 Civ. 6276 [ADS], U.S. District Court, Southern District of New York) (1980)" (6).

Betty Wedman, R.D., from Chicago, Illinois, who was threatened with a libel suit by a food company for a statement she made, has stated, "From personal experience let me emphasize the need for daily, detailed logs of conversations that could be used in a court of law, if litigation were pursued. Keep records and be widely read; check out your facts with reference books and other professionals, and you need not be intimidated by the foods industry, drug manufacturers, physicians, or patients "(6).

Malpractice insurance coverage will usually cover your court costs and up to a maximum amount for a settlement for nutrition-related libel suits. Check with your insurance agent or policy concerning all items covered.

CONCLUSION

The dietitian's main concern should always be the welfare of his or her patient. Excessive measures need not be taken to practice differently just out of fear of liability. By offering quality, humanistic care, good management practices and taking the steps to document their services, practitioners should be able to conduct business with a minimum fear of risk.

REFERENCES

1. Bhide, A. and H. Stevenson: "Why be honest if honesty doesn't pay?," *Harvard Business Review,* September/October, 1990.
2. The American Dietetic Association, *Code of Ethics for the Profession of Dietetics,* 1988.
3. Baird, Patricia, and Barry Jacobs: "Malpractice: Your Day in Court," *Food Management Magazine,* February 1981.
4. Reidy, Elizabeth and Daniel Reidy: "Malpractice Law and The Dietitian," *Journal of The American Dietetic Association,* October 1975.
5. "News Notes," *Courier* newsletter of The American Dietetic Association, May 1990.
6. King, Kathy: *Starting A Private Practice,* Study Kit # 3, The American Dietetic Association, 1982.

Chapter 24

Jobs with Physicians and Allied Medical Persons

Becky McCully, M.S., R.D.

Presenting a professional image is imperative if an entrepreneur is to work successfully with other professionals. This includes a positive attitude, the ability to communicate without distracting gestures or habits, a neat and updated appearance and dress, consideration, cooperation and tact. Showing respect for another professional's expertise and expecting others to respect yours is important.

MAKING CONTACTS

Making contacts to find work or to network with professionals can be accomplished in many ways. Remember to keep visible and audible. Be seen in public frequently. Be careful not to limit opportunities. Be broad-minded in thinking and explore all possibilities as future contacts. Develop a filing system or use your computer to record all contacts. Include names of individuals, what was discussed, the reaction of the person contacted, telephone number, address, date, and a recommended follow-up procedure. Add personal information about the individual such as their children, an upcoming trip or a remark, to trigger your memory the next time you contact the person. This helps the person feel you are taking a personal interest in them.

When making contacts, always have business cards available. Anything else with your name and phone number such as handouts, fliers, brochures, and so on would be helpful to leave. Remember to keep visible!

Who Should Be Contacted?

The number and type of contacts one chooses to make are essentially unlimited. Below is a list of potential organizations and people to approach, but the list should be individualized according to your interests.

- Professional health organizations and associations, such as American Heart Association, American Diabetes

Association, American Lung Association, Arthritis Foundation, etc.

- County and State Medical Associations

- Education centers (vo-tech schools, community colleges, nursing schools, etc.)

- Clinics and hospitals

- Women's and men's groups (business and professional organizations, etc.)

- Fitness centers

- Sports facilities and teams

- Individual physicians

- Newspaper, television and magazine editors

- Church groups

- Civic organizations

How To Make Contacts

There are three ways to make an initial contact--an introductory letter, a telephone call, or a personal conversation--and each can be appropriate for different situations.

Introductory letters. Although a letter is not as personal as a conversation, it is an effective way to introduce yourself and what you have to offer. It allows time to preplan and edit the message. The letter should vary according to the particular needs of the person being addressed. Keep the letter simple, clear, and concise. Additional information about yourself such as a resume, brochure, or letter of reference could be included. Brochures are also available from the Consulting Nutritionist Practice Group of The American Dietetic Association, which explain the services provided by a nutritionist.

Telephone contacts. Whether networking or marketing your business, decide what needs to be said and outline the points to be emphasized before making the call. It may not be possible to talk directly to the individual in charge. Be concise and yet give enough information so the person will want to schedule and appointment for you. Be flexible in offering times to meet. Offer to go to the physician's or owner's office, or suggest a luncheon meeting at your expense. If the individual is interested, an appointment time will be arranged. If not, neither of you has invested much time.

Be conscious of voice tone on the telephone. Voice sound and the spoken message are the only tools for making a first impression. Speak clearly and slowly.

Personal conversations. Whenever possible personal contact is most beneficial. You are seen, heard and have the opportunity to leave printed material. Plan and organize the entire presentation. Dress appropriately. When contacting a physician, a business suit would be appropriate. Even if the meeting is with an individual at a sports or fitness center, your dress should still present a professional image. Dress to feel comfortable for the specific interview.

Body language speaks loudly. Practice role playing and, if possible, have a friend film it. This allows you to observe individual mannerisms, gestures, and body movements. Constant movement such as swinging a foot, shifting weight, wringing hands, and so on are distracting and will take away from the presentation.

It's a good idea to take pertinent materials that can be left with the person contacted. For example, if contacting a physician, include a business card, diet prescription blanks (see Figure 24.1), samples of progress notes designed to provide patient information to the physician, newsletters that you have prepared, a list of types of services provided, and so on. If the physician specializes, it would be helpful to include articles on nutrition intervention related to the specialization.

When approaching an owner of a fitness center or clinic director about providing group services, present a brief overview of the particular program. For example, if you are offering a weight reduction class, show, but do not leave, a schedule of class topics, a brief summary of information to be presented in each class, and handouts that would be distributed to class participants. You could leave a brief list including the purpose of the class, fee structure, facilities needed (such as available space, blackboard, etc.), and what will be required of the participants. Also, it may be beneficial to have a list of the many services you offer to leave.

OPTIONS FOR WORKING WITH PHYSICIANS

There are many options for working with one or a group of physicians. A creative arrangement with a physician allows you to get a taste of what private practice is all about without the risk of opening a free-standing practice initially.

Besides individual consultation on therapeutic, normal, and sports nutrition diets, suggested programs could include weight control groups, diabetes education programs, seminars on specific diseases such as cardiovascular disease and hypertension, wellness and prevention programs, cooking classes for various types of diets such as low calorie, low sodium, and diabetic.

Development of handouts, information sheets, newsletters, and articles is also a part of a well-designed nutrition program. Although these are not directly income producing, they are effective educational and advertising tools and, therefore, indirectly produce income. Such creative tools are enriching to a program. Be sure to include your name, address, and telephone number on all printed materials. They will become very inexpensive advertising.

The attorney who assisted in the preparation of the simple physician agreement (see Figure 24.2) strongly suggests that in cases where long-term association with a physician or clinic is envisioned, that the

Figure 24.1

Business Card and Diet and Prescription Blank
(*Source:* Reprinted by permission of Rebecca L. McCully.)

Rebecca L. McCully, M.S., R.D.

Consulting Nutritionist

Cardiovascular Clinic Office
Pacer Development Center
3300 N.W. 56
Oklahoma City, Oklahoma 73112

℞

CARDIOVASCULAR CLINIC
Becky McCully, M.S., R.D.
Consulting Nutritionist

_____
Patient's Name

_____
Patient's Number

Diagnoses:
_____
_____
_____

Additional Information:
_____
_____

_____ M.D.
Physician's Signature

Diet Recommendations:
_____Cholesterol Reduction Diet
_____Diabetic Guidelines
_____ _____Calorie Diabetic Diet
_____Mild Sodium Restriction (2 grams)
_____ _____mg Sodium Diet
_____Calorie Control Weight Reduction
_____PSMF
_____Low Sodium PSMF
_____Other: _____
_____

Educational material to send patient:
_____Cholesterol Programs
_____Diabetic Programs
_____Hypertension Programs
_____Weight Control Programs

---

nutritionist consult an attorney for preparation of a formal contract. The investment in a more detailed contract may pay for itself many times over.

An Employed Position

If the physician strongly desires your services for his or her practice, it is possible the physician will be willing to take considerable more financial risk than if there are questions regarding the importance of nutritional services. The physician may work out an arrangement to hire you as an employee.

Although this is different from opening a practice, it can be advantageous. There is virtually no risk to the nutritionist, and it gives the opportunity to try consulting with patients and developing programs for patients before opening a practice.

If the physician hires the nutritionist as an employee, benefits such as health insurance, malpractice insurance, paid vacation, use of office space, equipment, office supplies, and receptionist or secretary are usually offered. The patients are financially responsible to the physician and the physician pays the nutritionist a salary. Although this type of working relationship may be beneficial in gaining experience, it has many limitations.

The nutritionist is dependent upon the physician to refer enough patients to use the nutritionist efficiently without open blocks of time. (Other physicians are not apt to refer their patients to a nutritionist who is employed by a physician.) With this arrangement the nutritionist may be expected to see patients when they come to see the physician and, consequently, will not have much control over the daily schedule. The physician may or may not have specific nutrition guidelines the nutritionist is expected to use. The nutritionist may have to compromise personal philosophies to work for the physician.

Independent Contracting with a Physician

It is common for practitioners to work as independent contractors in a physician's office. This arrangement gives much greater flexibility of time and

---

Figure 24.2 Sample Physician Contract

CONTRACT

This agreement entered into this _____ day of _____ , 19 _____ , by and between _____ , hereinafter referred to as "Nutritionist," and _____ , hereinafter referred to as "Physician."

It is agreed by the parties hereto that Nutritionist shall provide professional services to the clients and patients of Physician.

COMPENSATION. Nutritionist shall be compensated for professional services provided pursuant to this contract at the rate of _____ dollars ($ _____) per hour.

PROFESSIONAL SERVICES. "Professional services" as used herein shall be defined as being provided on a contract labor basis and shall consist of the following: (a) nutritional consultations with Physician's patients; (b) development of literature; (c) development of nutritional programs for patients; and (d) public speaking engagements on behalf of Physician.

HOURS. Nutritionist shall perform the above-enumerated services in the office of Physician between the hours of 1:00 P.M. and 5:00 P.M. Monday through Friday each week unless modified in writing.

DURATION. This contract shall be in effect for a period of one year from the date of execution and may be renewed by agreement of the parties.

Nutritionist

Physician

scheduling and more opportunity to control your business. It also may involve more financial risk or investment of personal capital.

Practitioners contract with physicians in a variety of ways. A contract may be for a predetermined number of hours per week or it may vary with the patient load. Another option is to have a percentage of the nutritionist's fee be charged for the use of the office space. Finally, the nutritionist may pay the physician a flat rental fee for the use of the office and facilities. The physician will continue to refer patients to the nutritionist but incurs no financial responsibility if the patient does not show.

Working with a Group of Physicians

It is also possible to work as an employee or independent contractor with a group of physicians in a medical complex. This option offers more variety and sometimes more professional challenge as one works with the different philosophies of physicians. Be sure the physicians specialize in areas of medicine compatible with your interests. Generally speaking, family physicians, cardiologists, internists, diabeticians, obstetricians, and allergists will be able to utilize the services of a nutritionist more fully than specialists such as surgeons, urologists, and dermatologists. Orthopedic specialists who work with athletes are a growing market also.

WORKING WITH REGISTERED NURSES

Numerous types of programs benefit from combined efforts of various health professionals. Consider combining the consultation services of a registered dietitian with a registered nurse. One example would be a diabetes education program. The expertise of each specialist can mesh beautifully to form a well-rounded program. A diabetes program could be designed in a variety of ways including a two-or-three-hour class, a weekend seminar, a series of classes meeting daily for a week, or a weekly class meeting for a specified number of weeks. This program could be presented in a clinic, hospital, community service program, or on a college campus.

The nurse could cover information about the disease itself, the mechanisms of oral hypoglycemic agents and insulin, insulin injections, and complications of diabetes. The dietitian could present the principles of the diabetic diet, recipe conversion, eating out, traveling, and shopping for the diabetic diet. A cooking demonstration also would be helpful.

Another program that could be developed by a registered nurse and a registered dietitian is a hypertension control program. This could be offered through a clinic, a hospital, or made available for individual patients to be held in a centralized location such as a church, hotel conference room, school auditorium, clinic, and so on.

Suggested topics to be included in a hypertension control program to be discussed by the nurse are the disease process of hypertension, medications and how they work, complications of uncontrolled hypertension, and instructing people in how to take their own blood pressures. The nutritionist could present various aspects of nutrition intervention with hypertension including sodium restriction and calorie control. Film strips, pamphlets, and dietary flashcards are good tools for teaching specific dietary principles. Discussion of seasoning foods without the addition of salt, how to cut calories, and eating in restaurants would all be applicable.

Pregnancy programs developed by nurses and nutritionists have numerous possibilities. The nurse could present information on pregnancy, delivery, and caring for an infant. The nutritionist could discuss nutritional needs during pregnancy and lactation, as well as infant nutrition.

Another component of a pregnancy program could be an exercise specialist. This person would plan exercise programs for women during pregnancy and after delivery.

WORKING WITH FITNESS SPECIALISTS

There are various areas of fitness involving specialists who could work well with nutritionists. Examples of these specialists include physical therapists, physical education specialists, and exercise physiologists. Each of these specialists focuses on different areas of fitness an may be located in institutions such as hospitals, fitness centers, nursing homes, or physical rehabilitation facilities. These specialists could utilize a nutritionist as a consultant or partner to develop coordinated nutrition/fitness programs. Health clubs, public school systems, senior centers, wellness programs, corporate fitness centers, and facilities designed to teach educators are all marketing outlets for your programs.

YWCA/YMCAs and community groups may contract with a nutritionist. Programs for weight control, preschool or teenage nutrition problems, sports, and wellness are all possibilities.

Contact the person responsible for coordinating all programs to determine the primary age groups and the needs of people who primarily utilize the facility. Get feedback about the types of programs the coordinator feels would be most appropriate.

OTHER GROUPS

There are numerous opportunities for development of nutrition programs with people not in the health profession. Examples include directors of cooking schools, libraries, and recreation centers. Consumer specialists who work for grocery stores and restaurants are also potential clients.

Cooking School Directors

A director of a cooking school may be interested in offering a variety of health oriented cooking classes. These classes could include cooking for your heart, low sodium cooking, low calorie cooking, diabetic cooking, low cholesterol cooking, healthy snacks to prepare, and so on.

When setting your fee, consider the mechanics of the class. Will you only be teaching and cooking, or will you be doing the preprep and clean up also? Will you help advertise the class or will the cooking school absorb this cost? These factors must be considered before quoting a price for conducting the class.

208

If doing a series of classes, one should design a creative logo and style of writing recipes. This helps to establish an identity. Again, be sure your name, address and telephone number are on each recipe.

Libraries
Frequently libraries offer classes to patrons on various subjects. Consider doing book reviews on diet books, having discussion groups on various nutrition topics, conducting weight control classes, diabetic classes, and so on. These classes may not prove to be financially lucrative, but your name will be exposed to the public, and this may be a good referral source. Remember to keep visible!

Recreation Centers
Recreation centers frequently attract people interested in exercise and good health. Consider approaching recreation centers with the idea of offering some fun activities centered around nutrition such as nutrition crossword puzzles, quizzes, and games. These could be incorporated with healthy snacks to be served at the center.

Grocery Stores
Many grocery stores now make nutrition information available to customers. This may be in the form of grocery store tours, a series of nutrition booklets, healthy recipes using ingredients sold at the store, or creative advertising of new products that can be worked into special diets.

Consider suggesting color coding products in a store according to the nutritive value, sodium content, caloric content, and so on. Another idea is to provide nutritious food demonstrations in the store. Again, this could advertise many of the products available at the store to be used in special diets.

Other Dietitians
Involvement with the local and state dietetic association and Consulting Nutritionist Practice Group is important. It provides support from other dietitians and keeps one visible as well as helps keep one up to date with what other dietitians are doing. Sharing information and working with other dietitians is extremely helpful.

Various Businesses
Many employers are interested in providing employees with programs to promote their health and job performance. Consider a wide variety of companies that could be interested in fitness, cooking, nutrition or wellness programs for employees.

Chapter 25

Computers in Nutrition Practice

Cecelia Helton, MA, R.D., updated by
Kathy King Helm, R.D.

Computers are not new to the field of dietetics, however, many of us are just learning to appreciate the myriad of functions they can perform. According to Ellyn Luros, R.D., president of Computrition, Inc., her company now has software that can do everything she did (nutrition-calculation wise) in her internship and first two years of work. Recipes can be calculated for cost and nutrients in minutes. A patient's allergies and food preferences can be allowed for on menus. Drug and nutrient interactions are caught before the patient is served. Repetitive tasks can be handled easily by computer.

This could scare some practitioners. It will replace some. However, for most dietitians, it will free them to do more care on the floors, or other work in the food service.

WHAT CAN A COMPUTER DO FOR A PRACTITIONER?

Before investing in the expense of computer equipment, the software, and training to learn how to use the system, decide what you want the computer to do. Too many small business owners buy a computer because they think they must need one. But, they have no idea (other than for bookkeeping and nutritional analysis) what to do with it. What an expensive and limited investment!

Nutrient Analysis

Nutrient analysis of recipes, menus, and food intakes is probably the most familiar computer function to dietitians. Before the use of the computer, it was so time consuming to analyze foods for nutrient levels that it was not done with any regularity, except perhaps in research settings.

Today many practitioners offer nutrient analysis to institutional settings such as jails, nursing homes, and hospitals. Nutrient analysis is used to help write menus, to document the nutritional value of the foods offered, and to calculate the nutritional value of food eaten by any one resident.

Many private practitioners also use nutrient analyses while working with individual patients, corporate clients, or athletes and sports teams. Clients are impressed and fascinated with computer printouts that show "scientifically" how nutritious their diets are. The truth, of course, is that the results are only ball park figures. The foods analyzed may not have been

210

representative of the client's normal eating patterns. The amounts and ingredients of foods may even be thiry percent or more wrong because of the guesswork involved in a layman's food diary or recall. And, finally, the database used to analyze the foods may not be complete enough, so entire foods are left out of the calculations, or their ingredients are estimated. To help avoid these pitfalls as much as possible, a practitioner should instruct the client on how to measure foods (ideally by weight). A week's record could be recorded with three representative days chosen for analysis. Take care to find   analysis software that has an accurate and adequate database.

Nutrition Histories

Nutrition histories, fitness, and lifestyle computer questionnaires can be developed or purchased for use by the patient or you in your office. The questionnaire results can be used to motivate the patient by showing specific areas for needed improvement, or where he is doing well.

Nutrition Assessment

Handheld and portable laptop computers make nutrition assessment, and enteral and parenteral or BEE (basal energy expenditure) calculations available at a patient's bedside.   These tools are crucial to critical care dietitians, and for outpatient consultants who also use the diabetes, renal or exchange programs.

COMMON QUESTION: Computer Replacing a Dietitian

I see so many weight loss and wellness programs run by laymen and nurses who feel they can do nutrition counseling because they can nutritionally analyze a person's diet. Am I overreacting or am I being replaced by a floppy   disk?

I always tell dietitians that if they can be replaced by a floppy disk, they are not doing dietitian-level work. I tell potential consultant accounts that the nutritional analysis of a person's diet is an easy way to arrive at "ball park" estimates of the days analyzed. But the interpretation and application of the results, along with the motivational counseling, behavior change training, medical score interpretation, and individualized nutritional care are really what a trained nutritionist has to offer.

We have to market ourselves and perform to standards that are above the competition.   Kathy King Helm, R.D.

Word Processing and Desktop Publishing

Word processing capabilities of a computer are well known. Articles, menus, newsletters reports, letters, individualized diets, and other written items can be typed, viewed on the screen, corrected or changed, and then printed. If the item is stored on software, it can be recalled and reused or corrected as needed. Lists of names and addresses of patients, colleagues, customers, or whomever can be sorted and then merged with a letter to give a bulk mailing that individualized look. Labels or envelopes can be printed to match the headings. By preprogramming nutrition care plans onto software, a practitioner can individualize or adjust a plan for each patient and then print it for a personalized presentation. Software with artwork and typesetting, as good as the quality produced by print stores, is available if you have a computer with adequate memory and a laser printer.

Business Management

Business management is greatly simplified through use or software with financial spreadsheets and accounting capabilities. More detailed and complete records can be maintained of customers' buying habits and sales figures. The computer can calculate food orders, cost analysis per vendor or menu item, inventory control, employee scheduling and paperwork, and of course many other bookkeeping functions. Detailed records can be prepared more regularly and compared with past incomes, expenses, and forecasts.

Bookkeeping records can be sent by telephone using a modem and your computer to your accountant for auditing and tax preparation. Software is available that will turn your computer and its modem into a facsimile machine (FAX). You can then send or receive printed material over the phone line and communicate more quickly in the business world.

Patient and Client Records

Records of all sorts can be "filed" on computer software. In fact, unless you feel you must have a folder to hold the patient's pertinent information, there is no reason not to put all information on software (with a backup copy). When a patient arrives for an appointment, you could retrieve his record on the screen with its chemical scores, medical diagnosis, nutritional history, assessment, care plan, appointment summaries, and financial records. The information can be used from the screen or printed as needed. After the appointment is over, the practitioner can update the payment record and input changes in status (chemical scores, percent body fat, habits, attitude, etc.) and future goals, including the date of the next appointment. Each patient can be assigned a patient number or his last name can act as the file code. The practitioner could recall files by diagnosis name or code, referring physician's name, or whatever.

Other types of clients, such as wellness programs, restaurants, consultant contracts, and so on, and their key people can be listed. Reminders for appointments, reports, and marketing can be keyed in. Follow-up letters, proposals, and reports can be typed into the computer using word processing software, and as many copies as needed can be printed in minutes---each originally typed.

Teaching

Teaching nutrition to patients or clients can be carried out on a computer. Topics such as energy balance for weight control, sports nutrition, and menu planning, also diabetic or other clinical diet guidelines or behavior change lessons can be programmed onto software in a self-instruction format.

A computer may be used for evaluating the effectiveness of your nutrition counseling sessions. By pre- and posttesting a patient in a nonthreatening environment, the patient and you will be able to tell whether the patient and his family understood the most important points. The posttest will act as a summary.

Researching Literature and Reports

Researching is another function that can be carried out on a computer. Through use of a modem and the appropriate software, through your telephone you can access information in much larger databases at libraries, government offices, and banks. Companies in the business of placing journal reports, medical literature, media articles, stock reports, and so on, on databases for sale to subscribers can be accessed for a fee. When practitioners want to write an article or book on a subject or appear on the media, they can have the most recent information at their disposal.

SELECTING A COMPUTER SYSTEM

The most crucial question to ask yourself when thinking about purchasing a computer system is, "How do I plan to use the computer?" Your response to this question is the key to the size of memory in the computer, whether the monitor is in color, whether there will be an audio component, and the type of software you'll need. It is very beneficial to take samples of the kinds of projects you want to run on your computer into the computer store for the sales people to see. Trained sales people, knowledgeable friends with computer expertise, and computer instructors can be give you advise that will help you decide the system to buy. Currently, not all software is applicable to all computer systems, so it is important to match appropriate software to the right computer. Quality software is essential in obtaining the maximum use from your computer and investment.

Guidelines for Evaluating Software

The first step in evaluating software is to become aware of available programs that appear suitable for your needs. Keep in mind that new programs are being developed daily, and some are definitely better than others. Since it is difficult to evaluate software from a written description, before buying ask to try a copy of the software and run the program on an appropriate computer system. **As you run through the program, ask yourself the following questions:**

1. What is the objective of this program? Is it what I want?

2. Are the instructions clear?

3. Is the format appropriate and interesting?

4. Is the content accurate?

5. Does the program output provide useful information that is easy to understand?

6. Is the cost of the program worth it?

Since most types of software or its stored information can be destroyed by various elements, such as air pollutants, spilled liquids, magnets, heat, bending, power failures caused by severe weather conditions, and so on, it is legal to make a copy for your own use. A copy can be made if it is necessary to use the program more effectively (1). Computer software is usually protected though a copyright by its owner.

Selecting Hardware

When selecting your computer, deal with a local, reputable company who is willing to provide good service, training, and maintenance. Talk to other people who own and use the machine you want to buy and ask how happy they are with it. Find out as much as you can about the operation and reputation of the equipment that is compatible with the software you want. Many books, magazines, and professional articles compare and review the major brands of computers The choice is a matter of your own personal preference.

The basic equipment included in a computer system is:

1. Keyboard (similar to typewriter keyboard)

2. Monitor (screen or CRT cathode ray tube)

3. CPU---central processing unit (the brains of the computer)

4. Printer (to turn information into "hard copy")

Salespeople also suggest purchase of a surge protector device to keep power changes from erasing data or programs.

Monitors differ in appearance, type face, and size. Some display information using black letters on a white background and others called monochrome use bright green print on a dark green background. Monitors with the capability of using a wide range of colors are also available. Characters can be in upper case only or both lower and upper case. Some features enhance the display of information, which is important since eye strain and fatigue are common complaints of computer users.

The CPU is the working brains of the computer. Always find out the number of "K's" (size of a computer memory) available before buying. One "K" is equivalent to 1000 bytes or characters of information storage. It is important to remember that your CPU must have a "K" that is equal to or greater than the software program you wish to use.

Printers vary with respect to:

214

1. Number of characters printed per second

2. Number of characters per horizontal inch (that is usually between 10 to 12 and comparable to pica/elite type on the typewriter)

3. Number of lines per vertical inch

4. Number of lines printed per minute

5. Type of print (dot matrix, or fully formed characters--letter quality, or laser postscript or not)

There is a wide range of print quality, so you need to decide which is most appropriate for your needs. Again, be certain that the printer you purchase is compatible with your other hardware and corresponding software.

By the time auxiliary equipment, print paper, and floppy disks are added, the purchase price is significant. Selection of the right equipment and software is prudent.

COMPUTER ADVANTAGES

Computers require time and commitment to work well but the effort is worth it. Most of us are not born "computer friendly." It's an acquired skill. The major advantage that computers provide is greater volume of quality business output. In today's market, computers can help give you an edge in offering more information and service than your competitors.

REFERENCES

1. "Computer Savvy. Copying Software: Legal or Not" *Forecast of Home Economics,*April 1983.
2. Downs, J.: Computers at Home, *The Community Nutritionist,* January-February 1983, 2:24.

section 6

Developing Your Professional Practice

Words of Wisdom:

"If you don't invest very much, then defeat doesn't hurt very much and winning is not very exciting."

Dick Vermeil

"Never, Never, Never Quit."

Winston Churchill

Chapter 26

Office Policy and Dealing with Clients

Kathy King Helm, R.D., updated by Alanna Dittoe, R.D.

There are many other factors beside the quality and amount of nutrition information given to clients that influence their opinion of your services. Clients are usually expecting their association with you and your office to be courteous, organized, efficient, reasonable in cost, and timely. Actually, our clients' expectations are no different from our own.

CREATING AN EFFECTIVE OPERATION

Competition is growing for the consumer's dollar and a business owner cannot afford to turn clients off with inadequate service. *Personalized* care of clients should begin when they first call to ask about your services or schedule an appointment. Attempts should be made to impress clients with the nondietetic functions of your operation.

Establish office hours and days and try to follow your schedule as closely as possible to help develop an image of stability and continuity. As long as clients can leave a message for you, it is not necessary to be available in the office, in person, five days a week. In the beginning, try to condense your patient instructions and interviews with other clients to only a few days per week. The remaining days can then be used to hold down another job while you start your business, or give you time to market your business, write, or whatever.

Telephone coverage for your business is extremely important. The telephone is your clients' major link with you. During normal business hours Monday through Friday, clients should be able to either reach you by phone or leave a message with a secretary, answering service, or voice mail machine. If you cannot answer the phone yourself, be sure to take the time to instruct the secretary or answering service in exactly what to say and what information to ask for. Have someone call to check for you occasionally. Messages on telephone answering recorders should be well prepared--keep trying until you record a message that people will not only listen to but, most importantly, respond to. A higher level of service is perceived when calls are returned promptly.

Some hints that may be important to you concerning your telephone answering service include the following:

1. Do not allow your services and fees to be given to clients unless the person is trained to properly "market" your business. Have them say, "I will be happy to take your name and number and have the nutritionist call you back."

2. Caution your answering service or secretary about giving out your private home phone number and address.

3. When you are out of town, instruct your answering service to tell people that "She (or he) will be in the office to return your call on Monday, July 10; can she (or he) call you back at that time or is this an emergency?" If you have another dietitian who knows your practice, you might have the answering service say, "Mary Jones, R.D. is covering all calls and I can have her call you if you wish." **If it is an emergency,** leave the number of another dietitian or the local hospital clinical nutrition department.
   If it is a personal message, leave a number where *your answering service* can reach you or leave a message.

When scheduling appointments with new patients, use the conversation as an opportunity to "market" your services. Take the time to ask several questions about the patient and his or her nutritional needs, pertinent lab values, and referring physician's name. Request that the patient bring a copy of the most recent lab results and if applicable the physician's written referral to the appointment. Explain what the patient will receive in the way of individualized care and information. State approximately how long the appointment will take and how much it will cost. Make sure that the patient knows the directions to your office, the suite number, where to park, if it is a problem, and the date and time for the appointment. Request that the patient try to give 24 hours' notice if the appointment has to be changed or cancelled.

The office setting should be quiet, comfortable, and professional. The office furnishings are usually not as important as the atmosphere, hospitality, and service provided. However, because of the image they want to portray and their clients' expectations, some private practitioners spend extra for more affluent looking office space and interiors. One practitioner reports that in a survey of her office patients, the majority mentioned the office coffee as the best amenity. Offering tea, coffee, water or whatever either in an office or home office setting can be "that little extra" that makes patients feel more at home.

The chart system for your office can be as expensive as a computer system or the color-coded systems, or as simple as a manila folder for each patient, or all the patient interview sheets kept in one notebook. Because of the importance of documentation of a patient's progress, it is best to have the patient's nutrition chart available for all visits. The patient's medical chart is usually only available when you work in a medical office.

The information to include in the patient's chart is name, address, work, and home phone numbers, their physician's name, the referring physician's name (if different), and a copy of the diet prescription, if available, pertinent lab values, a diet evaluation, action plan, and goals. The follow-up sessions should have any changes in lab values and other objective measurements listed, as well as more subjective comments, both pro and con. After the initial instruction and when something significant happens to a patient, the referring physician should be notified, and the contact documented.

Publications for your clients enhance the service and will contribute to the positioning and image of your practice. It is probably not necessary to copyright your diets, unless you feel it would keep clinics, physicians, and clients from photocopying them. Any booklets, programs, etc., that you write should definitely be copyrighted.

Include the cost of handouts and diets in the fee for the instruction. Many consultant nutritionists keep a supply of books, booklets, and other educational items they know patients want to buy. However, in most states, sales tax must be collected, and a sales tax or even vendor's license may be necessary.

An easy way to have diets that all use variations of the exchange lists is to print one style of the lists and change the top cover page. If the paper size is a standard 8 1/2" x 11" or 8 1/2" x 14" printing costs are less. The typeface should be easy to read, not script; some people with poor eyesight also have trouble reading single-spaced elite type. Printing 100 pages at a time on white paper with black ink usually is the most economical, compared to colored ink and paper and small batches of printing. However, many practitioners feel the flair of color is worth the added cost, especially on the cover pages.

Information overload is a common problem. Avoid giving clients too many publications. Start with several at the initial visit and assess what each client needs or wants. Patients and their families: (1) get confused by material that is not specifically for their diet, and (2) can only absorb a small amount of information on a new subject at any one time. Patients lose sight of the most important points of the diet when so many new points are made in the additional booklets. Save the less specific material and the larger number of booklets, for the few clients who want them and will use then appropriately.

Many practitioners report that their patients are impressed when they started using folders to hold take-home materials. The folder usually has pockets on the inside to hold the diet and any booklets. On the outside of the folder, print the company name or logo for easy identification of the contents and for advertising purposes. Attach a business card to the folder to provide your address and phone number.

Diet manuals are readily available to all practitioners today. In writing your own diets, you may choose good ideas from several manuals and from your experience. If you are unaware of your local medical community's nutritional biases, try to purchase diet manuals from the local hospitals or make an appointment with a hospital dietitian to discuss them. Pages should not be photocopied directly from a manual unless it was designed for that purpose or you request permission from the copyright owner.

In private practice it is not necessary to have a large variety of different diets, such as in the hospital. Practitioners report the most common nutrition publications are the following: weight loss, diabetic, hypoglycemic, low salt, low cholesterol, hyperlipidemia diets, allergy, high potassium, normal pregnancy, and good nutrition for the healthy individual. Specialties in your medical community may dictate that other diets be developed.

DISTINCTIVE SERVICE

Private practitioners and outpatient counselors know that their consultative sessions and handout materials need to be different and better than those provided by free hospital clinics or by physicians' office nurse or secretary. Practitioners must create this difference or patients and clients will balk at paying the fee. The key words are "quality," "individualized," and "personalized."

Many dietitians, though not all, think it is important to use different terminology in private practice from that used in acute care settings: "diet" could be "nutritional care plan" or "food plan," and "diet order" could be "nutrition prescription." Some practitioners call the people they instruct "clients" instead of patients, especially in more wellness-oriented settings. Always remember, care should be taken to differentiate patients from their illness. In other words, a person is not a diabetic or a hypertensive, but instead, *person with diabetes or hypertension.*

Whether a consultant wears a white jacket or lab coat is a personal choice. Some patients appear to feel intimidated by the authority signified by the white and like to feel more familiar with their counselor. While others expect the white jacket/coat which shows you are the nutrition authority. (Helm's note: I've always felt that I could put my patients more at ease without the "whiteness." If they couldn't tell I was an authority in nutrition by the time they left, a white coat wasn't going to help me.)

COLLECTING FEES AND ENDING A SESSION

The end of the interview is a good time to talk about rescheduling a visit, or to discuss why it is not necessary. This is a good "ending" subject and lets the client know that the visit is over. As you are winding up, be sure to incorporate some system to collect the fee. You may simply state, "I will make out your receipt now--how do you want to pay for your instruction?" or "The fee for the initial visit is $____ and revisits are $____ . I will give you an itemized receipt that you can attach to your insurance company's form along with a copy of the referral slip from your doctor. You can try to get reimbursed for our visit." If you have a secretary or receptionist, be sure to train her or him on how to collect fees.

If a patient continues to linger after the closing of the session and you have other commitments, you can either relax and take a minute longer, or you can try standing up and walking slowly toward the door to show him out and simply state, "I want to thank you very much for coming. I am sorry to rush, but I have another patient waiting."

220

COMMON QUESTIONS

I can't get physicians to refer patients to me and the patients who call me from my brochure and newspaper ad don't show up. What can I do?

Your services could be so new that physicians and prospective patients haven't learned how to use them yet (even when you try to tell them). Or, there could be some more painful answers like you haven't and don't know how to establish credibility (check Chapter 10), your appearance or personality may not meet the expectations of your target markets, or you could be saying the wrong things or "right" things in the wrong way.

Before you change too many things on your own, I would go talk to someone who markets him or herself as a business consultant. Long term this could save you a lot of time and money. You can usually find a person like this in the Yellow Pages, through contacts in professional or business groups or the SBA. Talk to the person over the phone and if you like him or her, get an appointment.

In preparation for the appointment, write down what you say to prospective patients over the phone and to physicians when you interview with them. Go over your marketing strategies like the prices, promotion, products and location(s) you use for your business. Take copies of your brochure and ads. Listen to what the person suggests as solutions and try them out, since you have nothing to lose. Don't get discouraged! We all have things to learn.

One Maryland dietitian, who had this same problem, had to work on lowering her voice because she sounded like she was twelve years old over the phone instead of twenty-nine. An advisor told a short, young-looking women to buy suits instead of wearing such feminine dresses in pastel colors that lacked any "power." Similarly, a male dietitian who consulted to major hospitals and corporations for very big fees found that he was most successful in landing the accounts when he dressed in expensive suits and shoes like the successful corporate president he was.

One dietitian opened her business charging the same higher fees as a practitioner who had been in business in the area for many years and was very well established. It took a while for the new dietitian's business to grow because there was price-resistance since she was new and unknown in the community. Does this mean every dietitian should start with low prices as a marketing strategy? Of course not! It just means it takes time for a business to become established. If the level of service matches the price asked, and the target market needs the service or product, and can afford it, the business will grow.

Once you try a few new ideas and they seem to be working, go back to see the physicians who have not been referring to you and start building a rapport with them and their office staff. Use some of the ideas mentioned in Chapter 20 on Promotion. Good luck!

My patients aren't returning after the first visit. What might be wrong?

There are many reasons why patients don't return. Some reasons are in your control; others are not. The reason physicians overbook and some dentists and psychiatrists charge for no-shows is because a certain number of patients will not keep appointments That point known, there are still professionals who do not have as bad a problem as others, and there are times when each of us experiences it more frequently.

After allowing for bad weather, business advisors will tell you that it is significant whether patients don't show at all or they call to reschedule. Not calling or showing is of course more symptomatic of a problem.

Some of the more obvious reasons patients do not return are:

- They feel no commitment to the care plan because you did not involve them enough in developing it, or it did not fit their true lifestyle.

- It was not their choice to make the appointment and they only gave lip service while there.

- The patients did not understand the importance of follow-up and how it would improve their chances for successful behavior change.

- They followed your suggested guidelines and did not get results--or they got results without following it.

- You did not impress them with the consultation, your manner, or something about the office visit. (Some patients will not take advice from traditional-thinking, or young or inexperienced counselors.)

- The fee was too high for what they felt they received or for their present income.

- The consultation style and approach may have been too threatening, embarrassing, or too familiar to suit the patient. (We do not always hit it off with every patient.)

- The instruction materials may have been too confusing.

- The patient may believe his present habits fit his needs better, and he is not willing to change. Maybe the suggestions weren't reasonable--or maybe they were but not at this time.

Areas you may want to evaluate and improve if you deem them a problem are:

- Are you marketing and describing your services well over the phone when the patient calls for an appointment? Fees should be mentioned up front along with what you have to offer and what commitment you expect from the patient. The patient should feel he knew what to expect.

- Are you impressing upon your patients the importance of follow-up visits?

- Is the patient's visit a pleasant one? Is he greeted and given good, timely service?

- Are you up to date and knowledgeable in nutrition and counseling? Can you offer a variety of solutions and are you flexible enough to make changes when they are needed? Are your counseling sessions organized and professionally handled?

- Do you have the appearance of a credible, competent, stable professional? Can you change your appearance to look more like what is "expected" by your clientele?

- Are your fees too high or low for what you offer or for your local community? Could you offer more, package it better?

Two of the best ways to take the mystery out of this process is by sending a note to remind patients a week in advance when it has been a while in between appointments and by calling all patients a day ahead to remind them of the appointment and to ask how they are doing. Calling a patient can serve several purposes: the patient may feel more at ease about stating a problem, he may decide to make a greater commitment because of your apparent interest, or he may cancel future appointments on the spot.

EMPLOYEE CONSIDERATIONS

If you decide to budget an office employee into your business, there are several considerations to think about:

1. How will the secretary/receptionist spend her or his day--write a job description.

2. In the beginning can he or she work mornings or a short week to help keep overhead lower.

3. Decide how much you can afford to pay. It may be worth paying a little more to keep someone who speaks well on the phone and is courteous and efficient in the office.

4. Decide what skills are most important for the running of your office before you start to interview applicants.

5. Talk to your financial advisor about what "perks" if any to offer as present or future incentives to your employee(s).

6. Discuss with your accountant or CPA the difference in costs to you for an employee versus contract labor, such as, payroll taxes, social security, worker's compensation, added paperwork, pension plan, etc.

To assure that the person represents you well, take adequate time of your own to train your new secretary well. You should decide whether to teach him or her how to market your business on the phone or just to take messages. Some practitioners have had a problem with their enthusiastic secretaries trying to do diet counseling over the phone, using their own remedies. To help avoid this problem, office policies need to be determined and procedures established to carry them out. A poor employee can harm your business, so do not hesitate to terminate someone who does not work out.

Although there is added expense in having an employee, a person who can perform such duties as typing, mailing, screening phone calls, confirming patient appointments, scheduling new patients and revisits, collecting fees, and greeting clients can be as valuable as your right arm.

Several private practitioners have hired Dietetic Technicians to work in their offices to conduct initial interviews with patients and fill out the needed medical, chemical and nutritional data. They are very happy with the DTRs and highly recommend that other dietitians consider hiring them too. It may take time to find the right person(s), but it is worth it, if in the future you generate more income and a better-functioning business.

CONCLUSION

Other than having a good background in nutrition, it is just as important that a consultant have good management and business skills in order to succeed. A practitioner should strive to produce distinctive service and provide up-to-date information with a flair.

224

Chapter 27

Counseling Expertise

Paulette Lambert, R.D.

The challenge for the next decade is to get more people eating good food. The development of communication skills is a necessity to promote a change in our clients' eating habits. No longer can we provide lists of foods to avoid along with a sample menu and feel that we have functioned as a professional counselor. A receptionist with no training can do as much; we have to do a lot more.

Our success as consulting nutritionists depends on our ability to help clients learn and apply new information and skills. What occurs in what we call the "counseling session" determines our success. Dietitians who become counselors need to realize that their level of counseling expertise determines the quality of their output. When counselors have problems getting their businesses established it may be for several reasons. One reason may be their lack of counseling skills.

Developing high quality counseling skills is a time-consuming, complex task. It often means changing old well-established but unsuccessful counseling habits or beginning with no applied experience. Do not expect yourself to achieve perfect skills within a few weeks or months. It takes time to practice the new techniques learned through course work, seminars, and self-study. There will always be room for improvement and a need for continual change.

The day-to-day job of counseling clients can be extremely stressful and draining. One needs the ability to be able to "turn off" your business when not working to protect yourself from frustration and burnout.

This chapter intends to share some new techniques and resources for producing successful counseling sessions. Successful practitioners have their own style of patient counseling. The amount of information, number of sessions, commitment to wellness, behavior modification, or psychology is a counselor's decision and varies with each patient.

QUALIFICATIONS OF A COUNSELOR

Not everyone has the personality and patience to be good at counseling. The personal attributes usually associated with a successful counselor include: empathy, optimism, good communication skills, sensitivity, patience, creativity, teaching ability, and enthusiasm.

Although good counseling skills can be learned, you are usually most successful   in doing things that fit your personality and that are comfortable for you. In research originated by General Electric on executive potential to initiate and manage change, they found that   each person preferentially accesses one of four areas of the brain, although some people can access two or more, one area is usually dominant. In the study it found that people who use the left cerebral area are authoritative and tend to become physicians, while nurses use the right limbic brain area (considered authority-phobic). Dietitians could use either depending upon whether you counsel patients or manage a kitchen (1).

Nutrition consultation, as a specialized skill, requires a rich background of experience in the profession. You need skills in more than one area, and must be studied and practiced. These include academic, clinical, administrative, behavioral therapy, psychology, and interpersonal communication skills.

Clinical judgment is imperative to good nutrition counseling. The American Diabetes Association's position paper on consultation emphasizes a minimum of three years experience in clinical, administration, and education. Without this practical experience, a clinical nutritionist has not been able to practice long enough to be proficient at counseling or to have developed sound clinical judgment. A consultant must be aware of common drugs and their side effects, know how to do simple assessment tests, and be aware of the laboratory chemical values as they relate to nutrition.

Relationship-building skills are necessary for effective counseling.   Before counselors can develop plans for a client's behavior change, the counselor must understand the client's needs (2).   The development of a "helping relationship" that projects empathy, understanding, and trust needs to precede any development of plans and strategies.

The nutrition counselor understands the client's concerns because he or she encourages them to talk about themselves and their feelings. A client needs to feel safe in reporting failures so as to adjust the care plan to make it more successful.

Being a good nutrition counselor involves possessing interpersonal skills that promote positive outcomes in counseling. A successful counselor is one who genuinely cares about and is committed to her or his patient.

Although a counselor wants to be warm, caring, empathetic, and so on, it is important that the counselor remain professional. Exercise caution. There is a point in counseling where becoming very close and familiar with patients may jeopardize your ability to act as a counselor to them. Occasionally, having a patient as a friend is certainly no problem, but if you notice it happening with a large number of clients *with a resulting decline in counseling effect,* reassess your needs as a counselor.

Several solutions may keep your private and professional lives more separate. Spend more time making or seeing friends in your personal time, or seek help.   Read about handling this counseling problem or talk to a counselor yourself.

226

Several other traits are helpful in being successful in nutrition counseling. A positive attitude keeps the client and you interested in continuing to work together. Changing eating behavior is difficult, with many barriers to overcome. One needs to be positive and even tempered to deal with the phenomenon on a   day-to-day basis. Being assertive in a caring way and not being afraid of dealing with issues that inhibit progress is important. Nutrition counseling is not passive but a very active procedure and is doomed if otherwise.

Behavioral therapy skills are important to counselors. Along with the ability to dispense information, a practitioner needs to be able to promote behavior changes in clients. Nutrition counselors need to be proficient in skills in behavioral therapy. As Ohlsen has commented, "true dietetic counseling must involve discrete counseling skills, not merely dissemination of information" (2). The focus of behavioral therapy is to do something to promote a change in behavior. Behavioral therapy skills include being able to define a problem, design plans and strategies to treat a problem, and to evaluate and make necessary changes. Behavioral therapy uses various techniques such as behavior modification, stimulus control, and cognitive restructuring to assist in helping the client change his behavior.

For example, if your client admits having many failed attempts at weight control, find one eating behavior that is causing the biggest problem and come up with a solution the client can do . . . fast and easy. Start with one incremental step and avoid giving the patient one more complicated, overwhelming diet consultation. For many clients it may be merely reducing their fat intake or changing the evening snack that gives them weight loss success.

An understanding of psychology is important to a counselor. By understanding peoples' motivations for different behaviors, a good counselor can then offer alternative suggestions for satisfying needs in non-self-defeating and food oriented ways. An appreciation for psychology also helps in perspective--in other words, the counselor becomes part of the solution, not part of the problem. As an example, if the counselor fails to comprehend a patient's frustration with changing his diet and lectures him, any possibility of helping the client may be lost.

Teaching skills help ensure that the patient learns the new information. The content must be geared to the patient's level of understanding. A patient is often "turned off" by language and nutrition information that is either over his head, or too elementary and thus unchallenging and uninteresting. Presentations should be organized, since random discussions are hard to recall. A good teacher knows how to help patients reach their goals by using a variety of teaching methods and only the information the patient "needs" to know. As a patient's needs change a good teacher should be flexible enough to adjust the patient's care plan to handle new problems. If a patient doesn't respond to one type of approach, try another.

The ability to sell is a vital skill often overlooked. Selling is based on meeting the client's needs. Selling means convincing someone of the importance of something to them. For example, a client may not realize why the physician wants him to lose weight in relationship to decreasing his blood sugar. The counselor needs to convey benefits to the client.

In her book, *The Woman's Selling Game,* Carole Hyatt defines selling as skillfully negotiating, persuading, influencing, and enlightening people to change behavior (3). In nutrition counseling you sell the client, his family, the physicians, and all others involved in counseling. You sell the program and the changes the client needs to make in order to be successful. If you look at the many fad diets that materialize each year, you soon realize the power of the ability to sell.

THE ROLE OF THE NUTRITION COUNSELOR

Traditionally, the role of the dietitian was to be an educator, a teacher. With the role expanded to nutrition counselor, we now need to see ourselves in a more complex role: that of a trainer. The trainer role includes both consideration of the client's needs and the application of training technology. Together they produce a change in behavior.

The nutrition counselor is more effective today than in the traditional role. Training involves active, not passive learning. The client actually does something. Traditionally, we used to give out information and hope the client would change his eating habits. Now, the trainer provides information, talks it over with the patient, the patient practices, and responds. Emphasis is on the benefit to the client. The trainer's role is to guide, not dictate the consultation. Training is a balance between client- and content-focused instruction. The following example (See Table 27.1) compares traditional, content-focused teaching to trainer, client-focused instruction (4).

Table 27.1 TRAINER VS. TRADITIONAL INSTRUCTION*

Trainer (client-focused)	Traditional (content-focused)
1. Information given determined by assessment of individual needs.	1. Information given is determined by availability.
2. Practice is provided—active learning.	2. Information is given—passive learning.
3. Only needed information is given.	3. An abundance of information is given.
4. Success is determined by the ability of the client to function independently.	4. Success is determined by how much and how well content was delivered.
5. Instruction is based on premise that virtually all people learn what they need to learn, allowing for adequate time.	5. Instruction is based on the assumption information was delivered, and only some clients will be able to learn material.
6. Learners' mastery is practiced and then observed.	6. Learners' mastery is assumed.
7. Instruction is paced according to the individual accomplishments.	7. Instruction paced according to subject matter.

*An instruction is never totally client- or content-focused but a balance between the two.
Source: R. Shortridge: *The Percepteur,* A manual of training behavior for professionals, Dairy Council of California, 1980.

228

When counseling is totally dominated by client requests and tangential topics, little behavior change will take place. A session totally dominated by counselors who provide only information, without listening to client concerns, can be equally unproductive. The ideal is a mix of client and counselor interaction (5). Two very good books on the subject of counseling are Linda Snetselaar's *Nutrition Counseling Skills* (5) and Patricia Hodges' and Connie Vickery's *Effective Counseling (6)*; please refer to these resources for more in-depth discussion.

Client expectations of what the counselor will be like can greatly influence how receptive he or she is to counseling. If a client expects the counselor to be domineering and antagonistic or friendly and helpful, the client may react to the counselor as if he were actually playing that role (5). Through experience counselors learn to perceive what the client is expecting from them. Qualified counselors then try to correct or validate clients' preconceived beliefs.

Clients also come to nutrition counseling sessions with feelings about themselves that may act as barriers to behavior change. A young obese woman may say that she wants to lose weight, but may be so fearful of the attention she may receive from men when her weight goes down, she puts up barriers (regains lost pounds) to keep her "safe." A man with hypertension may come for instruction because he knows he should be careful with his food intake. However, he may choose not to be responsible because of his relationship with his wife. For example, he may want her to feel responsible. A counselor learns to perceive a client's needs so that those needs can be either satisfied or altered. The client is then motivated to change and take *responsibility* for his own *constructive* behavior.

Counseling Theories

Counseling theories and personal philosophies influence the way in which a counselor conducts a session. Snetselaar lists four theories commonly used in nutrition counseling (5):

1. *Client-centered therapy* assesses clients' needs and perceptions and changes behavior through promoting more positive, confident, and realistic attitudes about self. Realistic, attainable goals are set to build clients' self confidence.
2. *Rational emotive therapy* encourages clients to confront and alter their inner self-talk and self-thoughts to ones that promote positive behavior. Clients learn not to punish or belittle themselves for less than ideal behavior.
3. *Behavioral therapy* believes that clients' environments shape their behavior; therefore changing experiences and role models should alter the clients' behavior.
4. *Gestalt therapy* emphasizes confronting the barriers to behavior change so that clients can regulate their actions with present needs. Clients identify and confront the "deeper" reasons why they believe and act as they do.

In practice Snetselaar feels that most counselors use a combination of theories and determine what to use according to the clients' needs or their own biases.

In addition to these theories, counselors are very concerned about being able to "read" clients and "speak their language" in order to establish or enhance communication. Study of body language and nonverbal communication is imperative to achieving good counseling skills.

Some counselors use the techniques outlined in *Frogs into Princes,* called Neurolinguistic Programming (NLP) to interpret how a client communicates (7). Some individuals speak in terms of wanting personal attention or wanting to "feel" better; others want to "look" differently or want written directions; and still others want "verbal" input and feedback. Telling a " visual" person who wants to look thin that he will "feel" so good when his weight is down may not interest him nearly as much as working with him on imaging.

Wellness Approach

A counselor may choose to incorporate emphasis on the "wellness" approach in nutrition consultations. This approach believes that nutrition information should not be separate from other life-style decisions. Counseling sessions could include evaluation and discussion of the client's fitness and exercise program or referral to a fitness specialist.

The counselor may identify a client's inability to handle stress or a dependence on alcohol, drugs, or smoking. A counselor could encourage the client to consider a change in behavior and perhaps refer him to another program or specialist for those problems. To be qualified to discuss these other topics a nutrition counselor must be familiar with health risk factors and their effect on health. A counselor should take course work and seminars on wellness, health education, and exercise physiology.

VARIOUS APPROACHES ALL "SELL"

Experienced nutrition counselors bring a wealth of practical knowledge. Counseling sessions are usually a mixture of what has worked in the past along with a few ideas that the counselor has always wanted to try. Here are examples of different approaches:

•   Many practitioners do not feel that a dietary program should be given at the first counseling session. They feel that the initial session should be used to collect data, teach patients how to measure foods for computer analysis, make assessments, and determine habits and needs. A later session is used for more formal instruction. One practitioner's program consists initially of three, one-hour sessions over several weeks, followed by short sessions scheduled as needed. Another practitioner sees a patient initially for thirty minutes to instruct him or her on filling out the computer food intake record then begins counseling at the next session.

•   Some practitioners offer instruction in "packages." A consultation for diabetes or heart disease is sold in a group of three visits to assure understanding and compliance. A weight loss program may be eight to twelve weeks of individual or group sessions.

- Other practitioners provide written nutrition instructions at the first visit of approximately one hour and schedule follow-up visits every one to two weeks and set no limitations on the duration of therapy.

- Practitioners may incorporate a variety of activities in their programs: computer nutrient analysis, menu planning, grocery shopping, skinfold analysis or impedance body analysis, individualized fitness program and workout, and long-term follow-up. Sometimes the nutrition consultant handles all of these functions and other times he is in association with a fitness specialist.

- Practitioners sometimes choose to send their patients questionnaire/ interview sheets in advance or ask that they arrive a little early so that session time is not spent filling them out. Others want to fill out the questionnaire with the patient in order to interpret insinuations and body language (see Figure 27.1).

THE SESSIONS

Before beginning with a new patient, a counselor should prepare for the role of diagnostician by reviewing all available data on the patient (5). If the patient's chart is accessible, it should be reviewed. However, in private practice or outpatient clinics it is usually necessary to start your own chart and put in chemical scores, intake analysis, anthropometric results, interview sheet, progress notes, etc. as you have them (See Figure 27.2).

The Introduction
The patients' first exposure to you and your office begins to form their opinion of your ability to help them. Trust and respect for the counselor are important motivators to patients. Small, fairly simple actions on your part can help engender good feelings in your patients. Try to start counseling sessions on time. Be sure to introduce yourself and be friendly. It sounds so elementary, but many counselors and medical professionals are so consumed with their counseling or the patients' diseases that they forget that it's the person they are working with (5).

The Interview
The session begins with an explanation of the counseling relationship describing enough so that the client knows precisely what will take place (5). If the client has other expectations, this is the time to have them known during the assessment phase, you act as a diagnostician and evaluates the client's nutrition status and relates food intake data to behavioral indicators (5). **Assessments can be made of many categories of information (also see Figure 27.3) (9):**

Figure 27.1

Sample Nutrition and Medical Evaluation Form

Name _____ Date _____

Address _____ Phone _____

Physician _____ Diet _____

Age _____ Sex _____ Marital status _____

Height _____ Weight _____ Percent body fat_____

Desired weight _____ Recent change in weight?_____

Occupation_____Hours work/day _____

EXERCISE

At work_____ During leisure_____
Discussion:

MEDICAL DATA

Personal history: (List any medical problems, past or present.)

Family: (List major medical problems of family members.)

Medication: (List any medications taken recently, include vitamins, antacids, aspirin,
             birth control pills, etc.)

BIOCHEMICAL DATA

Hct_____ Hb_____ Albumin, serum_____

Fasting blood sugar_____ mg% GTT_____

Chol._____ Triglycerides_____HDL_____LDL_____

Other:

Figure 27.1 (Continued)

NUTRITION HABITS

1. Are you on a special diet?_____ If so, which one?_____

2. Is your appetite good_____ fair_____ poor_____?

3. Who prepares your meals?_____

4. Whom do you eat your meals with?_____

5. How many times per week do you eat out?_____

6. Where do you eat out?_____

7. How many alcohol drinks per week?_____ Kinds?_____

- Biochemical studies
- Anthropometric studies
- Vital and health statistics
- Socioeconomic data
- Additional medical information

A client's behavior must be assessed (5,10):

- General health practices
- Attitudes, beliefs and information
- Physical activities
- Educational achievements and language skills
- Economic considerations
- Environmental considerations
- Social considerations

Motivation must be assessed since it is essential for compliance. Motivation is the desire to change (behavior, in this case) in return for perceiving a positive gain. In order to counsel effectively, you must pay attention to the content of the instruction as well as how well you access motivation in your clients. Clients are motivated by their own needs more than by the counselors' desires (4). Therefore, in order to assist the somewhat motivated clients, you need to perceive their needs appropriately and the clients need to perceive the changed behavior as important to them. Clients also become motivated when they see results. To that end it is important for the counselor to identify and set intermediate, more easily reached goals with the client.

Figure 27.2

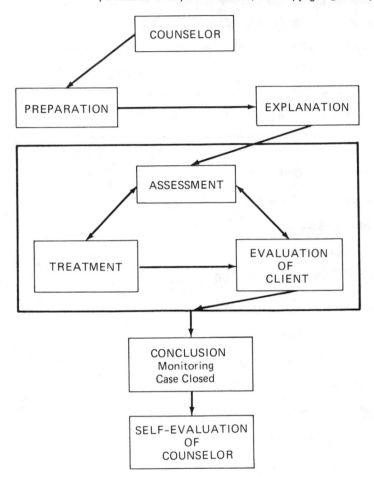

Model for Nutrition Counseling
(*Source:* Linda Snetselaar, *Nutrition Counseling Skills.* Reprinted with permission of Aspen Publishers, Inc. Copyright © 1983.)

Nutritional care or treatment plan can be developed once assessments are made and problems are identified. In the treatment phase the counselor assumes the role of both expert and mutual problem solver (5). Most novices at counseling tend to follow one extreme or the other--- expert or empathizer. Patients may be overwhelmed by the counselor who knows everything and makes all of the decisions. On the other hand, as mentioned earlier, counselors may become ineffective if they become too friendly or liberal with clients and their diet limitations. Clients often seek counseling to get assistance in setting limits for themselves. A good balance of the two roles is optimal.

In the treatment phase problems, behaviors, inconsistencies, and wrong beliefs are matched with possible solutions or alternatives. Desired

234

Figure 27.3

Figure 19.4   Possible Factors to Include in an Assessment
(*Source:* Reprinted by permission of The American Dietetic Association.)

Anthropometrics	Laboratory (can include)	Diet and Nutrition
1. Height in cm	13. Serum albumin in gm/100 mL	22. Protein intake in gm
2. Weight in kg	14. Total iron-binding capacity (TIBC) in μg/100 mL	23. Caloric intake in kcal
3. Usual weight in kg		24. Nitrogen balance in gm
4. Sex (male/female)	15. Serum transferrin in mg/100 mL [Trans = (0.8 × TIBC) − 43]	25. Obligatory nitrogen loss in gm
5. Ideal body weight (IBW) in kg		26. Net protein utilization
6. Weight as percent of IBW	16. Lymphocytes as percent	27. Basal energy expenditure (BEE) in kcal/day
7. Weight as percent of usual weight	17. White blood cell count in no./mm³	28. Caloric intake as percent of BEE
8. Triceps skinfold in mm	18. Total lymphocyte count	29. Skin test results in mm
9. Arm circumference in cm	19. 24-hour urine urea nitrogen in gm	
10. Arm muscle circumference in cm	20. 24-hour urinary creatinine in mg	
11. Triceps skinfold as percent of standard	21. Creatinine height index as percent of standard	
12. Arm muscle circumference as percent of standard		

changes or goals are ranked, and a program for step-by-step counseling is developed by the practitioner. For many reasons if the counselor determines it's necessary a patient may be referred to another health professional.

When assuming the training role, the nutrition counselor works hard to interpret the identified problems to the patient. In an orderly fashion, solutions are offered that would be acceptable to the patient---considering all that is known about him now. The patient has enough time to react and provide input of his own.

Good counselors attempt to keep instructions as simple as possible. People remember more of the information they hear in the beginning of the instruction so top priority items are discussed first.

Behavior or belief changes are discussed with the patient (and his family) in a manner that will produce positive results for that individual. For some patients it may mean confrontation in order to explore underlying reasons for present actions or beliefs (10). Other patients respond well to logical explanations of cause and effect; as long as they agree with the logic they will try to make changes. Patients may sometimes need to be led initially when they don't trust or believe anything. In this instance the counselor says, "Let me show you how it will work for you, if you take responsibility for yourself and follow the steps I suggest to you." Most patients who come to see nutrition counselors have already decided to give the counselor "a chance" to help. The important determinants are whether the patient and his family understand and respect what the counselor says, and whether the changes are reasonable given the patient and his lifestyle.

Factors associated with compliance

- Belief that following a diet is necessary for good health

- Supportive family members

- High level of concern over consequences of noncompliance

- Eagerness to reject the sick role

- Feeling comfortable about ability to cope with the diet

Factors associated with noncompliance

- Living alone

- Lack of symptoms that belies need for diet regime

- Failure of consultant to communicate purpose of diet treatment adequately

- Multiple restrictions that require changing one's lifestyle

- Poverty or unemployment

When teaching nutrition information, a counselor produces his best results when he uses a variety of tools and methods (11): We remember 10 percent of what we read, 20 percent of what we hear, 30 percent of what we see, 50 percent of what we see and hear, and 80 percent of what we ourselves say. To increase compliance combine visual aids, verbal instructions, written instructions, and learner feedback.

Counselors determine on a patient-by-patient basis whether to use an exchange list, a point system, or another method. To improve adherence and understanding it is important that the patient receive only the instruction materials and handouts that apply to his lifestyle changes or eating pattern--not every free booklet on low fat foods or diabetes. If the patient or his family expresses an interest for more recipes, etc., at follow-up visits, additional materials can be offered.

To conclude a session it is suggested that counselors summarize the agreed upon goals for the next visit and *let the patients reiterate* the most important points they should remember about the session. Except in very rare cases patients need follow-up visits in order to make permanent changes in their behavior. They also like to be told that they may call with questions or concerns at any time.

236

Evaluation/Follow-Up

After clients have been counseled, they are ready to apply and practice the suggestions at home and work. Practice gives the patient the opportunity to try new ideas and behaviors. Patients may be asked to prepare a week's menu or list the lower sodium entrees on a favorite restaurant's menu. The counselor uses the follow-up sessions as a time to reinforce the positive behaviors and provide immediate feedback on any completed projects, behavior records (see Figure 28.4), or questions. In evaluating clients, counselors again become diagnosticians (5). If no solution to the problem has been reached, counseling reverts to the assessment or treatment phase. Sometimes the clinicians may decide to refer the client to a more experienced practitioner or other health professional (5).

Ending Care

In concluding counseling care, a practitioner and client should come to mutual agreement that the client is ready or that any benefits from counseling have been derived. Monitoring the patient with appointments (or phone calls) every three to six months helps identify and solve problems that tend to appear when living in the real world. Again, counselors usually offer to be available by phone or appointment if a problem arises.

It is now believed that the concern for a patient's dependency is often unwarranted. While the goal of the counseling is to provide clients with long-term, self-management goals and skills, many clients may need to remain in some form of continuous treatment to maintain the change in eating habits. By being available by phone and appointments after structured care has ended, a counselor can help a patient better handle relapses and new problems. Also, clients that were unmotivated earlier may feel comfortable about re-entry into counseling at a later date.

Self-evaluation

Since a practitioner's success as a counselor depends to a large extent on the patients' abilities to make lifestyle or belief changes, a counselor needs to evaluate his patients' performances. It is the patients' responsibility, not the counselors to make changes in their lives. The counselor's responsibilities are to make the patient aware of the foods and lifestyle habits necessary for good health, to help the patient identify and alter barriers, and to facilitate changes in motivated patients. A counselor can build on experience to improve present skills.

Documentation

Records should be kept on each patient and his progress. The information is not only important and useful to the consultant, but it may prove essential in a malpractice suit. In courts of law the statement is often made that if the service wasn't documented it didn't happen--where is the proof?

Whether a practitioner uses the SOAP method of recording or just states the pertinent facts is not important. The most important point is for objective changes such as improved chemical scores or anthropometric values to be documented along with behavior and belief changes.

CONCLUSION

Creating realistic expectations of what your clients can do and guiding them through the changes are of the utmost importance. Change is difficult to achieve and cannot be done in a short time. The belief, held by many health professionals and clients, that lasting changes in food behavior require only a few interviews is an illusion. Change has a complex nature. Nutrition counselors and clients should not feel as if they failed when a perfect, smoothly functioning set of skills are not achieved in a few weeks. Lasting change, the goal of nutrition counseling, is most likely to occur when the nutrition counselor can teach the client the specific steps for learning and problem solving.

Professional commitment, along with hard work, will assist you in refining and improving your counseling skills. The experience should reward you as your professional effectiveness improves.

REFERENCES

1. Hospital Forum: Katherine Benziger, May-June 1990, pg. 15-20.
2. Snetselaar, L., H. Schatt, L. Iasiello-Vailor, and K. Smith: "Model Workshop on Nutrition Counseling for Dietitians," JADA, 1981, 79:678.
3. Hyatt, C.: *The Women's Selling Game*, Warner Books, 1979.
4. Shortridge, R: *The Percepteur*, A Manual Of Training Behavior for Professionals, Dairy Council of California, 1980.
5. Snetselaar, Linda: *Nutrition Counseling Skills*, Aspen Publishers, Maryland, 1983.
6. P. Hodges and C. Vickery: *Effective Counseling*, Aspen Publishers, Maryland, 1989.
7. Bandler, R., and J. Grinder: *Frogs Into Princes*, Real People Press, Moab, Utah, 1979.
8. Danish, S., M. Ginsberg, A. Terrell, M. Hammond and S. Adams: "The Anatomy Of A Dietetic Counseling Interview," *JADA*, 1979, 75:626.
9. Mason, M., B. Wenberg, and P. Welch: *The Dynamics of Clinical Dietetics*, John Wiley and Sons, New York, 1977.
10. Egan, H., L. Iasiello-Vailor, and K. Smith: "Confrontations: A New Dimension in Nutrition Counseling," *JADA*, 1983, 83:34.
11. "Compliance Dilemmas: The Renal Diet From Patient and Dietitian Perspectives" presented by James D. Campbell and Anne R. Campbell at ADA Annual Meeting, San Antonio, TX, 1982.

Chapter 28

The Wellness Movement

By Kathy King Helm, R.D., updated by Wendy Perkins, MSW, MPA, Executive Dir. of Wellness Promotions, Boulder, Colorado

Wanting "wellness" and other self-help information is a megatrend of the American people for the 1990s. Many people are excited about taking more responsibility for their own health and lives, while others are becoming more aware of their responsibility out of financial necessity. Health professionals are being seen not only as providers of care but, increasingly, as providers of information. The media regularly offer proof that substantiates that a person's cardiovascular fitness, stress management, and general health can be improved through lifestyle changes made by the individual.

WHAT IS WELLNESS?

The term "wellness," although we consider it new and futuristic, is what many people have been saying for ages should be health care's major concern---prevention or keeping well people (the majority of us) asymptomatic. Wellness involves striving for a state of health that is not just absent from disease, but optimum. People get into wellness programs not to be healthier but to enjoy their lives, spend more quality time with their families and feel better.

Most wellness leaders assert that wellness is a multidisciplinary approach to health. It is not just exercise or nutrition or stopping smoking or handling stress or making better choices. It is all of these and more. What wellness programs offer depends upon variables such as client needs, available financial support, and the leadership of the program. Typically, wellness programs in the United States include encouraging physical fitness, good nutrition, and healthy lifestyle choices. However, it is not uncommon for only one of these areas to be stressed more heavily, often to the exclusion of the other two.

Advocates of the wellness movement are quick to make the distinction between *wellness* and *holistic* since the latter's reputation is tarnished by so many questionable "treatments" that have used holistic as a banner. Charles Sterling, Ed.D., Executive Director of Cooper's Institute for Aerobics Research in Dallas, Texas states, "*Holistic* is associated with treatments of all sorts used to attain good health. Wellness is a lifestyle approach to realizing your best potential for physical health, mental alertness and serenity. It is not about extending your life or curing disease" (1).

In his book, *High Level Wellness*, Dr. Don Ardell explains that traditional medicine usually stops treatment when a patient's disability or symptoms no longer exist. Wellness starts taking place when patients become educated about their bodies and good health, when they practice new health habits and take responsibility for their own bodies by keeping them healthy. Dr. Ardell also asserts that besides nutritional awareness, stress management, and physical fitness, wellness includes environmental sensitivity and self-responsibility (2).

The Wellness Mind Set

For traditionally trained health professionals, the wellness concept may require a new mind set about their role as health providers. No longer does the medical professional do all of the work and make all of the decisions for a passive patient. Patients are taught that the responsibility for their well-being is theirs. The health provider becomes teacher, friend, and information specialist, as well as provider. Patients may decide to take care of themselves *without* input from health providers, as seen in the home pregnancy kits, screening tests in malls, and with the trend to make some prescription drugs available over the counter.

Wellness doesn't involve quick, curative measures, such as drugs and surgery; instead one works with something much more challenging---the human mind. The wellness-oriented medical specialist works with changing habits, giving guidance to people who may feel well, are energetic, and are excited about life.

Health professionals who are not wellness-oriented have problems understanding how they are supposed to help this individual since there isn't anything to cure. People must motivate themselves, but the professional can help by using the **three components of successful behavior change:**

1. Raise peoples' awareness, as with stress tests, blood pressure, blood chemistries, fitness testing, diet evaluation and so on.

2. Provide skills and knowledge to change behavior.

3. Provide reinforcement and cultural changes (cafeteria alterations, bike tracks, follow-up visits and so on.)

Without these three factors change does not happen.

The biggest challenges that nutritionists have with wellness is learning about the normal individual and then making normal nutrition exciting to the listener or reader. Good marketing is essential. Merely having fantastic handout information will not have people flocking to the door. The presentations must be interesting, stimulating, creative, timely, and packaged well. For the first time in our nutritional careers, our effectiveness may depend 80-90 percent upon our personal skills instead of our knowledge. Successful program directors are aware of that fact and are looking for nutritionists with unique skills in effective leadership, marketing, and public relations.

240

WHY WELLNESS NOW?

The wellness concept is growing and coming into its own now because of problems in our present medical system and because statistics are finally being generated by reputable sources that show positive results.

The way medicine has been practiced: acute care with passive patients and with little-to-no cost containment has reached its limits in public acceptance. The public is being repeatedly made aware of the fact that some eighty percent of all symptoms will go away given rest and good food. When sick, people want to know if they are in that eighty percent and can go home to wait it out. Many physicians believe that iatrogenic medical care and misdiagnosis may cause far more discomfort to a patient than the flu or infection that precipitated the medical visit. If they are truly ill, most patients still want the medical system to take care of it.

Many patients want good, prudent state of the art medical care from caring health professionals who *involve the patients* in the decision making. After the symptoms disappear, growing numbers of patients want to know what they can do to keep the symptoms or illness from recurring. Patients and their families are usually scared and often motivated at this time. Family members have become more aware of the relationship of heredity to their own health and are sometimes more willing to adjust their life habits to help avoid problems later.

According to popular news reports health care costs in some areas of the country have risen between 400 percent and 600 percent since 1965. The cost of health care insurance for employees has become a major concern of employers. The average annual expenditure in 1965 for health insurance was $625 per employee. However, in 1984 that average was $1,000-$1,500 per employee and $2000 or more in 1990. Ford Motor Company calculated in 1977 that it spent $2,100 per employee (3). General Motors reports that it spends more on health care for its employees than on steel for its cars (4). Inflation on cost of goods has been fueled by spiraling insurance benefit cost for employees. Historically, there have been few questions about the necessity of medical care procedures and tests and the overgrowth of hospitals, their equipment, and the length of patient stays. No one, including patients, insurance companies, or businesses, checked costs. As expenses went up, patients still expected care, insurance companies had to raise premiums, and businesses paid them and passed the cost on to the consumer. Now, the entire system is questioning value and necessity for dollars spent.

MEASURABLE RESULTS

Trying to measure the results of a wellness program has proved difficult. Some changes such as attitude improvement and better quality of life are so subjective that they are not easily quantified. The indices that are use are aerobic fitness, absenteeism, medical claim costs, sick days, accidents on the job, and productivity. However, these indices also involve many variables other than a wellness program.

241

Companies with employee wellness programs are becoming more plentiful every day. On-going programs are starting to report their preliminary results: Kimberly-Clark reports a seventy percent reduction in accidents (5): Blue Cross of Western Pennsylvania reports that for 136 persons who used insured outpatient psychiatric benefits, their medical claims dropped from $116.47 to $7.06 per month; New York Telephone showed a one-year medical cost savings of $1 1/2 million; a Goodyear plant in Sweden reports that after offering an employee fitness program, absenteeism by participants fell by fifty percent; and, General Motors Alcoholism program reports a forty-nine percent reduction in lost work hours and twenty-nine percent reduction in disability costs (5). The results are encouraging and indicate that altering one's lifestyle may produce measurable, as well as, very personal, health improvements.

CORPORATE WELLNESS PROGRAMS

Businesses are understandably interested in the boost in productivity output, and morale that good lifestyle changes can produce. The financial savings produced by some companies are also very impressive, though many other businesses have tried and failed to duplicate such dramatic reductions in costs.

When wellness programs are introduced into the workplace, it is imperative that employees are approached correctly, especially when unions are involved. The motives for encouraging wellness can be misinterpreted, or sometimes interpreted correctly, as coming from the management for purely financial reasons (instead of their purported humanitarian ones).

Some companies have begun programs that spread some of the savings around. They offer bonus plans when fewer sick days are used, mental health days off, bonuses for exercise participation and stopping smoking, all in the hope of changing lifestyles. Some companies use peer teachers to train and encourage their colleagues, while others use competitions or private professional counseling.

Consulting nutritionists can perform a variety of services for a corporate program: counsel clients, adjust cafeteria menus, teach other staff members, give speeches, write newsletters and brochures, make videos, and so on.

WELLNESS IN HOSPITAL SYSTEMS

Hospital systems are interested in the wellness concept for several major reasons. It offers public relations opportunities to improve the image of the hospital in the community. It may reduce health care costs for self-insured institutions or give premium breaks to those who have an outside insurer. It can offer the opportunity for greater income generated by community and corporate outreach programs. Some hospitals develop programs to placate administration, staff, or physicians. Eventually, results must be generated that substantiate the value of the program and warrant the capital expenditure and continuing expense.

Creating an in-house wellness program presents many challenges for an institution. Obtaining financing is usually not as difficult as gaining consensus about program staffing and defining *wellness.* Depending upon who runs the program and how involved the medical staff is, program emphasis too often begins to look very similar to the director's philosophy of wellness. A general practitioner wants to screen everyone medically, identifying illnesses and curing them. A cardiologist develops a cardiac rehab and aerobic exercise wellness program, assuming that if your heart is okay, so are you. A psychologist emphasizes counseling and stress management and wants us to believe that good mental health conquers all. Many nutritionists emphasize food and exercise, but are often hesitant to forge new roads in programming or philosophical change. The exercise physiologist sees wellness in terms of fitness. The most successful programs use an integrated approach to wellness, treating equally the importance of nourishment, being physically fit, and making lifestyle choices.

The complexity of the hospital staff coupled with the medical hierarchy and the bureaucracy often make the development of hospital wellness programs tedious and complicated. The need for good communication is paramount. Strong leadership is important. Most importantly, the program developers should never lose sight that it is the client who should be at the center of the program. For that reason, it is often beneficial to include a client or two on the development staff. Why create a program that doesn't fit the needs of your clients? It is also very helpful as a communication tool to have a business prospectus or plan written that describes the goals, purposes, target audience(s), staffing, plan of action, and timetable for the program.

Wellness Programs Come in Many Forms

Facilities for wellness programs vary from the very elaborate with exercise equipment, pool, masseuse or masseur, jogging track, and meeting rooms to only an office for one or two people to coordinate the programs for a staff of consultants.

Special events offered by wellness programs include sponsoring races, health fairs, and wellness retreats as well as media spots on health topics. Classes and seminars cover topics such as alcohol, stress, and smoking, all facets of sports, prenatal, parenting, making good choices in life, healthful cooking, weight loss, aerobic and strength exercises, wellness nutrition (the prudent diet), vegetarian diets, relaxation, and flexibility exercises. In a corporate setting, there are also programs on self-esteem, communication, team building, time management, and wellness as a whole person/ whole organization effort.

WINNING A NUTRITION POSITION IN WELLNESS

Most wellness programs assume that nutrition is a necessary component. However, that assumption does not necessarily include having a registered dietitian as the only professional giving out nutrition information. Today, ethical information on basic nutrition is readily available. Dietitians face job

243

competition in wellness settings even in some hospitals from at least nurses, social workers, health educators, physiologists, and physicians. However, dietitians who distinguish themselves in teaching skills, program and marketing creativity, and keeping abreast in nutrition knowledge will always have jobs.

Several years ago a hospital in Denver decided to cut expenses at their wellness program and only keep the positions that were generating a profit. That left only the dietitian on staff. Eventually, she built up her staff and wielded much more professional weight because she had demonstrated fiscal responsibility.

Wellness programs are looking for dietitians who have good communication skills (writing and speaking), who believe in and know about wellness and who are innovative and creative in programs, materials, and teaching skills. Dietitians must be assertive leaders while interacting and appreciating what other health professionals have to offer. *Appreciation of the team approach is vital.* It is also important that dietitians acquire business savvy so that they understand the "larger picture" of the organization, are politically effective, and understand and contribute to financial goals.

Seeking Leads and Making Contacts

Hospitals and corporations are usually very good about advertising available positions on their staff. However, to be associated with a wellness program during its beginning developmental stages, contact should be made early. In other words, it may be necessary to "cold call" on an institution to establish your interest. If you are already an employee at the hospital and want to apply for the job, you may find that you will still have to sell yourself and convince the wellness director that you can do well in the new position.

Tools that can be used to promote yourself for the position include a good resume written with emphasis on skills and experience that would be useful in a wellness program, copies of published articles, booklets, or teaching materials you've written, copies of newspaper articles, brochures, or flyers that have promoted your public speaking, and, finally, a proposal either oral or written on what you could do for their program. If you do not have enough information to offer suggestions on the first visit, offer to write a simple proposal after you meet outlining what you could do for them. Try to return the proposal within a week so that they feel that your work is timely and efficient.

Dietitians are hired as employees for programs and therefore acquire all of the benefits of a salaried person. They are willing to accept the fact that the institution owns the developed materials and programs (unless negotiated otherwise).

Wellness programs also hire consultant dietitians either by themselves or as part of a group of consultants. These dietitians prefer to take more risk and the responsibility for their own vacations, insurance, and continuing educations, and so on, in return for more money and freedom. Consultants are often paid to bring expertise that is not easily found or creativity that inspires a program. Usually the materials created belong to whoever paid for their development. Some consultants prefer to create them

244

on their own time and then sell the materials or license the rights to use them to an institution.

Services to Offer

Dietitians offer a variety of services to wellness programs. These services include nutrition counseling, presenting classes and workshops, providing in-service classes to the wellness staff as well as other medical people, and conducting weight loss classes with an exercise specialist or psychologist. Others work with the cafeteria to change recipes and menu items to ones lower in fat and sugar and to include more fresh foods or "gourmet natural." Some wellness programs are also interested in dietitians who have media experience and can do media interviews, cable, and video programs. Dietitians with writing skills and experience are in demand by programs that plan to produce educational materials for sale. Computer expertise has opened doors for some dietitians when some wellness programs have wanted to produce their own software. Many hospital or corporate fitness weight loss programs have also employed dietitians.

Wellness Promotions of Boulder, Colorado is "a team of experts that can guide a company through the process of designing, delivering and evaluating health and wellness programs to fit management and employee wants and needs." Run by Wendy Perkins, MSW, MPA a social worker with extensive business, marketing and program development experience, this company helps businesses enters wellness where their needs are met best---every organization is different.

Jean Storlie, MS, R.D., started her career in wellness at LaCrosse,Wisconsin and first became known as a program developer and co-author of weight loss books with Dr.Jordon. She later worked at the Cooper's Aerobic Center, Dallas, Texas and then was hired by Rush-Presbyterian-St. Luke's Hospital to start their subsidiary division "Arc Ventures," a wellness and health promotion company. Today, Jean has her own consultant firm in Madison, Wisconsin in nutrition communications, health promotions and sports nutrition for individuals, local and national corporations and public relations firms. She also teaches graduate courses in sports nutrition and wellness at Rush University.

MARKETING AND PROMOTION ARE MUSTS!

Wellness programs must recognize early on that their competition for clients is in the private sector. They do not have the luxury of a "captive audience"; unlike a hospitalized patient, wellness participants are not ill and do not require immediate treatment. Therefore, employees and the community have to be enticed and excited about the programs being offered or they will go elsewhere, if they go at all.

It will take a while for the image of a center to become established and market itself. It will take a while for the staff, classes, and programs to become known. More time and money must be spent up front to acquaint prospective clients with you and what you offer. It may be necessary to give free introductory "brown bag" talks to nurses on the patient floors or to employees at a bank, visit community meetings, or give a prerace seminar.

To promote an individual program, such as a new weight loss series, marketing tools could include: an easy to remember name and logo, colorful posters, brochures, and folder covers for handout materials, and a personal letter to all physicians promoting the classes. T-shirts could be displayed that will be given out at the class. Paycheck stuffers could promote the program, as well as any other newsletter or communique. Ads could be purchased in local newspapers. Public service announcements are also effective through local media, and occasionally, a local newspaper or magazine writer will ask for an interview and take photographs.

Marketing is so important and critical to the survival of your programs. Don't leave it to chance and don't assume that someone else has it all under control. Stay on top of marketing!

WHY WELLNESS PROGRAMS FAIL

Even wellness programs with good financing and staffs can have problems and eventually fail. In surveys conducted by Robert Allen, Ph.D., and reported in "The Corporate Health-Buying Spree: Boon or Boondoggle?" reprinted from *Advanced Management Journal*, he found **six factors that contribute to failure:** (l) Fragmentation of effort--timing, organization, or marketing were off; (2) overemphasis on initial motivation--lack of long-term effect or follow through; (3) misdirected emphasis on illness--trying to motivate by avoiding disease instead of encouraging the positive potential of a healthy lifestyle; (4) appeal to individual heroics--there is a need for a supportive environment that is not competitive; (5) overemphasis on activities as opposed to results--a successful program produces lifestyle changes, not just good attendance; (6) a "we will do it for you" approach rather than a better "together we can do it for ourselves" attitude--avoid passive programs (3).

In opposition to Allen's guideline #4, Denice Ferko-Adams, R.D. has found that the competitive environment is very positive for behavior change in her weight loss/wellness programs in numerous corporations around Pennsylvania. Eighty-six percent of the employees who join the two-month program complete it with the each employee losing an average of 9 1/2 pounds. Many lose far more weight as they stay with the guidelines established and practiced in the program, supported by their peers with new cafeteria selections and new foods at home.

THE COMING AWARENESS

The people who are well are seen today as an untapped market and potential source of revenue. Perhaps someday, they will be seen as the medically exciting and unique individuals that they are. Why should someone have to be ill to be studied and helped to a better quality of life?

REFERENCES

1. Fitness Leadership Program Manual: Cooper Clinic Publisher, Dallas, Texas, March 1983, pp. 21-25.
2. Ardell, Don: *High Level Wellness,* Bantam, New York, 1979, p. 1.
3. Allen, Robert F: "The Corporate Health Buying Spree: Boon or Boondoggle? *American Management Association* (Society for Advancement of Management), New York, 1980.
4. Fitness Leadership Program. Cooper Clinic, Dallas, Texas, March 1983 pp. 21-25.
5. "Kimberly-Clark Health Management Program Aimed at Prevention." *Occupational Health and Safety,* November/December 1977, p. 25.

Chapter 29

Sports and Cardiovascular Nutrition

Marilyn Schorin, Ph.D., R.D., updated by
Karen Reznick Dolins, M.S., R.D.

These are exciting times to be a sports or cardiovascular nutritionist. Opportunities for dietitians in these areas abound and continue to grow. Dietitians are finding positions at sports and fitness centers, wellness programs, cardiovascular clinics, spas, and as consultants to sports teams and athletes at all levels and abilities. They are also being hired as consultants to food manufacturers and as media spokespersons for health or fitness-related products or services.

Crowds in health clubs and wellness programs, and the proliferation of bikers and runners on the streets show the public's awareness of the benefits of a healthy lifestyle. Clients' ages and levels of physical conditioning as well as their motivations vary, posing a bold challenge to a dietitian's professional capabilities. Young athletes may be more interested in maximizing performance with foods and timing of meals. While adult clients seek ways to become fit, prevent disease, and use nutrition and exercise to control their weight.

These two specialties are discussed as one because both have a strong exercise physiology component and deal closely with cardiac output. In practice, many places of employment offer both sports and cardiovascular rehabilitation services making it necessary for the dietitian to know in depth information about both. Dietitians' growing interest in this area of practice is mirrored by the growth in membership in the Sports and Cardiovascular Nutritionists (SCAN) Dietetic Practice Group of The American Dietetic Association. SCAN is now ADA's second largest practice group, boasting thirty-eight hundred members nationwide.

RECENT FOCUS ON NUTRITION AND FITNESS

A series of relatively recent efforts by government agencies has focused attention on nutrition and physical fitness. In 1985 we saw the inception of the National Institutes of Health's National Cholesterol Education Program (NCEP) that identifies RDs as the preferred educators of the public on diet to lower blood cholesterol (1). The Surgeon General's "Report on Nutrition and Health" issued by the Department of Health and Human Services in 1988

248

advised Americans to reduce their intake of fat and cholesterol and identified diet as the cornerstone for treatment of coronary heart disease (CHD) (2). The National Research Council of the National Academy of Sciences issued their recommendations in 1989, specifying a reduction of total fat intake to thirty percent or less of calories, saturated fatty acid intake to less than ten percent of calories and cholesterol intake to less than 300 milligrams daily to reduce the risk of atherosclerotic cardiovascular disease in the general population (3). "Healthy People 2000," a document released by the U.S. Department of Health and Human Services in 1990, outlines health goals for the nation over the next ten years and identifies nutrition and physical activity as priority areas for improving the nation's health (4).

The interest in nutrition benefits extends beyond the scientific and medical communities. More coaches, athletic trainers and athletes from high school and college to professional and Olympic levels are enlisting the aid of qualified sports nutritionists to use nutrition to help achieve a competitive edge. A recent ruling by the National Collegiate Athletic Association (NCAA) states that university and college athletic programs can provide athletes with only one training table meal a day instead of three. Expect it to be enforced by August 1, 1996. This offers the opportunity for sports nutritionists to educate athletes and coaches better about what to eat.

WHAT KNOWLEDGE AND TRAINING IS NECESSARY?

We are acutely sensitive to the propensity of marginally trained lay people or health care professionals with no background in nutrition to advertise their dubious expertise in our field. It follows, then, that we must be as insistent with our peers, requiring them to be well trained in the nutrition specialties they purport to practice.   The dietitian who is an expert in sports and cardiovascular nutrition must have at least a basic knowledge of each of the areas listed below.

Baseline subjects for sports and cardiovascular specialists include:

- Nutritional science
- Biochemistry
- Physiology, especially exercise physiology
- Cardiovascular disease etiology and treatment
- Sports rules, training, common injuries, verbiage
- Counseling skills
- Communication skills

Specialized knowledge or advanced training is expected in at least one of these categories.   There is no degree or certificate necessary to call oneself a sports or cardiovascular nutritionist. However, most practitioners have had special training (in a fitness or cardiac disease course, CPR , or sports injury class), or additional degrees in exercise physiology, athletic training, or nutrition with a sports nutrition emphasis.

Nutrition

First and foremost, of course, is a working knowledge of nutrition science and food composition. Sports and cardiovascular dietitians must not only be conversant with general information about foods taught in most nutrition courses, but must keep tabs on particulars such as which cuts of beef offer the lowest saturated fat content and which types of fish are the best sources of omega-3 fatty acids. They must know the nutrient composition of specific brand names. For example, which brand of cereal can be recommended for its high soluble fiber content as well as being low in sugar and sodium? Which foods in a fast food restaurant would provide a high school athlete with the most amount of carbohydrate with the least amount of fat?

Always be up on the latest. Recommendations regarding optimal carbohydrate concentration in sports drinks, for example, has changed in recent years. While earlier studies showed that a 2.5% carbohydrate solution was ideal for quick gastric emptying, we now know that 7.5% carbohydrate solutions are absorbed into the intestines more rapidly and therefore get to body tissues in a comparable length of time. The sports nutritionist should be familiar with ergogenic aids and their contents being promoted to athletes. He or she should know the carbohydrate content and sources (sucrose, fructose, glucose polymers) of the various sports drinks on the market and the practical differences between them.

The mass media picks up on research published in credible medical journals and turns it into news. Articles frequently appear in the newspaper the day after a study has been published, and the implications of such studies are often exaggerated. Physicians and patient alike may ask your opinion on a story relating intake of oat bran or garlic to blood cholesterol levels. You will gain their respect if you are ready with a knowledgeable answer.

Biochemistry

Sports and cardiovascular dietitians need a working knowledge of the metabolism of macronutrients and the interrelationships among energy-providing fuels. A sports nutritionist should know which substrate is being used for fuel at a particular intensity of exercise. If they have not kept up with lipid metabolism, some advanced training or assiduous review is critical. The biochemistry of exercise is a fascinating, but complex subject, yet it is essential to grasp its intricacies in order to explain sports nutrition in terms appropriate to each client. It is difficult to advise very learned athletes and fitness enthusiasts on their nutritional requirements without a comprehensive understanding of this field.

Physiology

A clear understanding of muscle morphology is necessary when talking to athletes, coaches, and trainers. The specialist in this field must know terminology like red and white muscle and fast-twitch and slow-twitch fibers

250

when conversing with medical and exercise specialists. The cardiovascular nutritionist will be familiar, of course, with digestion from a background in dietetics, but this dietitian will need more advanced knowledge of cardiovascular and respiratory physiology as well as hormone physiology.

Cardiovascular Disease

The dietitian whose clientele will be primarily cardiac patients or those at high risk of cardiovascular disease will require greater proficiency in the diagnosis and treatment of heart disease, enhancing interaction with other professionals involved in the patient's care as well as maximizing the quality of client counseling. Ideally, the various drugs used to treat angina, cardiac arrhythmias, and hypertension should be recognized, with an emphasis placed upon familiarity with nutrient interactions caused by these pharmacological agents. The specialist's effectiveness is increased by awareness and mastery of other modalities of treatment of coronary artery disease and atherosclerosis, such as techniques for stress reduction, smoking cessation and exercise prescription.

Sports Knowledge

The best way to become successful as a sports nutritionist is by knowing the sport and the people in sports. You can have all the nutrition knowledge in the world, but if you can't make it apply to the sport you are targeting, you are of no use to an athlete or team.

Make sure you know the rules of the sport. For example, some sports have weight requirements, and by knowing when they have to be met enables the nutritionist to target fluid intake in the period before an event. Learn about training schedules: do athletes train throughout the year or is there a season? How many hours in a day do they train? What does their training regimen consist of? Do they cross train? What types of injuries are they prone to? Is nutrition considered an important adjunct in recuperation from injury? When dealing with professional athletes, this point is crucial.

Know the commonly accepted guidelines for body weight and body fat in an athlete's sport. Know that it may be different for various positions on the team. The sports nutritionist can make him or herself more valuable to a sports team by being able to measure body composition and determine appropriate body weight based on percent body fat. Keep up on the latest research in the area of sports drinks. Be able to discuss the benefits of different beverages, including water, and which sports will benefit the most from them, and how to select one.

Advertisements for nutritional supplements are attractive to athletes interested in enhancing their performance and gaining the "competitive edge." The sports nutritionist must be able to discuss this issue with the athlete without appearing judgmental and respecting the athlete's belief system. Remember that placebos often work! Visit the local health food store at regular intervals to keep in touch with the latest in ergogenics. It helps to know, for example, that MCT oil (medium chain triglycerides) is being promoted to athletes as a "fatless fat," a quick energy source that won't be stored as body fat. By advising the athlete that MCT oil packs the same 9 calories per gram as any other fat, you may help them avoid an economic rip-off. For the athlete supplementing amino acids, it makes an impression when you can demonstrate that the supplement with 5000 milligrams of amino acids provides fewer than 1 ounce of tuna fish with 7000 milligrams or 1 cup of skim milk with 8000 milligrams.

Know the energy requirements of the sport and which energy systems are used. A power lifter is not going to deplete their glycogen stores so advice in this area is less valuable to them than to a basketball player. Baseball players and sprinters do not rely on endurance to win.   When addressing them, hydration issues or possibly weight control for the ball player will be a more relevant topic.

Counseling

The dietitian who concentrates on sports and cardiovascular nutrition needs to have well-honed counseling skills. Like all aspects of dietetics, counseling achieves its greatest impact when these two factors prevail: (1) the client is highly motivated and (2) the nutritionist knows how to structure the care plan into small, manageable steps. Male and female athletes are motivated by improvements in performance; they constantly seek the competitive edge. Nutrition has been touted to them as a type of snake oil in which anything from carbo-loading to bee pollen may provide that edge. Their motivation is, fortunately, not usually a problem.

On the other hand, the client at high risk for cardiovascular disease may feel "fine" and therefore, resist making any dietary changes. A skilled counselor can dispel resistance, increase motivation, build confidence in the client's ability to make dietary changes, and promote maintenance of positive salutary changes.

Communication

Through a concerted effort to expand one's audience, the sports and cardiovascular dietitian can reach many people via methods less direct than individualized counseling.   Communications skills become vastly more important when one does not see the client face-to-face.   In   direct counseling, the skilled dietitian can determine whether the nutritional recommendations are understood through gentle probing and observation. When the message is relayed through an indirect medium, expertise in writing and public speaking is demanded. Some modes of communicating with clients include:

- Individualized counseling

- Classes on specific topics

- Lectures

- Articles written in lay publications

- Radio and television appearances

Commonly used approaches include seminars, supermarket tours, or food demonstrations on one's specialty. Classes may be offered through hospitals, adult education programs, junior colleges, or health clubs. More corporations welcome the opportunity to provide on-site instruction for their employees, set up under the auspices of the corporate health or personnel departments as part of corporate wellness programs.

Should the nutrition specialist prefer to avoid the constraints of regularly scheduled meetings, lectures offer an alternative avenue for educating the public. Finding an audience for lecturing is usually easy. Examples include business and professional clubs, religious and community groups, and self-help groups for topics related to nutrition and the heart. While the "Y"s, sports or fitness clubs, coaches conferences, school groups and amateur sports groups want speakers on sports nutrition. Some lectures may be given for free to help market oneself, to attract referrals, or to get to know local athletes and their coaches. At other times a fee may be paid by the sponsoring organization.

WHO IS THE CLIENTELE?

Sports and cardiovascular nutritionists have limitless opportunities. This section will be directed at five specific groups of people who provide excellent targets for our services. These are:

- Professional athletes

- Recreational athletes

- School age athletes

- Patients with high risk of cardiovascular disease

- Patients with confirmed ischemic heart disease

Professional Athletes

The glamour certainly lies with the big names. Who wouldn't want to play a role in the success of such superstars as Michael Jordan, Joan Benoit Samuelson, Lanny Wadkins, or "Flo-Jo" Joyner? Although such opportunities are not out of the question, there are of course very few of these superstars to go around. Also, there are many other health professionals, coaches and trainers who want the chance to work with the big name athletes and are willing to do it for free or a greatly reduced price. So competition is sometimes stiff to get your foot in the door. Dietitians with professional football, basketball, hockey and baseball teams are usually paid good hourly fees, however, there are no full time positions and often only sporadic hours at the beginning of a season and as-needed thereafter. It's not unusual to be "paid" with a T-shirt, season tickets, or just a gate pass when the teams or athletes can't afford any other compensation.

Recreational Athletes

Most of us will have a better chance of earning a livelihood by focusing on the legions of athletes outside the realm of the top pros. Recreational athletes are overflowing our biking and running clubs, walking trails and pools. Communities abound with health-oriented adults determined to live longer and healthier. Sports and health clubs provide a source of motivated clientele who may wonder why pounds aren't dropping off as they drip buckets of sweat while working out on the stairmaster or exercycle. Other clients work out on their own and just want to know how to lose body fat and stay motivated on a diet.

Practice settings and financial arrangements vary. Some nutritionists find it helpful to set up shop within a fitness facility or sports medicine clinic, while others benefit from setting up a referral system and counseling in their own offices. Practitioners may choose to work in a facility in a salaried position, at an hourly rate, or set their own rates and pay a percentage to the facility to help cover any overhead. Group lectures can be a practitioner's main source of income or it can be a marketing vehicle offered for free or at a reduced cost to introduce large numbers of people to the practitioner's services. Whichever way you choose, working with the recreational athlete can be stimulating and financially rewarding work.

CASE STUDY

When Nancy Clark, M.S., R.D. was beginning her practice she wanted the credibility that comes with being part of a large medical practice. Therefore, she contacted Dr. William Southmayd, the medical director of Sports Medicine Brookline, one of the largest athletic injury clinics in the country. He welcomed this opportunity to include a nutritionist on the medical team, and they were able to agree to terms.

Nancy set up shop in the clinic and quickly realized that despite the high traffic flow, she would have to do more than simply put out her shingle and wait for physician referrals. She embarked on a promotional campaign to the patients coming through the waiting room with a brochure explaining the benefits of sports nutrition counseling. She coached her professional colleagues to look for possible nutrition related conditions like anemia, stress fractures and slow to heal injuries.

She increased her national visibility through speaking, writing sports nutrition columns for several lay magazines, and authoring two books, *The Athlete's Kitchen* and *Nancy Clark's Sports Nutrition Book.*

Nancy finds it invaluable to remain visible to her target markets by joining local bike or running clubs and practice a healthy lifestyle. She also encourages everyone who wants to become a sports nutritionist to be patient. It takes time to build a client base.

School Aged Athletes

Young athletes provide a wide open market for sound nutritional advice. In the fall an athlete may be using protein powders to bulk up for football while the winter months may find him eating less than one meal per day trying to

254

make weight for wrestling. Young girls in gymnastics and ballet often skip meals in order to control their weight. However, before practice many may succumb to vending machine fare for a quick "pick me up," while after practice there is fast food with its high fat content. A balanced dinner at home may only be picked at.

These students need help not just in deciding what and how much to eat, but also when. Salient suggestions that the nutritionist can offer regarding food choices and timing of meals can make a difference in both their athletic and academic performance. These budding sportsmen and sportswomen must be shown that focusing on weight without regard to body fat is an ineffective way to achieve an athletic body.

Nutrition services are not typically included in school budgets. Funding for services may come from a parent, a Booster Club or the PTA, if there is funding. When money is tight, group talks are the most efficient vehicle for getting the message to the greatest number of people and it gives an opportunity for nutrition misinformation to be aired. Many sports nutritionists give their time to schools without pay or with only modest payment because of the fun and satisfaction of working with the kids. It's also a good place to hone skills before trying to work with the top athletes and it may lead to more paying client and job referrals.

CASE STUDY

Merle Best, M.S., R.D., a sports nutritionist is a consultant to professional and amateur athletes in the New Jersey area. She became interested in the high school athletes out of concern for this impressionable age group. She realized that sports nutrition could be an effective vehicle for teens to develop good health habits.

Merle has her own business, but to help establish her credibility, she has a good working relationship with a sports medicine group. In developing her client base, she reached out to athletes on their own turf by holding on-site sessions at local high schools. To grab the young athletes' attention, she also brought the sport group's athletic trainer who had been a wrestler. Individuals were charged a small fee and were encouraged to bring a coach or parent free of charge. Merle finds that coach and parent support is essential to the success of the program. The group session was directed at weight control and hydration issues. Athletes in need of more in-depth follow-up were seen individually for an additional fee.

To be a more effective sports nutritionist, Merle suggests," Always calculate a young athlete's body fat to help change his or her focus from body weight to body fat. And when counseling young athletes, always reserve time at the end of the session to include the parent. Then allow the athlete to explain the program to the parent which effectively reinforces the learning process."

Merle urges dietitians interested in a career in sports nutrition to develop a strong referral base by networking with other health professionals interested and working with sports, with athletic trainers and coaches. Each state Interscholastic Athletic Association has a listing of area schools with their coaches and athletic directors. *

HIGH RISK CARDIOVASCULAR DISEASE

The American Heart Association estimates that 101.2 million Americans have blood cholesterol values above 200 mg% (6). Registered dietitians working with cardiologists in clinics and in private practice have endless opportunities to provide information to physicians and patients alike on the role of diet and exercise in prevention and treatment of CHD. Dietitians excel at translating scientific recommendations into practical, individualized suggestions for lifestyle changes. Their counseling and motivational skills are instrumental in enhancing compliance. National Cholesterol Education Program (NCEP) publications outlining steps for dietary treatment make excellent marketing tools for the RD hoping to expand a practice.

CASE STUDY

Karen Reznick Dolins: I began my private practice while working at a major medical center as a clinical dietitian. A physician with the affiliated medical school was opening a hyperlipidemia clinic and needed a registered dietitian. I made the contact, and I was off and running. When the medical school opened a cardiac rehabilitation facility, I was offered the opportunity to open a private practice in nutrition counseling.

I cut my hours back to part time at the medical center, but my private practice soon took up so many hours, I resigned as clinical dietitian. I maintained my contacts with the dietary department and the hospital physicians, both of who continue to refer patients.

Once dependent on my private practice for a living, I broadened my referral network by writing to all area cardiologists. Each letter was followed up with a phone call, and invaluable contacts were made. One medical group of six physicians preferred to have an in-house nutritionist. As this large practice provided great opportunities, I agreed to spend one day a week at their office on a fee-for-service basis.

Physicians continue to be a major referral source for me. I see a number of physicians as clients, and they in turn become referral sources. When the NCEP guidelines were published I took advantage of them by sending a copy to all of the physicians I work with, highlighting the areas about the value of the RD. Now that I am well established in my community, many of my clients are referred by others whom I have helped. My practice has grown over the years to include a variety of corporate clients, athletes, and a teaching position at a local university.

I tried advertising in local papers early on, but found it to be unproductive. I find that word-of -mouth advertising is my best promotion.

To enhance my skills, I took advantage of a nutrition counseling workshop offered by the local chapter of the American Heart Association. In addition to making me more proficient in this area, the workshop gave me the opportunity to network with other RDs involved in this type of counseling.

My advice to other RDs developing a practice in this area to be sure you have a strong referral network. Thanks to the attention focused on the efficacy of cholesterol lowering in recent years, few would argue with the benefits of nutrition counseling for these patients. The field is wide open. Go for it!

CONFIRMED HEART DISEASE

Cardiovascular disease remains a major cause of morbidity and mortality in the U.S. with an estimated sixty-eight million people, more than one in four Americans, effected (6).   Personalized nutritional counseling is vital for these patients. An intensive approach with a Step 2 diets defined by the NCEP and the AHA is required . Dietary cholesterol intake should be under 200 mg. daily and saturated fat less than seven percent of calories. A registered dietitian can individualize this strict prescription according to the patients preferences making it more palatable. Working one-on-one helps compliance. The dietitian must be patient and flexible, often working slowly to decrease the saturated fat and cholesterol content of the diet and achieve the above goal. These patients may be on a prescribed exercise program and coordination between the dietitian, exercise therapist, and cardiologist will achieve maximal results.

CASE STUDY

Joyce Sokolik, RD. developed her expertise in cardiovascular nutrition while working with the multiple Risk Factor Intervention Trial (MRFIT). Designed to measure whether men at high risk for premature death from coronary heart disease would benefit from a multi-factor approach to risk factor reduction, the program gave Joyce invaluable experience with this population. This credential gave her the edge she needed to get her foot in the door with a cardiology group.

Joyce follows up on all medical referrals with a letter to the referring physician. She finds it helpful to include an educational component in these letters, citing recent studies   to improve their knowledge and her credibility.

Joyce has expanded her practice to include group counseling sessions and supermarket tours in addition to individual counseling. She promotes her practice directly to the consumer through ads in a local newspaper and the telephone book.

WHERE TO GET INFORMATION

Although the demand for adequate formal training is emphasized above, equally important to success in this field is keeping up with new information and materials. Included in this area are professional meetings, reading selected journals, and networking with colleagues in this field. Sports and Cardiovascular Nutritionist (SCAN) of the American Dietetic Association, represents a broad group of Registered Dietitians who are working in this area. They publish a quarterly newsletter and hold an annual symposium..

American College of Sports Medicine, headquartered in Indianapolis Indiana, represents over fifty different professions involved in sports, exercise, and fitness. They also hold an annual meeting and publish a monthly journal. A suggested bibliography follows:

REFERENCES

1. U.S. Dept. of Health and Human Services: *National Cholesterol Education Program: Report of the Expert Panel on Detection, Evaluation, and Treatment of High Blood Cholesterol in Adults, NIH,* No. 89-2925, 1989.
2. U.S. Dept. of Health and Human Services: *The Surgeon General's Report on Nutrition and Health,*DHHS (PHS) No. 88-50211, 1988.
3. National Research Council: *Diet and Health: Implications for Reducing Chronic Disease Risk,* Nat'l Acad. Press, Washington, DC 1989.
4. U.S. Dept. of Health and Human Services: *Healthy People 2000,* 1990 Supt. of Documents, Govt. Printing Office #017-001-00474-0.
5. *Lowering Blood Cholesterol to Prevent Heart Disease:* Concensus Conference, JADA 253:2080, 1985.
6. *1991 Heart and Stroke Facts:*American Heart Association, Dallas, TX.
7. Ernst, N.D., Mullis, R., Sooter-Bochenek, J., et al: *The National Cholesterol Education Program: Implications for Dietetic Practitioners from the Adult Treatment Panel Recommendations,* JADA 1988, 88:1401.

SUGGESTED BIBLIOGRAPHY

Biochemistry
Harvey, R. and P. Champe: *Biochemistry--Outline Review,* Medical Exam Publisher, Garden City, NY, 1984.
Stryer, L.: *Biochemistry,* Freeman, San Francisco, 1988.

Nutrition and Cardiovascular Disease
Kris-Etherton, PM (Ed): *Cardiovascular Disease: Nutrition for Prevention and Treatment,*Sports and Cardiovascular Nutritionists Practice Group, American Dietetic Association, Chicago, IL, 1990.

Sports Nutrition
Benardot, D. (Ed): *Sports Nutrition: A Guide for the Professional Working With Active People,*2nd edition, Sports and Cardiovascular Nutritionists Practice Group, American Dietetic Association, Chicago, expected publication date June 1992.
Berning, J., and S. Steen (Eds): *Sports Nutrition for the 90's: The Health Professional's Handbook,* Aspen Pub., Rockville, MD, 1991.
Clark, N.: *Nancy Clark's Sports Nutrition Guidebook, Leisure* Press, Champaign, IL, 1990.
Coleman, E.: *Eating For Endurance, Bull* Pub., Palo Alto, CA, 1988.
McArdle, W.: *Exercise Physiology: Energy, Nutrition, and Human Performance,* Lea and Febiger, Philadelphia, 1988.
Peterson, M. and K. Peterson: *Eat to Compete,* Yearbook Med. Pub, 1989.
Smith, N., B.W. Roberts: *Food For Sport,* Bull Pub., Palo Alto, CA, 1989.

258

JOURNALS/ NEWSLETTERS

Pulse, The newsletter of the Sports and Cardiovascular Nutrition dietetic
Practice Group, free with $20 annual membership, 4 issues per year.
Write for subscription to SCAN c/o ADA 216 W. Jackson Blvd.,
Chicago, IL 60606-6995.

Sports Nutrition News, J Fishman, Ed, P.O. Box 986 , Evanston, IL 60204.

Sports Medicine Digest, P.O. Box 10172, Van Nuys, CA 91409;
800-365-2468.

Sports Science Exchange, Gatorade Sports Science Institute, P. O. Box
9005, Chicago, IL 60604-9005.

Medicine and Science in Sports and Exercise, bimonthly, free with membership in the American College of Sports Medicine.

International Journal of Sports Nutrition, quarterly, Human Kinetics
Publishers, Box 5076 ,Champaign, IL 61825-5076.

Continuing Education Courses In Sports Nutrition

Diet, Exercise and Fitness, by Ellen Coleman, M.S., R.D., Nutrition
Dimension, P.O.Box 301147, Escondido, CA 92030. Approved for 10
CE hours by ADA.

Chapter 30

Media Savvy

Health professionals who are comfortable with consultations and public speaking can be unnerved when entering the unfamiliar world of radio and television. Interviews with the print media are usually more relaxed, but you seldom have control over what is quoted. Why then, become involved in something so challenging or risky? Because you want to communicate with a great number of people. How else can you discuss nutrition with a million people for five minutes or warn your entire city about a new diet fad?

First chances, much less second chances, aren't always easy to get in any of the media avenues. Because so many people recognize the value of media exposure there is stiff competition in becoming a guest, especially on national programming. Local media and some cable stations are not so difficult. Jack Hilton, author of *On Television!* states, "The electronic media have replaced print as the basic source of information in this country, and the ordinary person is severely limited in the ability to get before a microphone and camera. In fact, even the extraordinary person has found it difficult to reach an electronic forum with regularity" (1).

Even considering all of the benefits, media work is not for everyone. Radio and television work require that the person have an original personality or something to say, and of course, the ability to say it. The pace is usually quick and just when you feel you are adjusting, it's over. There are times when the station or paper never again has time for another interview, and you never know why. They have time for the chef, the fortune teller, the gardener, and the police officer, but not the dietitian. At least not you. Was it something you said? Were you too straight? What could you have done differently?

PRACTICE MAKES PERFECT

Experts usually suggest that you plan, practice, and seek training or professional advice if you are really serious about pursuing the media on anything but an occasional or strictly small-time basis. It also helps to have experience. But how can you get it, if no one will give you a chance to start?

Practitioners have trained by first going to small local radio stations and newspapers to learn the ropes and the style that sells. If writing style is a problem, hire an editor to review your work or follow the other suggestions in Chapter 31. If speaking off the cuff is not comfortable, take communication course work or a seminar, pay a tutor, or practice with another person using a tape or video recorder. It is also beneficial to watch, listen to, or read the media. Train yourself to begin thinking of angles that will make your project (or you) more newsworthy. Review media topics below:

Food demonstrations on
Low-cholesterol cooking
Vegetarianism
Low-salt dishes
Eating out on a low calorie diet
Natural food sources of vitamins

Discussion on
Fiber and cancer
Obesity in children and adults
Persons' nutrient needs after 60 years old
Sports nutrition
Breast feeding
Hyperactivity in children
Foods for the storm box
Snacks for long auto trips
Water and water impurities
Nutrition cultism
Vitamin or mineral supplements
Caffeine
Calcium and bone disease
Qualifications to become a Registered Dietitian

To prepare for call-in talk shows read newsletters such as *Nutrition and the M.D.* and *Tuft's University Diet and Nutrition Letter.* Read lay publications, such as *American Health, Prevention,* and local or national newspapers, to get a better idea what your audience is reading.

Jack Hilton offers some good suggestions to consider before joining the talk show circuit, even on the smallest scale. He states, "Watch every talk show you can. Get a feeling for the rhythm, and for how much can be said. Note how questions tend to be repeated from show to show. Make up a set of questions and answer them in the microphone of a tape recorder. Listen to your voice. If you hear a continuing series of crutch words or sounds, practice talking without them" (1).

It is usually less stressful to be interviewed by a newspaper writer, but answering with concise clear statements is just as important. The fact that the interview is relaxed should not be construed as an invitation to ramble or become too familiar so that statements are made that you *hope* will stay "of the record."

LEGALITIES, LIABILITIES, AND CONTROVERSIES

When you appear on or write for the media on the subject of nutrition, you are representing yourself as an expert and as a member of your profession. Obviously, the better you do, the more credible everyone appears. However, there are legal and liability implications involved that you must be aware of:

261

1. As a nutrition expert, you have the right (and perhaps civic responsibility) to state the facts on an issue as you know them and as your peers would, given thorough research. If someone sues you for what you say, *they have to prove* that you intended malice.

2. If you are introduced as an officer or representative of your local, state, or national dietetic practice group or professional organization, you are speaking not only for yourself, but also for that organization. It is therefore very important, especially when you want to take a very controversial stand, that you think it out ahead of time. Then either only represent yourself by not implying otherwise or make sure that the organization is in total agreement with your statement *before* you make it.

To help avoid problems with controversial subjects, research the subject thoroughly and then state fairly both sides of the controversy. Quote higher sources to defend your statements. Afterward, you can either state your opinion with your reasons or quote a higher source and give their reasons.

A personal experience by the author helps illustrate the viewers' interest that can be generated by controversy:

> After years of doing media work in Denver on subjects that I thought were interesting and sometimes controversial, I learned a valuable lesson. One week Judy Mazel, the author of the *Beverly Hills Diet,* was a guest on NoonDay, the NBC TV program where I was a weekly guest on nutrition. She appeared about 15 minutes before my segment and was lively, vivacious and a "media event." After her segment, the hostess asked if I could quickly look over the book and critique it for my segment instead of talking about what I had planned. I told her I needed more time to do an adequate job, but suggested we give a "promo" for next week's segment where I would give a critique. At least people might wait a week before they bought the book.

> That next week I spent three times more preparation time than normal in developing my critique of Ms. Mazel's book. I even called several PhDs to get their comments on some of the erroneous statements made on physiology and digestion. The show went very well, but the viewer response to the station was much greater than I expected.

> A physician friend, whose opinion I respected, said it was the best show I had ever done, and he gave me a quick review. He stated that the hostess and I first got everyone's attention because we issued a warning about the book. Then my arguments began to crescendo as each became stronger than the preceding one. At the moment when I had everyone's attention I quoted a higher source that lent greater credibility, and the hostess and I made light of the author's poor knowledge

of the subject. I hadn't realized what had transpired, but I was glad it was pointed out to me so that I could use it again. My reviewer also told me that I should stop covering such "milktoast" subjects and go after the "hot" or controversial ones.

I took my friend's advice and immediately went after the Nestle issue, Dr. Adkins and other similarly qualified authors, stagnant schools of thought in nutrition, and the Cambridge Diet Plan (our station received its first threatening phone call for my segment on that one). To prepare for the subjects, I called national headquarters' offices to talk to people, requested printed materials, and read other professionals' reviews. I even had a personal interview with the president of Cambridge International at my home the evening before the televised program on the diet. Phone calls and letters increased to the station and to me, and the station loved it.

BY-LINES AND PROMOTION

We miss many good opportunities to market ourselves in the media because of our hesitation to ask for and contractually negotiate by-lines and promotional credits. A by-line is a written acknowledgement in a newspaper, magazine, or other article that you were the author or at least a contributor. There have been times when dietitians have written magazine articles assuming they would be given credit, only to find that no one or someone at the magazine was listed as the author. The magazine rewrote the article to make it appear the dietitian was merely interviewed.

A promotion on radio or television usually consists of a short statement that people can contact you directly (presumably for more information) through the Yellow Pages, or a place of employment, or by a phone number offered over the air. Do *not* assume that any of this will be offered to you automatically and the media person can refuse your request, but at least ask. To help establish on-going relationships with media professionals, it helps if you accept the fact that they will not quote you each time they call. But if *you* write an article or column, that is a different matter.

DEVELOPING YOUR SALES STRATEGY

There may be many motives for wanting to pursue the media: personal challenge or promotion, business exposure, consumer crusading, or all of the above. Whatever the reason, you must demonstrate that your cause is of interest or benefit to many people. But a worthy cause is not enough in itself. Unfortunately, the importance of your cause may be less important than the style in which you sell it.

You must have something new to say about the subject, something you have discovered yourself, engineered yourself, or dramatized in a newsworthy fashion (1). Appearing each March to say that this is National Nutrition Time wouldn't gain much attention if it weren't for the creative dietitians willing to appear on the media or the school children's colorful projects or the "new" nutrition facts used to catch the audiences' attention. Television stations and newspapers love stories with visual content. It doesn't have to be spectacular, just interesting or dramatic.

Becoming involved in "causes" to get media exposure (along with other personal and professional benefits) is a tactic long used by individuals in the know (2). In many business, notoriety or popularity often equates with power or clout. Sometimes doors open to us first because of our popularity or the draw of our name, before our great expertise in nutrition even is considered!

Some suggestions that may help develop a sales presentation include (1):

1. **Is there a way to demonstrate a perceived benefit to many people?** Could you orchestrate an effort by restaurants to give their unserved food to the homeless? Is there a local fruit or vegetable that everyone grows that is in season and high in nutrients? Is your local water contaminated; is there a lead problem?

2. **Is there a way to package your cause that makes it seem new, even if it's old?** New research or study results may prove your point. A selling point in a media appearance consists of a good strong headline, plus a specific example or anecdote that supports the headline. It's not enough to talk about nutrition generalities, you must add the information that falls in the "I never knew that before" category (3). For example, "Our nutrition consulting business specializes in working with adolescent obesity. Did you know that if both parents of a child are overweight, the child has an 80% chance of being obese too? We are very concerned about that fact and want to teach kids and families how to break that cycle."

3. **Is there a dramatic way to illustrate your cause (before and after pictures, charts, films, slides or testimonials)?**

4. **Can you demonstrate a particular expertise in talking about a subject of continuing public interest?** (This is a favorite ploy of professionals who do not advertise widely, but who like broadcast exposure as way to build a practice.) (2)

How to Get in the Media

You can always call up and ask if you can be on a show or talk to a reporter. By first doing your homework and observing the media, you should know whom to contact, what kind of programming they offer and what topics are current. In radio and television first start with the program host (1). If that person is unavailable or won't talk to you, speak to the producer. At a newspaper ask to speak with the editor of the section most likely to be interested in what you have to say.

If the show or paper prefers to have requests made in writing, write a good one page cover letter, sample newspaper column or whatever and attach your bio or resume to support your credibility. Follow that up with a phone call. Try to call at least an hour or more before any show or deadline time so that the person will have time to speak with you.

You will need to let them know your ideas, what you have to offer, and why the audience would be interested. Make sure you have thought of several news "hooks" (unique features about your story) that will draw their interest. Remain flexible in case the reporters or station people have a new twist or approach that they like better, that still includes you. If the person doesn't like the idea at all, ask why. Offer to rethink the concept and offer a new proposal. Do not, however, ask for recommendations for other media contacts or approaches for you (1). The information may be offered, but it is not their responsibility to be your public relations counsel.

Gail Levey, R.D., was consulting at the NewYork City YMCA and Heart Association. A reporter from WCBS-TV called to ask if she would do a news segment, and she reluctantly agreed. The interview went so well, she has since been a "regular" on CBS News, the McNeil/Lehrer Report, quoted in the New York Times and a regular contributing author to four national magazines.

"Gentle persistence is the key" to finally getting in the media, according to Jeffrey Lant, author of *The Unabashed Self-Promoter's Guide: What Every Man, Woman, Child and Organization in America Needs To Know About Getting Ahead by Exploiting the Media* (2). No one should be discouraged if turned down; just keep persisting until someone is interested or the idea finally proves that it isn't right for you. See Figure 30.1 for a sample media biography.

Before Arriving for the Media Interview

When you work with the media you are selling yourself and your ideas. Be comfortable, prepared, rehearsed, and confident about your appearance. You will not be able to read a prepared speech, so reference material, notes, props, or whatever else you plan to refer to should be accessible, easy to read, and familiar to you. Go prepared! Or don't go.

Many media consultants encourage interviewees to choose only three major points that they would like to emphasize. Props, notes, charts, and so on could revolve around those points. All artwork and lettering should look professionally prepared, not homemade. The possibility of "freezing" or getting off the subject is much smaller when you simplify the interview, and your expectations are more realistic. The audience will remember what is, if it is clear, simple, and restated several times in different ways. After you make the main points, feel comfortable in discussing whatever is brought up or additional points that may be of interest.

Wardrobe is important since first appearances are crucial in all forms of the media. Don't wear anything so flashy that your clothes draw attention away from you. Don't overdress or underdress. Clothing you would expect to see on a bank vice president or TV newscaster will be good at any hour (1).

On television the color and print of an outfit are important. Try to avoid stark white or black. Instead use colors like gray, royal blue, purple, red, yellow, and beige. Patterned items, if you wear them, should be quiet, very small, and only one at a time. Avoid wearing herringbone, bright flowers and too busy-looking clothing.

Jewelry can be a problem on television because it can reflect into the camera or keep hitting a lapel microphone. Wedding rings and watches are usually fine, but bracelets, pins, necklaces, or chains may have to be taken off. Eyeglasses, especially with metal frames, can reflect the light. However, if you can't see without them and you don't wear contacts, don't take them off. They may ask questions about the slide they are showing on the monitor or a cameraperson may try to signal to you.

The Interview

When an interviewer meets a knowledgeable guest, the guest usually gets more freedom to carry the conversation. But this is not always the case, especially when the interviewer feels loss of control. So be aware and empathetic to needs other than just your own.

Try to be relaxed and don't forget to smile. Hold something in your hands if you like, but don't play with it or mutilate it. Before an interview on radio or television begins, it's usually possible to take a few minutes with the host to mention the items you feel are most important to discuss. Usually the details on props, slides, charts, or whatever, are worked out ahead of time with the host or an assistant, but if not be sure that the host is aware of them and when they are to be used. It is also appropriate to ask if the host is familiar with the topic you plan to speak on. If he or she is not, offer several key points that might be of interest.

Be careful not to explain everything ahead of time because the host may unintentionally make your points in his or her introduction and cause you to panic. (This happened to the author in Little Rock while on an initial spokesperson tour for Butter Buds. On the break before my segment as I spread out my props I told the hostess, a former Miss America, my three points. On the air she introduced me, then gave *my* three points while she pointed to my props, smiled and turned to me. I was sick. I'm seldom at a loss for words, that time taught me a lesson.)

There are interviewers in all forms of the media who enjoy controversy and antagonizing guests, but this is not usually the case. The best way to handle this type of person is to be well prepared and to remain calm. In radio and television the audience will usually side with the person they like and respect the most. At a newspaper writers will write whatever they want anyway. So, keep the discussion lively, but keep to the facts as you know them. Try not to be drawn into emotional controversies that have no satisfactory answers. Don't be afraid to have an opinion, however. Sometimes the best answer is to say that you don't have an answer to the problem. When you take telephone calls over the air from the public, there is risk involved, but remaining calm is the best defense along with a sense of humor and *being well prepared.*

On media spokesperson tours just about anything can and does happen. If you decide to go into this line of work, keep a sense of humor. There will be times that the interviewer tells you *on the air* that your product is no good or only for rich yuppies or whatever. That is why it's so important to choose very carefully which products you represent . . . because you may have to defend them.

Interviews are cut or lengthened *while you are on the air or two seconds before you start.* You may be told you have thirty seconds instead of the scheduled two minutes in which you must entertain the audience and introduce your product, yet not be commercial. You are trying to please the audience, the station, the client, the public relations firm, your professional peers and yourself---the pressure is intense at times. That is why they train you to give public service messages that position your product in a good light or as the answer to a problem. For example,"A new study of snack foods shows Americans eat too much fat," and you have a low fat cheese and other ideas for snacks. Or, "Caffeine can make people nervous and have sleepless nights," and you discuss herb teas without caffeine, along with other caffeine-free beverages.

Handling The Session

Be very aware of time limitations. Make your answers interesting and to the point. Unless it is the only appropriate answer, don't just answer with a yes or no. Use examples to make your selling point. And, it's very important that you listen to questions and conversation instead of just thinking about your next statement because you may be caught off guard with a simple, "What do you think about that, Ms. Jones?"

Bridging is a conversation tool used by anyone who wants to change the direction of questioning. The best guests don't evade the difficult questions --they restructure them. Before answering a question you don't like or that doesn't fit your needs, volunteer additional or different information introduced by a lead-in clause such as: "Let us consider the larger issue here . . ., " or "Instead of that, you should be aware that . . ., " or "Another issue the public is even more upset about is . . . " (l).

Trained guests volunteer much more than the required information when they like a question. No question is sacred, and none need be answered slavishly. It is possible, through bridging, to bring up more interesting issues than you are being asked by the interviewer (1).

The A or B Dilemma is where the interviewer asks a question and only gives two or so answers to choose from, both of which put you on the spot. An example would be, "Why do dietitians have such unrealistic ideas about what people eat? Is it because of poor training or aren't they observant?" What would you say? Probably, the best answer either is disagree with the original statement or avoid the trap by offering an alternative not given by the interviewer.

Don't echo any negative words like "rip-off" or "cancer-alley"(3). Don't restate hostile questions used by the interviewer.

Whenever you are on the premises of a media interview be cautious of the things you might say or do. When in a radio or television studio always be aware that a "live" microphone or panning camera may be picking you up. On the premises is not the time to mention to a colleague or friend that the hospital kitchen was just closed by the Health Department or that a patient is suing you for malpractice.

After the interview

Obviously, after interviews take a moment to thank interviewers for their time and express a desire to do it again sometime. If no offer is forthcoming, offer to be a resource person, leave your card, and plan to call again in a month or two.

REFERENCES

1. Hilton, Jack: *On Television!: A Survival Guide For Media Interviews,* Amacom, New York, 1980.
2. Lant, Jeffrey: *The Unabashed Self-Promoters Guide: What Every Man, Woman, Child, and Organization in America Needs to Know About Getting Ahead by Exploiting the Media,* JLA Publications, 1983.
3. Berg, Karen and Neal Rosenau: *CommCoreMedia Skills Workshop manual,* New York, 1990.

HERMAN

"I know you want to play Hamlet, but for this one television commercial you're a stick of celery."

268

Chapter 31

The "Write" Way to Get Published

Susan Tornetta Magrann, MS, R.D.,
updated by Kathy King Helm, R.D.

Don't skip this chapter because you think you don't have the skills to be a writer.

Writing talent is not something you are born with like curly hair or brown eyes. Learning how to write is like mastering any new skill whether it is skiing or developing healthy eating habits. It is the mark of a truly educated person, a necessary communication tool for the professional practitioner. You need motivation guidance, and practice, practice, practice.

WHY WRITE?

The abundance of inaccurate nutrition articles and books written by pseudo-nutritionists should motivate dietitians to pick up their pencils or learn to use word processing by computer. Complaining about nutrition misinformation will not solve the problem. Even instructing patients in a one-to-one situation won't have a tremendous impact. But dietitians writing interesting articles and books about sensible nutrition will. Just think how many people you can reach with one article---probably more people than you could counsel in a lifetime.

A second motivational factor is the self-satisfaction you will experience when you see your name and work in print. It is what will spur you on to write additional pieces.

Writing gives you a chance to be creative. It is like painting a beautiful picture or sewing a gorgeous outfit. You start out with a few basics---paper, pen, and an idea---and you can create a masterpiece.

Publishing can give you credibility with your readers and peers. People who write books or articles don't necessarily know more than their peers, but everyone thinks they do. Being published opens doors to speaking, media, top level committee appointments, tenure for educators, and it makes it easier to become published in the future.

And you can't overlook the financial rewards, but don't spend the money yet. The publications most likely to print your first articles probably will pay poorly. But they do provide the opportunity to get established and perfect your writing skill. Besides, many of these initial contacts can serve as a network to meet the right people from bigger---and better paying---publications.

Having had the experience of writing for a variety of publications helped me convince a large supermarket chain that I was the person best qualified to write a monthly nutrition newsletter for their approximately 200 stores.

There also are other financial gains from getting published. Most publishers especially those that don't pay well---are willing to print a brief statement about your background and the location of your private practice. This can attract potential clients or business contacts. You also include information about nutrition materials you developed and how they can be purchased. This is how one dietitian is marketing her self-published book.

THE RIGHT START

Ready to dust off the old typewriter? Good. But before you begin, you should *polish your writing skills.* Attend a publishing workshop, hire a tutor, or take a writing course at a local college. Or at least check out library books on the topic such as *Writing with Precision* by Jefferson Bates or *On Writing Well* by William Zinsser. Two major national writer's magazines---*The Writer* and *Writer's Digest*---also offer invaluable writing tips.

Reading newspapers, magazines, and books also can advance your writing education. Scrutinize what you read. Take a close look at the lead and the format of the article. Analyze what techniques the writer uses to capture your interest. If you spot a poorly written article, think about how you could improve it.

A writer whose style is worth particular study--is Barbara Gibbons. Check if your newspaper carries her syndicated column the *Slim Gourmet.*

WHAT TO WRITE ABOUT

Now that your fingers are itching to write, you must focus on an idea. It is easy to come up with good ideas if you keep your eyes and ears open. Nutrition is an "in" topic. Listen to what people are talking about. Read a variety of newspapers, magazines, and books. Watch the news.

Once you have an idea, you must make it uniquely yours by giving it a different slant. Editors want articles that are timely, and your slant can help update any nutrition subject. For example, more career women are waiting to become mothers. Why not slant your piece toward nutrition during pregnancy for the woman over thirty?

Major national or local news stories can make a nutrition topic timely. Actress Merle Streep's involvement in the alar controversy made it a "hot" topic. President Bush's dislike for broccoli opened the door for many articles on vegetables and on children who don't eat well. A recession makes food budgeting especially pertinent to the consumer.

Use your calendar to help inspire timely ideas. Waistline survival tips for holiday partying would be perfect for the December issue of a magazine. But you better think about Christmas in July since editors plan months in advance.

In developing your idea, keep in mind who your readers will be and what would interest them. For example, most senior citizens do not care about basic nutrition for infants. But they may enjoy a story on healthy snacks for visiting grandchildren.

You should be able to state your idea in one sentence. Make it specific. General ideas don't sell. You are more likely to spark an editor's interest with "Ten Tips for Looking Great in a Swimsuit" than a general article covering weight reduction principles.

People love to clip recipes and editors know it. So consider developing recipes to sell your message. Don't just write about the need to use less salt but include recipes that show how to make delicious low sodium dishes.

Make sure you choose a topic that is of personal interest to you. This will keep you motivated to do the research and survive numerous revisions.

THE COMPUTER AND WRITING

With the growth in popularity of the personal computer, a discussion on writing would not be complete without mentioning how one can be used. Software such as Word Perfect or Professional Write or Ami Pro can allow you to use the computer as a word processor. This gives you the capability to compose directly onto the computer screen, correct or reword the manuscript as necessary, and then print it when you are happy with it. The manuscript can be checked for spelling and grammar with the right software. It can be stored on software, later recalled on the screen, and revised by the word, sentence, or paragraph.

Time-consuming handwritten or typed manuscripts that must be completely redone when changes are made become problems of the past. There are even scanners that can read typed manuscripts and record them on software so that you can easily store or revise them. And you don't have to spend hours typing the manuscript into the computer.

A modem device and your telephone line can allow your computer to access stored information in larger computer databases. This would allow you to conduct literature, newspaper, or scientific journal searches for the most current information and could greatly reduce the amount of time needed for research. For practitioners who do not live close to a good medical or research library this capability for accessing information would be especially invaluable.

As computers become more popular, it will no doubt be possible to have an editor check and revise your manuscript on their computer and send it back to your computer---all without either of you leaving your home or office. See Chapter 25 for more information on computer usage.

FINDING A MAGAZINE /NEWSPAPER PUBLISHER

After your idea is clearly defined, your next step is to find a publisher. You can start by referring to a writer's directory book that should be available in your local library. *Writer's Market, Writer's Yearbook,* and *Literary Market Place* are the best known books. (See Recommended Readings at the end of the chapter.) They are updated yearly and contain the names of thousands of newspapers, magazines, and book publishers.

In addition, there are market listings in *Writer's Digest* and *The Writer.* You also can write directly to a magazine and ask if it accepts material from freelance writers; also ask them to send "spec sheets" or Writer's Guidelines.

The following is a sample of the information listed in the directories for magazines and newspapers.

1. Name and address of the magazine or newspaper and the editor's name   Your letter is more likely to be read if you send it to a specific editor. Since editors change frequently, check the masthead of a current issue of the publication.

2. Type of magazine   If your idea is about nutrition during pregnancy, you would focus on a magazine geared to women in their twenties and thirties. Obviously magazines aimed at senior citizens or men won't be interested.

3. Date established   Recently established magazines are more likely to accept your material since they have not built up a list of regular contributors. At the same time, they are more likely to fold before you ever receive payment.

4. Circulation   Generally, the higher the circulation, the higher the pay rate--but this will also mean more competition.

5. Pay rates and preferred length of articles   Editors work with a fairly set budget so there is not much room for negotiating fees unless you're well known or have a really "hot" story.

6. Terms of payment   "Payment on acceptance" means that the magazine will pay you as soon as the editors agree to buy your article. "Payment on publication" means they will pay you when your article appears in the magazine.   This could be several months or longer after you submit the article. "Kill fee" is a portion of the agreed-on price for an article that was assigned but the editor decided not to use. You are still free to sell your article to another magazine.

7. Rights purchased   When you sell your article, you are selling the publisher the rights to reprint these words: "First serial rights." First serial rights means the newspaper or magazine has the right to publish your article for the first time in their periodical. "Second serial rights" gives a newspaper or magazine the right to print your article after it has already appeared in some other newspaper or magazine. This term also refers to the sale of part of a published book to a newspaper or magazine. "All rights" means the writer forfeits the right to use his material again in its present form. This is also true for "work-for-hire" agreements because the writer has signed away all rights to the company making the assignment.

8. By-line   This means your name will appear on your article.

272

9. SASE (Self-Addressed Stamped Envelope)   If you do not include one, and most request it, the editor will probably not reply to your letter.

10. Lead time   Many editors request that seasonal material be submitted a specific number of months in advance. Editors have a lead time of several months so they don't want to see ideas for a Christmas holiday article in October.

SELLING YOUR IDEA

Now that you have pinpointed which publishers are most likely to be interested in your work, you must sell them your idea.

A Query Letter

Before you write your article, you should send the editor a query letter (see Figure 31.1). Most editors prefer that you do not telephone or send the complete article. The query letter is your sales tool. Since editors will formulate their impressions of you from this letter, it is wise to use quality 8 1/2" x 11" stationery and to make sure your typewriter or computer is printing well.

A query letter should contain these basic components:

1. Description of your idea, why it is timely, and your slant. Include an abstract of how you plan to develop your idea and a suggested length and deadline.

2. An explanation of why the editor's readers would want to read the article.

3. Why you are qualified to write the article and resource people you plan to interview. Include a statement about your professional background as well as one or two samples of published works. If you haven't been published, you need not mention this fact.

The ideal query runs one to two single-spaced pages--just long enough to develop your idea but short enough to be read quickly by the editor. Enclose a SASE and your phone number in case the editor wants to contact you. You should receive a reply in four to six weeks. If you have not heard by that time, drop the editor a note or telephone him, asking whether a decision has been made about your query.

You can send simultaneous queries and even get the assignment from two or more editors. You can accept more than one assignment for a topic as long as you write different articles. This may be frowned upon however if the magazines are in direct competition.To increase your chances of acceptance, you should become familiar with the magazine before sending a query. Either get copies from the library or purchase sample issues from the editor.

Figure 31.1 Sample Query Letter

Susan Magrann, M.S., R.D.
CONSULTING NUTRITIONIST
5252 LINCOLN AVENUE CYPRESS, CA 90630 PHONE: (714)

John Smith, Editor   Date
Today's Family
1410 First Street
Morristown, NJ 07960

Dear Mr. Smith:

Are your readers buying what they think they are buying when they go to the supermarket? Shopping today is fraught with mysterious codes and language.

Do fruit drinks or fruit-flavored drinks contain more fruit juice? Does the term "lite" mean low in calories? Is instant breakfast a nutritious meal? Does white bread contain any nutrients? The answers are all there on the products' labels.

I would like to take the mystery out of label reading by writing a 1000-word article covering the following points:

1. HOW TO INTERPRET A PRODUCT'S NAME. Included would be a chart of the legal meaning for various terms. For example:

If the Label Says . . .	It Means . . .
Fruit juice	100% real fruit juice
Juice drink	35 to 69% real juice
Fruit drink	10 to 34% juice
Fruit-flavored drink	less than 10% juice

Your readers will probably be surprised to learn that the term "lite" can refer to other properties of the food besides calories. "Lite" corn chips aren't lower in calories; they're thinner.

2. INGREDIENT LISTING. You can learn a great deal about the product's composition since ingredients are listed in descending order by weight. Included will be a description of hidden sources of sugar, salt, and saturated fats. If your readers check the ingredients for instant breakfast, they will find that in addition to sugar, corn syrup solids, another form of sugar, is also listed.

3. NUTRITION LABELING. The article will have a detailed explanation of what every line means on the nutrition label and will define the term "U.S. RDA."

As for white bread, the nutrition label shows that it does contain some nutrients, although less than what is found in whole wheat bread.

I hope I will have the opportunity to help your readers become better-informed consumers.

274

Besides being a registered dietitian, my nutrition articles have appeared in several publications including *The Jogger.* I also write a monthly nutrition newsletter for a large supermarket chain on the West Coast. Enclosed are two samples of my work plus my curriculum vitae.

Sincerely,

Susan Magrann, M.S., R.D.

Take a close look at the magazine's format, style of writing, and length of articles. Even study the advertisements. They can provide a good insight about what type of people read the periodical. If there are advertisements for children's toys and baby food, this will clue you that the audience is mainly young parents.

A Book Proposal

If you're interested in having a book published, the market listings will tell you what types of books a company publishes, how they want the material submitted, and what terms to expect if you're offered a book contract. The author's payment is called a royalty and is usually calculated as a percentage of the retail price of copies sold. For hardbacks, 10 percent is the usual base rate and 7 to 8 percent for paperbacks. Generally, the percentage increases if your book sells well.

You also can find a potential publisher by looking at books that cover a topic similar to the one you intend to write about. Check in the front of the book for the name of the publishing house. Because of the interest in nutrition today, there are publishers who are looking for dietitians with writing or recipe-development talents or someone with a "new" twist on diet and foods. Karen Mangum, R.D. of Boise, Idaho was contacted by Pacific Press because of her public speaking and good reputation. They had decided they wanted to publish a vegetarian cookbook, and she was chosen as author. The publisher paid for 80 colorful photographs in the book (sometimes the author must share the cost or pay for photos) and they footed the bill for an eight-city media tour.

If you're working on a book or want to be, you would send the prospective publisher(s) a proposal. The proposal should be about five to ten single-spaced pages and contain all the elements of a good query letter as well as a synopsis or outline of the chapters. Most publishers would also like at least two good sample chapters or some other published material that shows your writing ability. Send the proposal along with a large return envelope with postage so that it can be returned to you if they are not interested. For additional tips, refer to *How To Write "How-to" Books and Articles* as well as the *Writer's Handbook.*

Since your proposal can remain under consideration for many months, it is reasonable to send it to two to three editors at the same time but you must inform them that others are reviewing the same material by saying "simultaneous submission" or whatever you wish.

Don't get discouraged when selling your book idea. Published dietitians tell stories about the numerous proposals they submitted before a publisher showed an interest. Lack of interest may indicate that the idea needs to be reworked, but it could mean the "right" person had not seen it yet. Try to get as much feedback as possible from anyone who rejects it.

It is curious how some opportunities come so easily and others are hard to find. At an ADA Annual Meeting in the early 1980's Kathy King Helm, R.D. and Olga Satterwhite, R.D. were setting up their display in the Consulting Nutritionist's booth when Earl Shepard, an editor for Harper & Row, walked over and asked, "How would you two women like to write me a book?" Kathy said, "When do you need it and what do you want it on?" This book is the result of that chance meeting. Kathy states that none of her other book proposals have had such a pleasant beginning. Earl said he had been an editor for twenty years and made the offer because of a gut feeling.

Using A Literary Agent

You don't have to have a literary agent in order to sell your book. Many dietitians have sold their book ideas directly to a publisher.

Dietitians and other authors who have used agents state that they do it for several reasons: first, the agent is often able to negotiate a much larger up front advance on your book; second, the agent represents your interests during the contract negotiations to make sure you make all you should on foreign rights and future printings as well as assure the publisher performs as promised with cover design, promotional support and maybe even media tours. Dietitians can negotiate this for themselves, but often first time authors don't know what to ask for and where problems arise.

Some agents help their clients get exposure in the media and make the right contacts in the industry. Some agents have writing skill and a knack for helping writers refine their book concepts before a publisher sees them. A few publishers will not look at manuscripts that are not submitted through agents they know and trust. Because agents perform the important function of screening many of the thousands of manuscripts that are written each year and bring only the best ones to publishers.

On the down side, some agents are very popular and thus very busy; they may keep your work a year or more without giving you much feedback. Some agents show initial enthusiasm for an author's work but stop returning phone calls after awhile leaving the author in a quandary. Unless you're an established writer or have a very good book concept, it will be difficult to attract an agent. Since agents' fees are usually about ten to fifteen percent of your royalties plus some expenses, they want to feel certain you will earn enough money to be worth their time and effort.

Some agents work only on verbal agreements while others have written contracts. In either case if you feel the agent is not working well for you, you should have an understanding that you can take your manuscript and go elsewhere.

276

If you decide to pursue getting a literary agent, you can start by asking for suggestions from writers you know. *The Literary Market Place* contains a comprehensive listing of literary agencies.

Self-publishing

If you or your agent cannot find an interested publisher, you can always publish the book yourself. Of course, you have to invest your own money. But if you don't have confidence that the book will sell why should a publisher?

Ellen Coleman, a dietitian from California, originally self-published her book, *Eating For Endurance.* She decided to self-publish because editors felt the topic did not have a wide appeal and wanted her to dilute the material. Today, she has her book with Bull Publishing because of its wider marketing channels.

It is extremely important before you take this step that you accurately estimate your costs and determine how you are going to market the book. It may look attractive to sell 2,500 books at $20.00 each, but look at the items below to get an idea of the costs involved in publishing your own book, consider the following:

- $3,500 for computer, desktop publishing and grammar software and laser printer (or less money, but usually more time if you type your manuscript on a typewriter and take it to a typesetter to layout the book pages).

- $250-500 or more for a graphic artist to prepare the book cover; professors and students will do it for the best price.

- $50-250 each for use of copyrighted cartoons, graphs, photographs and illustrations are usually less, but not always. An artist or photographer may want his or her money up front or some will take a percentage of the book royalty.

- $6,500-8,500 to print 1,000 copies of a 300 page book, or $12,000 for 2,500 copies, or $16,000 for 5,000 copies (this includes page layout for printing, book cover in two colors, binding and so on). Some printers will let you pay for it over several months and others will want their payment when the inventory is delivered. Before choosing a printer, see samples of his work, and confirm your time lines. Although a printer at a distant location may give you a better price than a local one, consider the added costs of delivering the inventory and long distance calls, FAX and overnight mail to check last minute details.

- $450 or more per 1,000 direct mail promotion brochures you send out ($.45 each sent first class with a purchased label; $.35 each if sent bulk mail); Nutrition Graphics will send your promotion brochures in its spring and fall mass mailing packets for $695 for 10,000 and $395 for 5,000 (Contact: Carolyn Minsch, owner at 8911 Trujillo Way, Sacramento, CA 95826, (916) 363-2006); a JADA classified ad costs about $90 per month; and state and dietetic practice group newsletters charge $0-50 to run one ad.

- Consider selling you books through Pat Stein's NC/ES publication catalog for dietitians and other health professionals (NC/ES Box 3018, Olathe, KS 66062 (913) 782-8230), and CSPI in Washington, DC offers products and books at the back of each month's newsletter, you usually sell your book to them at a discount similar to that given to bookstores.

- $325 plus all your travel and lodging expenses to exhibit in the Member Product Display at ADA's annual meeting for one day; $1,200-3,500 for a large commercial booth for three days at ADA. Other conventions like Home Economists, Nursing, or Restaurant, vary greatly and there is the possibility you could share the booth with one or more entrepreneurs or publishers.

- According to Linda Hatchfeld, RD, author of *Cooking A la Heart* and founder of Appletree Press, Inc., if your book is for the public, there are three distribution channels you could use: **Wholesalers** who warehouse the book for you and fill orders from book stores, but do not promote it; you pay them 50-55 percent of the retail price for that service and they sell to stores at a 40-43 percent discount--they make 10-15 percent for warehousing your book. A **distributor** will market your book to retail stores through their catalog and sales staff on consignment-- they don't buy the books, they usually sell them for 42 percent off the retail price. Then they split the remaining 58%, 30/ 70% with you getting the 70 percent to cover printing-paper-binding (PPB) and your profit. On a book which retails for $10, that would mean $4.06 to you for expenses and profit. A **retail bookstore** will ask for a 40-43 percent discount from the retail price and perhaps the right to return any unsold copies.

- If your book is over forty-nine pages, you should consider getting an **"ISBN"** number (International Standardized Book Number) to print on your back book cover (as well as on software, videos, audio tapes with voice and some calendars). This number makes it easier for book stores to order your book or other item and it puts your book in the *Books In Print* book available at all libraries and bookstores. The cost is $100 for a fifteen to twenty-day turn around and $151.50 if you need a seventy-two-hour response. To get a number and more information call R.R.Bowker at 1(800)521-8110.

You can easily see in this example it could take almost 1,000 copies of a book just to cover initial expenses involved in publishing and marketing the book. That is why most people who self-publish try to print as many as they think will sell over a year or more in order to save on printing. After the initial costs are paid for, any remaining inventory is profit except for on-going marketing costs.

If your book is for the public and you want to sell it in B. Dalton or wherever, its important that the book sell well to remain on the shelves. Mary Hess, RD author of *The Art of Cooking for the Diabetic,*whose first

278

edition sold more than 350,000 copies, and *Pickles and Ice Cream* along with Anne Hunt, reports that her publisher said a trade book has about ninety days to "make it" in the large bookstores. After that the copies are sent back to the publisher and a new book is ready to fill the space. To have a book that really sells well is the exception, not the rule. Knowing this, you can see why initial marketing is so important!

Illustrations

Don't overlook the value of good illustrations in your book to increase sales. Unless you are talented, your best bet is to find a freelance professional artist and/or photographer. Contact other writers who have used local illustrators and get their recommendations. Or look in the Yellow Pages under "Artists--Commercial" and "Photographers--Commercial." There is also lots of good young talent at local universities and art schools.

WRITING YOUR MASTERPIECE

Congratulations. You sold your idea. Now you only have a *deadline* to worry about. This can cause panic---and an illness called "writer's block." Don't worry, it need not be terminal. There are measures to overcome the condition.

First, find a location--either at home, work, or at the library--where you can work without interruptions. If the phone is a problem, consider investing in an answering machine.

Second, select the best time for you to write and force yourself to stick to it. Most people have a specific tine of the day they feel most creative. You will be more productive by spending whatever amount of time you can spare every day at your "peak creative time" than trying to cram the assignment into a couple of 8-hour days.

Third, break your writing into small parts. This will keep you from feeling overwhelmed by the project.

Outline

Maybe the first day will be spent on your outline. It is essential to have some type of outline since it makes the next step--research--much easier. An outline helps you gather and organize all the pertinent information you need. While doing your research, you may decide to revise your outline.

Research

Begin your research by reviewing materials you have at home or work. Then you'll want to expand your information by going to a local library and/or medical library or by a computer search.

Interview dietitians and other professionals who are experts in the topic you're writing about. In addition to providing valuable information, they can direct you to reference books and articles.

Don't let the term *interview* scare you. It's just a fancy name for talking to someone. Most people will be flattered that you value their opinion. In order not to waste the expert's time prepare a list of questions before contacting him.

Writing

After research comes the hardest step for most people---writing. Some would-be authors are guilty of research overkill to delay the inevitable.

It is easier to write your first draft if you don't worry about its being perfect at this point. Just sit at your desk and put your thoughts on paper. Don't stop for any corrections or even crossing out words. Once you force yourself to do the first draft, your work will become easier.

Next, revise and fine tune your piece. The first revision will probably be the most extensive. Keep in mind you want your work to be clear, concise, accurate, and interesting.

Check that your lead sentence is a grabber. Unless you capture the audience's attention, they won't continue to read on. It can take a good deal of time to develop your lead but it's definitely worth the effort.

Next, take a close look at each word. Specific and short words crowd more meaning into a small space. Cross out unnecessary words and check for spelling.

Avoid overusing a particular word especially within the same paragraph. This is when a thesaurus or a dictionary of synonyms and antonyms is invaluable.

Now you're ready to study sentences. Do they flow smoothly? Is the length of your sentences varied? Generally, shorter sentences are easier for the reader to understand.

After sentences comes paragraphs. Each paragraph should contain a main idea. Avoid paragraphs that are too long. You can even slip in some single sentence paragraphs for a change of pace.

Look for a snappy ending. The reader will then leave the story with a favorable impression.

After your first revision, put your work away for a few days so you will be able to take a fresh look at it. Now you're ready to do your second, third, or however many additional revisions it takes to make it perfect.

Editing

If you lack confidence about your writing and feel it is near perfect, pay a professional writer to edit it. You can find someone by contacting a college that has a journalism program. There may be an instructor or a senior student who could help.

Depending on your subject, you also may want an expert in that area to check your work for accuracy.

Final Copy

The end is almost near. You are ready to type your final copy, or let your printer do it, if you are using a computer. Don't forget to follow the guidelines the publisher sent you. After you've cleaned up all those typos, you're ready to mail off your masterpiece.

Since you've invested so much time and energy creating this literary work, you don't want someone to steal your material. If you're not familiar with copyright laws, refer to Chapter 22 on protecting your ideas and interest.

The last step: relax.

You'll need to gather strength before you start your next writing project.

One final piece of advice. Resist spending all of your writer's fee on buying copies of your work for friends and relatives.

On second thought, why not? You should be proud of your accomplishment. And you thought you couldn't be a writer!!!

RECOMMENDED READINGS
Magazines
The Writer. Published Monthly by The Writer, Inc.
Writer's Digest. Published Monthly by Writer's Digest.

Books
Marketing Information
Literary Market Place. Bowker, Annual.
Writer's Market. Writer's Digest, Cincinnati, OH, Annual.
Writer's Yearbook. Writer's Digest, Cincinnati, OH, Annual.

Writing and Publishing
Getting Published: A Guide for Businesspeople and Other Professionals by Gary Bellien.   New York, John Wiley and Sons, 1984.
How To Get Happily Published by Judith Appelbaum and Nancy Evans. New York, Harper & Row, 1978.
How to Write "How-To" Books and Articles by Ramond Hull. New York, Writer's Digest Books, 1981.
How to Write and Publish a Scientific Paper. 2nd ed., by Robert Day. Philadelphia, ISI Press, 1983.
Magazine Article Writing by Betsy P. Graham. New York, Holt, Rinehart and Winston, 1980.
On Writing Well by William Zinsser. Harper & Row, New York, 1988.
The Publish-It-Yourself Handbook edited by Bill Henderson. Weinscott, NY, Pushcart Press, 1973.
The Writer's Handbook edited by Sylvia K. Burack. The Writer, 1982.
The Writer's Survival Manual by Carol Meyer. New York, Crown Publishers, 1982.

Style
The Elements of Style by W. Strunk and E. B. White. Macmillan Publishing Co., 1978.
The Most Common Mistakes in English Usage by Thomas E. Berry, McGraw-Hill Co., 1971.

Chapter 32

Continued Competency

The fact that we should stay current with new advances in the field of nutrition is often just taken for granted. However, staying up to date is not a task that can be accomplished by attending a meeting or two a year and skimming a journal monthly. The rate of change in nutrition and its related specialties is happening faster than we have ever experienced before, and it may continue that way for some time.

Money is finally starting to be earmarked for research in nutrition, thus generating new information regularly. Government changes in regulations and payments for patient services are demanding changes in nutrition documentation and expected output. "Outside" competition to nutrition practice demands that our expertise and practice improve to stay ahead. The use of high technology, the computer in particular, will require that we have an appreciation and working knowledge of new systems that should free our time and give us the opportunity to better use our expertise. New techniques and human behavior skills need to be employed to be more effective in our roles as counselors. The public expects and is demanding that we take stands on the issues and that we provide information. Remaining unchanged will drop us behind. Every dietetic professional will be challenged.

Merely getting seventy-five hours of continuing education credit every five years will keep a dietitian registered. But, depending upon the quality of the programs and the subjects chosen to attend, a practitioner may or may not learn anything new. A practitioner's goal should not be to stay registered, but instead to become an expert and remain one.

As the marketplaces continue to change, especially for entrepreneurs, it is imperative that a dietitian gain nondietetic experience and attend other disciplines' seminars and educational training. Also, lay literature and world and economy periodicals should be regularly reviewed. Nutrition can no longer be seen as a narrow field of study. It is an element of life intertwined and influenced by many other constituent parts.

In business the practitioner is again greatly affected by nondietetic influences. The local and national economies, consumer trends, insurance coverage, competition, and available financing are just a few of the concerns. The more knowledgeable an entrepreneur is about these items, the more prepared the person will be to handle business life.

Educators tell us that the mark of an educated person is one who knows where to look something up. If you subscribe to several newsletters and take the time to read the Periodical Reviews in the back of the Journal of The American Dietetic Association, scanning nutrition literature is relatively simple. It is not necessary to purchase all of the most expensive resource books as long as you have several available to you. World and economic news can be found encapsulated in the daily newspapers or weekly and monthly publications. Business news is found in magazines, trade journals, newspapers, and newsletters.

The following list of references is not meant to be a complete list or an endorsement. Practitioners have shared the names of references and resources that have been beneficial to them. You may have additional ones that fit your needs better. Before subscribing to the periodicals buy a few issues at the newsstand and look up journals in the library to see if you like them. Many publishers agree to trial subscriptions for shorter periods than one year. Newsletter editors often offer to refund a partial subscription price, if you are not satisfied. Take advantage of these offers and don't hesitate to stop publications that do not fit your needs or interests. Staying current can be costly both in time and money, so evaluate your references carefully. See Figure 32.1 for James C. Rose's article on the new dietetics.

Figure 32.1 The New Dietetics
(Source: Hospital Food Nutrition Focus, July 1985. Reprinted with permission of Aspen Publishers, Inc. Copyright 1985.)

THE NEW DIETETICS

For over 50 years, a few basic diet therapy regimens have consumed the majority of our labor hours. Calorie control, diet for diabetes mellitus, carbohydrate control, sodium control, and fat modifications have taken the front seat in terms of interest and deployment of resources. Our menus are devised in accord with the premises of these diets; our very world has depended upon providing services to those patients who require these types of services--patients with diagnoses of heart disease, diabetes, renal disease, and many others.

In the last decade we have become more sophisticated in our provision of nutritional care. We now focus more closely on laboratory values, on protein (nitrogen) and calorie ratios, and on measuring the relative risk of malnutrition. But the content of the diets we provide has really not changed. There are still low sodium products, controlled fat products, and "magic" mixtures that emanate from the nourishment control centers. The nutrients in favor may differ from setting to setting but our basic approach to treatment has been static . . .

America is in the bionic age. Artificial organs, transplants, and other such medical wonders are becoming commonplace in some settings. Few deny that soon the lifelong behavior modification requirements for diabetes mellitus clients will no longer be necessary--an artificial pancreas will eliminate the need for diet control. Artificial kidneys and new methods for treatment have revolutionized our basic theories of protein, electrolyte, and

283

fluid controls in renal disease. Liberality in treatment of the aged and increasing knowledgeability of consumers concerning nutrition have altered the requirements for our services. Sodium modification is no longer universally viewed as the treatment of choice for hypertension and coronary artery disease. Our crackers and butter theories are not now held in high esteem in all medical circles.

The implications for our industry are clear. Recognizing that many of our staff have insufficient current knowledge to bridge the gap from the old to the new dietetics, we have a responsibility to provide meaningful continuing education for the seasoned--not just the novice--practitioner. If we bury our noses in current staffing configurations and fail to look to the future promised by new research, we will be poorly equipped to have a role in the new dietetics . . .

Certainly, our entire future does not rest on research in the nutrient-brain matrix, but how many of our dietitians have even heard of the research? How many of us have enough familiarity with these activities to respond to the questions of consumers or physicians? If we are acquainted with the research, are we discounting it as "not yet proven" rather than preparing ourselves for potential opportunities?

Though it is true there may be no long-term future for dietetics in this particular area of research--drug therapy may replace diet therapy--are we ready and willing to look beyond our old realm, our old world? Are we prepared to adapt our entrepreneurial approach to the new reality of medical advances?

James C. Rose, R.D., DHCFA, LD
Editor

BIBLIOGRAPHY AND REFERENCES

Books

Chenevert, M.: *STAT: Special Techniques in Assertiveness Training,* CV Mosby, St. Louis, MO, 1983.

Chernoff, R., ed.: *Communicating As Professionals,* The American Dietetic Association, Chicago, IL, 1987.

The Competitive Edge: Marketing Strategies for the Registered Dietitian, The American Dietetic Association, Chicago, IL, 1987.

Covey, S.: *The Seven Habits of Highly Effective People,* Simon & Schuster, New York, 1989.

Hakuta, K.: *How To Create Your Own Fad and Make a Million Dollars,* Avon Books, New York, 1988.

Holtz, H.: *How To Succeed As An Independent Consultant,* John Wiley, New York, 1983.

Holtz, H. and T. Schmidt: *The Winning Proposal: How To Write It,* McGraw-Hill, New York, 1981.

Mackay, H.: *Swim With the Sharks Without Being Eaten Alive,* Wm. Morrow & Co., New York, 1988.

Matheson, B.: *Asking For Money: The Entrepreneur's Guide to the Finaning Process,* Financial   Systems Associates, Inc., Orlando, FL, 1990.

McCormack, Mark: *What They Don't Teach You at Harvard Business School,* Bantam, New   York, 1984.

McCormack, Mark: *What They Still Don't Teach You at Harvard Business School,* Bantam,   New York, 1989.

Pooley, J.: *Trade Secrets,* Osborne/McGraw-Hill, Berkeley, CA, 1982.

Questions and Answers About Trademarks, U.S. Dept. of Commerce, Patent and Trademark Office, Washington, DC, 1979.

Shook, Robert: *Why Didn't I Think of That!,* New American Library, New York, 1982.

Zemke, R. and K. Albrecht: *Service America!,* Dow-Jones Irwin, Homewood, IL, 1985.

Zemke, R.: *The Service Edge,* New American Library, New York, 1989.

Small Business Administration

ACE (Active Corps Executives): working business people who volunteer their time to consult with entrepreneurs and conduct seminars

SCORE (Service Corps of Retired Executives): retired business people who volunteer their time to consult with entrepreneurs

SBI (Small Business Institute): training and classes for entrepreneurs, plus publications

Small Business Administration offices are located in each state. Look in the telephone   book under "U.S. Government" and ask for the address and telephone number of the nearest office.

Newsletters and Journals

American Journal of Clinical Nutrition, 9650 Rockville Pike, Bethesda. MD 20014.

Consulting Nutritionist in Private Practice Newsletter, ADA Practice Group Newsletter.

Consumer Reports, 256 Washington St., Mt. Vernon, NY 10550.

Contemporary Nutrition, General Mills, Inc., P.O. Box 1113, Minneapolis, IN 55440.

Current Dietetics, Ross Labs, 625 Cleveland Ave., Columbus, OH 43216.

Dairy Council Digest, National Dairy Council, 6300 N. River Rd., Rosemont, IL 60018.

Environmental Nutrition, 52 Riverside Dr., Suite 15-A, New York, NY 10024.

FDA Consumer, 5600 Fishers Lane, Rockville, MD 20857.

Food & Nutrition, Box 51271, Boulder, CO 80321-1271.

Harvard Medical School Health Letter (The), 79 Garden St., Cambridge, MA 02138.

Health Letter (The Edell), IN Health, 475 Gate Five Rd., #225, Sausalito, CA 94965.

Hospital Food & Nutrition Focus, Aspen Pub, 1600 Research Blvd., Rockville, MD 20850.

Journal of American Dietetic Association, 216 W. Jackson Blvd., Chicago, IL 60606.

Journal of Nutrition Education, 2140 Shattuck Ave., Berkeley, CA 94704.
Journal of Nutrition For the Elderly, The Haworth Press, 28 E. 22 St., New
        York, NY10010.
Kiplinger Washington Letter, 1729 H St., N.W., Washington, D.C. 20006.
Lifetime Health Letter (Univ. of Texas), P.O. Box42032, Palm Coast, FL
        32142-0342.
Nutrition Action, The Center For Science In the Public Interest. 175S "S" St.,
        N.W.,Washington, DC 20009.
Nutrition and Health, Institute of Human Nutrition, Columbia University,
        701 W. 168th St., New York, NY.
Nutrition and the M.D., P.O. Box 160, Van Nuys, CA 91405.
Nutrition Today, 101 Ridgley Ave., Annapolis, MD 21401.
Nutritional Support Service, Journal of Practical Application in Clinical
        Nutrition, I2849 Magnolia Blvd., North Hollywood, CA 91607.
Obesity and Health, 402 So. 14th, No. 5, Hettinger, ND 58639.
Sports Medicine Digest, P.O. Box 2160, Van Nuys, CA 91405.
Sports-Nutrition News, P.O. Box 986, Evanston, IL 60204.
Topics in Clinical Nutrition, Aspen Systems, 16792 Oakmont Ave.,
        Gaitherburg, MD   20877.
Tufts Univerity Diet & Nutrition Letter, Box 57857, Boulder, CO 80322-7857.

INDEX